Dear Justice Miguel Márquez,

Thank you for supporting my social justice work at Santa Clara Law.

Best,

P. Gulati

# THE NEW IMMIGRATION FEDERALISM

Since 2004, the United States has seen a flurry of state and local laws dealing with unauthorized immigrants. Though initially restrictionist, these laws have recently undergone a dramatic shift toward promoting integration. How are we to make sense of this new immigration federalism? What are its causes? And what are its consequences for the federal-state balance of power?

In *The New Immigration Federalism*, Professors Pratheepan Gulasekaram and S. Karthick Ramakrishnan provide answers to these questions using a combination of quantitative, historical, and doctrinal legal analysis. In so doing they refute the popular "demographic necessity" argument put forward by anti-immigrant activists and politicians. They posit that immigration federalism is instead rooted in a political process that connects both federal and subfederal actors: the Polarized Change Model. Their model captures not only the spread of restrictionist legislation but also its abrupt turnaround in 2012, projecting valuable insights for the future.

Pratheepan Gulasekaram is Associate Professor at Santa Clara University School of Law. He has published widely on immigration federalism and the constitutional rights of noncitizens both in popular media platforms and prominent legal journals. Before entering academia, Gulasekaram clerked for the U.S. Circuit Court of Appeals for the Fifth Circuit in New Orleans. He earned his BA at Brown University and his JD at Stanford Law School.

S. Karthick Ramakrishnan is Professor of Political Science and Associate Dean of the School of Public Policy at the University of California, Riverside. He directs the National Asian American Survey and AAPI Data and has written numerous books and articles on civic participation and immigration policy. Ramakrishnan is founding editor of the *Journal of Race, Ethnicity, and Politics*, a Global Fellow at the Woodrow Wilson Center, and an appointee to the California Commission on Asian and Pacific Islander American Affairs. He earned his BA at Brown University and his PhD at Princeton University.

# The New Immigration Federalism

## PRATHEEPAN GULASEKARAM
Santa Clara University School of Law

## S. KARTHICK RAMAKRISHNAN
University of California, Riverside

CAMBRIDGE
UNIVERSITY PRESS

# CAMBRIDGE
## UNIVERSITY PRESS

32 Avenue of the Americas, New York, NY 10013-2473, USA

Cambridge University Press is part of the University of Cambridge.

It furthers the University's mission by disseminating knowledge in the pursuit of education, learning, and research at the highest international levels of excellence.

www.cambridge.org
Information on this title: www.cambridge.org/9781107530867

First published 2015

Printed in the United States of America

*A catalog record for this publication is available from the British Library.*

Library of Congress Cataloging in Publication Data
Gulasekaram, Pratheepan.
The New Immigration Federalism / Pratheepan Gulasekaram, Santa Clara University School of Law, S. Karthick Ramakrishnan, University of California, Riverside.
    pages  cm
Includes bibliographical references and index.
ISBN 978-1-107-11196-7 (hardback) – ISBN 978-1-107-53086-7 (pbk.)
1. Immigration – Government policy – United States.   2. Federal government – United States.   I. Ramakrishnan, S. Karthick (Subramanian Karthick), 1975–   II. Title.
JV8701.G86  2015
325.73–dc23      2015007705

ISBN 978-1-107-11196-7 Hardback
ISBN 978-1-107-53086-7 Paperback

*To Gina and Mila; Brinda, Omji, and Millan …*
*And of course, our Ammas and Appas*

# Contents

# Figures and Tables

# Acknowledgments

This book began, funnily enough, over a breakfast of dosas. One of us (Karthick) was traveling to Stanford for a conference and called the other (Pratheepan), a law professor at Santa Clara University, to see if we might be able to meet. We were longtime friends – we met each other on our first day at Brown University – but had only been in touch occasionally since college. We went to Komala Vilas, a South Indian restaurant in the area, to share a traditional breakfast of dosas, idlis, and sambar and to catch up on each other's lives. Although the visit was meant to be entirely social, we started talking about work and quickly realized that we were working on a very similar issue: the growth of restrictive state laws on immigration, which was then a relatively new line of inquiry. Even though we had both been researching the same topic, we were evaluating it from very different approaches – one largely empirical and the other largely based on readings of constitutional law and federalism. After a spirited discussion, we resolved to keep the conversation going. And we have done so, for more than five years. This sustained dialogue has so far been a very thoughtful and fruitful one, yielding three law review articles, two issue briefs, several newspaper Op-Eds, and now this book.

Since 2004, immigration policy, and the state and local role in defining that policy, has been a hot topic. It has dominated headlines, consumed hours of media commentary, and generated two Supreme Court opinions and several others in various federal courts. Immigration federalism has made national celebrities out of governors and local sheriffs and has provided plenty of academic fodder for scholars across many disciplines. It has also been a fast-moving phenomenon. In little more than ten years, trends have waxed and waned, and the political valence of state and local participation has shifted and continues to evolve.

While the initial interpretations of the surge in immigration law was that it was due to sudden demographic change – after all, undocumented immigrants were increasingly settling in new destination states like Iowa and Georgia – there is now a growing recognition that partisan politics and political actors play an important role. We count ourselves as among those who have helped shift this understanding, although in several academic and policy quarters the "demographic pressures" argument still holds sway. As we and others have shown, immigration policy has now become a highly partisan subject at the national and local levels, generating ideological battles waged in towns, counties, states, Congress, and presidential campaigns, and with major national organizations and political networks stoking those contests.

As we show in this book, the Republican intraparty rebellion on immigration occurred well before the start of the Tea Party movement in 2009. Since then, the issue of immigration policy in the states has taken many twists and turns, some wending their way through state legislatures and city halls, others working their way through the Supreme Court and actions by the White House. One net effect of all of these developments is that immigration federalism has become an indelible feature of the federal and subfederal policy landscape and will remain so for the foreseeable future. We hope that this book's multidisciplinary approach, mixing empirical investigation, doctrinal analysis, and legal and political theory, will help shed light on the origins of this recent period of immigration federalism, producing new insight on its political underpinnings and legal consequences.

There are several friends and colleagues without whom this book would not have been possible. We owe special thanks to Professors Hiroshi Motomura, Cristina Rodriguez, Michael Olivas, Jennifer Chacon, and David Rubenstein, whose detailed and insightful comments on our earlier publications on the topic indelibly helped shape our ideas. We also owe significant gratitude to the institutions that gave us the time, space, and resources to work on these projects: Santa Clara University Law School and the University of California, Riverside, in addition to the Russell Sage Foundation and the Woodrow Wilson International Center for Scholars.

We must also acknowledge the editors and staff at the New York University Law Review, the Arizona State Law Journal, and the researchers and staff at the Center for American Progress who published the law review articles and issue briefs that form the basis of portions of this book. In particular, portions of Chapters 3 and 4 first appeared in *The Importance of the Political in Immigration Federalism*, 44 Ariz. St. L. J. 1431 (2012); portions of Chapters 4 and 6 first appeared in *Immigration Federalism: A Reappraisal*, 88 N.Y.U. L. Rev. 2074 (2013); and portions of Chapter 5 first appeared in *Understanding Immigration Federalism in the United States*, Center for American Progress (Mar. 2014). Additionally, some of the ideas in Chapters 6 and 7 are further developed in our forthcoming article in the Florida Law Review, *The President and Immigration Federalism*, 68 Fla. L. Rev.

We also owe significant gratitude to the several scholars from our respective disciplines who offered their thoughts, encouragements, critiques, and provocative questions on our work. A deep and sincere thanks to Ahilan Arulananthan, Sameer Ashar, W. David Ball, Angela Banks, Eleanor Brown, Jessica Bulman-Pozen, Ming Hsu Chen, G. Jack Chin, Aixa Cintrón, Mat Coleman, Adam Cox, Tino Cuellar, Rose Cuison Villazor, Keith Cunningham-Parmeter, Meera Deo, Justin Driver, Stella Burch Elias, Lia Epperson, Patricia Fernandez-Kelly, Alexandra Filindra, David Fitzgerald, Kyle Graham, Lucas Guttentag, Zoltan Hajnal, Bill Ong Hing, Daniel Hopkins, Margaret Hu, Clare Huntington, Kevin Johnson, Bradley Joondeph, Jane Junn, Catherine Kim, Stephen Lee, Taeku Lee, Stephen Legomsky, Peter Markowitz, Lise Nelson, Manuel Pastor, Huyen Pham, Emily Ryo, Neil Siegel, John Skrentny, David Sloss, Sarah Song, Juliet Stumpf, Rick Su, Roberto Suro, Daniel Tichenor, Jonathan Todres, Tom Wong, and David Yosifon.

The ideas in this book benefited greatly from opportunities to present at various conferences and meetings, including the 2015 American Association of Law Schools Annual Meeting; various meetings of the American Political Science Association, Western Political Science Association, and the Politics of Race, Immigration and Ethnicity Consortium; the Conference of Asian Pacific American Law Faculty; the American Constitution Society's Conference on the Constitutionality of State and Local Immigration Laws; the 2014 Immigration Law Teachers Workshop; the 2012 University of California International Migration Conference; and faculty workshops and seminars at City University of New York, Princeton University, Woodrow Wilson Center, U.C. Irvine, Cardozo Law School, and Lewis & Clark Law School. And a special thanks to the Center for American Progress and the American Constitution Society for Law & Policy for giving us a platform to reach a wider audience through events and issue briefs.

Next, we owe a huge thank you to our research assistants and graduate students who have made our work immeasurably easier: Allan Colbern and Andrea Silva (PhD candidates at UC Riverside); Ulises Aguierre, Philip Brody, and Ralitza Dineva (SCU Law School 2015); Keelin Haddix and Mariko Kotani (SCU Law School 2014); and Rachel Wilf (Woodrow Wilson International Center for Scholars).

We also acknowledge the editorial staff at Cambridge University Press, especially John Berger for his enthusiasm and guidance in bringing this book to fruition.

Most of all, we want to thank our families for providing the love, support, and understanding we needed to complete this book. From Karthick – A deep and sincere thanks to my parents, who made the brave decision to migrate with preteens in tow, and to my home crew that subsidizes my work and provides critical encouragement in various ways: Brinda, Omji, and Millan. From Pratheepan – My unending gratitude to my parents, my incredible spouse Gina, my most precious baby girl Mila, and Miles the beagle, my faithful companion through many hours of reading and writing.

# 1

# Introduction

In December 2010, the U.S. Supreme Court heard oral arguments in *Chamber of Commerce of the United States v. Whiting*. At issue was an Arizona law allowing the state to revoke the business licenses of employers who knowingly hired unauthorized immigrants. *Whiting* was the first in a series of Supreme Court cases involving immigration-related laws at the state level, all of them passed by the state of Arizona.[1] The most prominent of these laws was SB 1070, a state enforcement law passed earlier that year, eliciting a lawsuit from the Obama administration and eventually leading to the *Arizona v. United States* decision. Although *Whiting* was less well-known, the stakes were nevertheless very high – not only for workers who might be affected by Arizona's law, but also for employers, labor unions, other states, and even the federal government.

Several disparate groups filed briefs in the Supreme Court supporting the Chamber of Commerce's campaign against the law. The Chamber represented the concerns of employers who were worried that, if Arizona's law were allowed to stand, they would need to contend with a proliferation of individual state and local laws on employer verification, each with its own set of requirements. In addition to the Chamber of Commerce as petitioner, other business organizations filed an amicus brief, arguing that a "patchwork of state and local laws undermines Congress's intent to establish a comprehensive and uniform national framework that limits the imposition of undue burdens on businesses."[2] The federal government also had a keen interest in the case and it, too, filed an amicus brief in support of the petitioner, arguing that federal law, especially the 1986 Immigration Reform and Control Act (IRCA), left no room for laws like Arizona's to take hold.[3] Indeed, another amicus brief by former members of Congress, including Romano Mazzoli who helped author the 1986 law, argued that Congress intended to expressly preempt the ability of states to impose employer sanctions, and that it intended any exception for state licensing laws to be interpreted narrowly.[4] Finally, labor groups and immigrant advocacy organizations were also concerned about heightened employer verification requirements, arguing that Arizona's law threatened to upset the careful balance struck by federal law, between the goals of deterring unauthorized employment, on the one hand, and avoiding employee discrimination and national origin profiling, on the other.[5]

On the other side of the issue, proponents of Arizona's employer sanctions law also had enormous investment in the case, and they filed amici curiae briefs in support of the respondent, the state of Arizona. These included the bill's author, Arizona State Senator Russell Pearce, other states intending to follow Arizona's lead by passing similar legislation, and restrictionist groups such as the Immigration Reform Law Institute (IRLI). IRLI, which described its interest in the case as a group that "frequently assists State and local governments in the drafting of legislation to deter unlawful immigration," argued that the 1986 federal immigration law explicitly allowed states to issue and revoke business licenses in connection with the hiring of unauthorized immigrants.[6] The brief filed by the Attorneys General of various states advanced a broader and more fundamental federalism argument, contending not only that Congress had carved out an exception for states to impose penalties via business licenses, but that such powers were part of the State's traditional and sovereign power over the "formation, licensing, and regulation of business entities."[7]

Clearly, a lot was at stake in the Court's decision with respect to immigration federalism. The Supreme Court was ruling on the constitutionality of Arizona's particular law on employer verification, but the decision would affect plans for copycat legislation in other states that were following Arizona's lead. Even more intriguing, the Court was making its decision under the shadow of Arizona's other laws on immigration that were facing court challenges, including the widely publicized SB1070, an omnibus enforcement bill that thrust the state into the center of the national policy debate on unauthorized migration. Ultimately, the Court ruled in favor of Arizona's employee verification law, and this decision prompted a new round of speculation as to whether the United States was entering a new period of immigration regulation, one where states would play a more robust role in regulating the livelihoods of immigrant residents.[8] *Arizona v. United States*, which followed a year later, would curb some of the legislative zeal around state immigration enforcement laws, but viable avenues for immigration restriction still remained.

Indeed, over the past few years there have been many other developments – some involving the Courts, others involving the Executive Branch, and many involving state legislatures and local governments – that indicate a period of great ferment with respect to immigration and federalism. Which begs the state level waned in frequency, and a growing number of states began to pass laws aimed at the integration of unauthorized immigrants. As this book goes to press, this integrationist trend is still continuing.

Before we proceed with an overview of the book, a few clarifications regarding our terminology are in order. First, although this book generally deals with the regulation of all immigrants, it is particularly concerned with state and local policy regarding undocumented immigrants. As such, we make a conscious choice here to refer to the population of persons who would be characterized in the Immigration and Nationality Act as "unlawfully present," "entrants without inspection," or "not authorized to be employed" as either undocumented immigrants or unauthorized immigrants. We do not use the term illegal alien or illegal immigrant, which others may use to describe this same population. In doing so we acknowledge that the choice of language is itself one that suggests a certain view of the conclusiveness and consequences of unlawful status.[12] Nevertheless, we believe our choice of description is descriptively, legally, and morally justifiable, and is coming into greater use in judicial and media terminology.[13]

Second, throughout the book we use the terms "restrictionist" and "integrationist" or "pro-immigrant" to refer to the types of laws enacted at the state and local level. We use the term "restrictive" or "restrictionist" to describe a range of policy positions, or persons advocating policy positions, geared toward greater immigration enforcement, increased state and local participation in that enforcement, decreased ability of unlawfully present persons to access public goods and benefits, and fewer discretionary possibilities to permit continued unlawful presence. In contrast, we use "integrationist" or sometimes "pro-immigrant" to refer to a range of policy positions, or persons advocating the same, aiming to provide fuller inclusion of immigrants, including undocumented immigrants, into American society and the polity, and favoring policies that would provide pathways to normalized legal status, access to public benefits, and the benefit of legal protections, such as anti-discrimination laws, at both the state and national level. And, as a general matter, we might expect integrationists to support more expansive national immigration policies, while restrictionists would generally favor limiting immigration or maintaining it at the status quo.

We should also clarify that it is not an aim of this book to present a judgment as to whether state and local participation in aspects of immigration policy is a good or bad development, or one that should be categorically heralded or decried. Instead we take subfederal presence in this regulatory field to be both a historical and practical reality. Starting from that point, we attempt to uncover the legal and political conditions that make such involvement possible and likely, and the consequences of the quality and quantity of that involvement for the future of immigration jurisprudence, law, and policy. To be sure, we argue in Chapter 6 that equality and nondiscrimination norms should play a greater role in assessments of both federal and subfederal immigration law. As such, we view certain restrictionist laws with greater skepticism than integrationist efforts.

## OVERVIEW OF THE BOOK

In this book, we seek answers to three central questions with respect to the recent flurry of state and local legislation on immigration. The first is a descriptive one: What are the kinds of laws that states have passed in this new period of immigration federalism? Next, what are the causes of this development, in terms of background factors and more proximate causes? And, finally, what are the consequences of these new developments in immigration federalism, particularly with respect to our understanding of the role of states and localities in our constitutional order? We seek answers to these questions by conducting a set of related inquiries, which we outline below.

In Chapter 2, we situate the current flurry of subfederal legislation in the larger historical context of immigration federalism in the United States, showing how Congress and the Supreme Court have played key roles in particular historical moments, to either permit or limit state involvement in regulating immigration. Thus, we take a step back to offer an abridged narrative of the political and legal development of immigration federalism in American history. The purpose of this review is to identify and describe the historical antecedents and doctrinal innovations in immigration federalism, and provide a basis against which we can evaluate the recent surge in subfederal involvement. This background seeks to clarify the constraints and possibilities – produced by an interplay of Congressional action and Court decisions – that were left open to states and localities as they embarked on a remarkable period of proliferation and variation, beginning around 2004.

Indeed, we make the case that this contemporary period represents a new, quickening phase in a larger period of immigration federalism, an era that is distinct from the first century of immigration law that was state-centric, and the second century of immigration law where the federal government became dominant. We argue that the era from 1965 onward constitutes a still-developing *third era of immigration federalism,* as courts began to grapple more seriously with questions of equal protection as it relates to immigration, and Congress waded more explicitly into defining what states can do with respect to regulating the welfare and livelihood of immigrants. We end this chapter with the period immediately preceding the September 11 attacks, discussing in detail California's Proposition 187, the predecessor to the several state and local restrictive efforts that dominated headlines over the past ten years.

Having provided this context and background, we then explain the various types of laws that states and localities have passed during this new period of immigration federalism. We first turn our attention to restrictive legislation in Chapters 3 and 4. In Chapter 3, we provide a description and classification of key types of laws at the state and local level that were dominant from 2004 through 2012. After establishing a descriptive sense of this new flurry of legislative activity (in essence, answering the question of "what" we are trying to explain), we examine the causes for this remarkable spike in state and local legislation on immigration, and ask why it was occurring in some places but not in others. In answering these questions, we critically evaluate the "demographic necessity" argument that was dominant in explaining why states and localities passed restrictive laws starting in 2004: This argument held that the combination of demographic pressures from new patterns of unauthorized migration, combined with federal inaction, created irresistible pressure for states and localities to act. As we detail in Chapter 3, we find this explanation to be seriously flawed, both theoretically and empirically.

After providing a thorough critique of the "demographic necessity" explanation, Chapter 4 offers our alternative explanation for why we have seen a flurry of restrictive activity in the past decade. This explanation, which we ground in a political process model that we call the Polarized Change model of immigration federalism, offers several advantages. Not only does our model hold up better empirically than does the conventional model, using both statistical and historical methods, it has the added virtue of explaining not only the rise of state and local policies but also the generation of a federal legislative stalemate, which is often cited as a cause for local action.

Our explanations of immigration federalism centered on politics rather than demographic change gains further credence when we consider the shifting policy momentum after 2012, as restrictive efforts at the state level became more rare and pro-immigrant integration efforts became more common. Thus, while the fundamental demographic realities of immigration settlement did not change appreciably after 2012, the political landscape certainly did as presidential candidate Mitt Romney's embrace of immigration "attrition through enforcement" led to spectacularly sharp losses among Latino voters. There were other political factors at play in the shift to more pro-immigrant legislation, which we detail in Chapter 5.

More broadly, Chapter 5 seeks to situate this integrationist trend within the Polarized Change Model of immigration federalism described in Chapter 4.

Consistent with that model, the shift toward more integrationist laws is also heavily influenced by a political process, with Democratic-leaning cities and states much more likely to pass such legislation. In addition, our data indicate that the size of the Latino electorate, and the immigrant electorate more broadly, makes it more likely that a jurisdiction will pass certain types of integrationist policies. Beyond these factors, the chapter argues that immigrant advocacy groups have adopted the kind of networked strategy of subfederal legislation previously seen among restrictioinist issue entrepreneurs. In an important contrast, however, the networked actors working on state-level integration have not worked against comprehensive immigration reform at the federal level, even when it has contained many enforcement provisions that they find unpalatable. Finally, during a time of congressional stalemate, the federal executive's actions on immigration enforcement have also pushed states and localities to reexamine their policies on cooperating with federal enforcement efforts and grapple with the effects of policies like the Obama Administration's 2012 Deferred Action for Childhood Arrivals (or DACA).

In Chapter 6, we pivot from answering the "what" and "why" questions of this new immigration federalism, to more fully considering its theoretical and legal implications. In the emerging legal study of immigration federalism, scholars and courts have struggled to determine how these recent state and local enactments fit into the kinds of legal doctrines typically used to assess such laws. Mainly, these assessments have centered on the propriety of state and local involvement in the subject area, given federalism debates between the virtues of decentralized policy experimentation versus the general notion that immigration regulation and enforcement are best left to the federal government alone. Our Polarized Change Model, however, suggests that policy proliferation in the immigration sphere is the product of a coordinated, networked system that is highly dependent on political factors. Recognizing the political underpinnings of these developments in immigration federalism may not undermine their usefulness or constitutionally. However, an accurate assessment of the new immigration federalism certainly conveys an image that is at odds with the hallowed view of federalism, as organic responses to local needs that are self-evident and driven by objective conditions.

Furthermore, we argue against the false equivalency of viewing anti-immigrant and pro-integration laws in the same light: the former often play on misperception and group stereotypes and explicitly call out particular groups for differential treatment. By contrast, many of the integrationist measures passed by state legislatures have couched their policies in universalistic terms, and often do not make reference to particular classes of persons. Thus, we argue that a legal framework grounded in racial

In the wake of these rulings, states were barred from financing their immigration systems with specific taxes on immigrants and transportation companies, leaving the continued existence of these state institutions to the general state fisc or the generosity of private charitable organizations interested in immigrant welfare and integration.[28] The resource strain on states and charitable organizations placed enormous pressure on Congress to enact federal law. In response, the federal government only began to develop its own capacity to deal with immigrants when it became clear that states were no longer willing to shoulder the financial burdens of doing so.[29] The combination of crucial factors – the end of slavery and southern political resistance, the striking down of taxation schemes that funded state and local migration control, and the increased political pressure and financial need for federal intervention – finally galvanized the federal government to assume primary responsibility over immigration.

### Ousting State Control over Immigration: Chy Lung v. Freeman

Just as the 1870s were an important period for shifting authority over ports of entry in the eastern seaboard, it was also a pivotal time for immigration federalism on the West Coast. In addition to the demise of slavery, and the striking down of state taxes on arriving immigrants, a few other important developments in the mid-to-late 1800s also informed the move in the American political order from state-centric to federal supremacy on immigration control. Even prior to the Civil War, the United States signed the Treaty of Guadalupe Hidalgo with Mexico in 1848, transferring portions of what was once Mexico to the United States, establishing the contours of the southern border of the United States, and conferring citizenship rights to about 80,000 Mexican nationals in those territories.[30] Meanwhile, the population of Asian, especially Chinese, laborers in the United States had steadily increased since the mid-century, with gold mining and work on railroads as the major economic drivers for this migration.[31] The federal government played a significant role in facilitating this migration through its treaty-making powers, although as we note below, pressure from states like California prompted Congress to pass legislation that curtailed this migration from China and, later, from other parts of Asia.

In the confluence of these legal, demographic, and economic forces, the Supreme Court began opining on the constitutional division of responsibility over immigration matters, firmly building the case for dominant, if not exclusive, federal control. In Table 2.1, we summarize the key Supreme Court cases with respect to immigration federalism, from those that ended the first

Table 2.1 *Significant Supreme Court immigration federalism cases (1875–1970)*

| Year | Case | Law at issue | Outcome |
|---|---|---|---|
| 1875 | Chy Lung v. Freeman | CA law requiring bond for certain arriving immigrants | CA law struck down |
| 1875 | Henderson v. Mayor of the City of New York | NY law requiring bond for arriving immigrants | NY law struck down |
| 1886 | Yick Wo v. Hopkins | San Francisco law regulating laundries | SF law struck down |
| 1889 | Chae Chan Ping v. United States | Federal Chinese Exclusion Act (exclusion provision) | Federal law upheld |
| 1893 | Fong Yue Ting v. United States | Federal Chinese Exclusion Act (deportation provision) | Federal law upheld |
| 1896 | Wong Wing v. United States | Federal Chinese Exclusion Act (punishment provision) | Federal law struck down |
| 1914 | Patsone v. Pennsylvania | PA law banning noncitizen hunting | PA law upheld |
| 1915 | Truax v. Raich | AZ law requiring businesses to hire mostly citizens | AZ law struck down |
| 1927 | Ohio v. Deckenbach | Cincinnati law barring noncitizens from operating billiard halls | Cincinnati law upheld |
| 1941 | Hines v. Davidowitz | PA alien registration law | PA law struck down |
| 1948 | Takahashi v. Fish and Game Commision | CA law denying commercial fishing licenses to noncitizens | CA law struck down |
| 1948 | Oyama v. California | CA Alien Land Law barring noncitizens from owning land | CA law struck down only as applied to U.S. citizen of Japanese dissent |

century of state-centric immigration laws to those in the second century of immigration federalism that established federal supremacy on "immigration law" pertaining to entry, exit, and enforcement, as well as the contours of state laws that regulated the lives of immigrants, or so-called "alienage law."

Even prior to the Supreme Court cases of the 1870s that galvanized some states to pressure Congress into covering the costs of immigration, a more basic anti-immigrant, anti-Chinese fervor from California also influenced the first federal forays into immigration restriction.[32] Starting in the 1850s, the importation of Chinese labor was critical to large companies that required cheap labor, but many others did not share that sentiment.[33] In attempts to combat this trend, the California legislature passed several laws attempting to deter, exclude, or raise money from the state's growing Chinese population.[34] These attempts were struck down by the state Supreme Court because they interfered with foreign commerce, an area reserved for Congress by the federal constitution.[35]

Despite the failure to succeed in judicial forums, California lawmakers and anti-Chinese interests pressed their case at the federal legislative level. Discussed in further detail below, their efforts against what they considered the debauchery of Chinese women made their way into the federal Page Act of 1875. And then, eventually, in 1882, the federal government passed its first laws restricting Chinese immigration, and imposed a federal tax on all arriving aliens to offset the costs to the states of maintaining their immigrant intake systems.

Distinctions between national and state preferences with regard to Chinese immigration became evident in the aftermath of a formal treaty between China and the United States. In 1868, the United States negotiated and signed the Burlingame Treaty with China to provide for the migration of Chinese laborers, who were necessary for construction of the transcontinental railroad, and reassured China that its citizens would not be discriminated against in the United States.[36] The 1868 Treaty was based on the following premise: "the inherent and inalienable right of man to change his home and allegiance, and also the mutual advantage of the free migration and emigration of their citizens and subjects, respectively for purposes of curiosity, trade, or as permanent residents."[37] It also purported to accord the citizens of China residing in the United States the same status and treatment "enjoyed by the citizens or subjects of the most favored nations." In fact, one of the purposes of the treaty was to reassure China about the safety and treatment of its citizens in the face of the rising tide of anti-Chinese state and local laws, particularly in California. Because of this apparent threat to discriminatory state laws, that language became hotly contested during Senate deliberations on the Treaty.[38]

Given the simmering anti-Chinese policy movement already afoot in California, the Burlingame Treaty galvanized significant backlash in the state, ranging from rioting and lynching, to legislative efforts to curb what many argued were the deleterious effects of Chinese migration on California's economy and society.[39] Indeed, partially in response to California's treatment of Chinese immigrants, Congress also passed the Civil Rights Act of 1870 (now codified at 42 U.S.C. § 1981) that, in one of it provisions, directed states to provide all "persons" the same protections as "white citizens" with regard to certain enumerated rights.[40]

Still, nativists in California would have their way. The state legislature, responding to a rising anti-Chinese fervor and displeasure with the 1868 Burlingame Treaty, passed a series of laws intended to oppose the federal invitation to Chinese immigration and to mitigate its effects. In 1870, the state passed an "anti-kidnapping and importation law" intended to prevent the immigration of Asian women, who were presumed to be prostitutes, immigrating and working against their will.[41] Accompanying the anti-kidnapping law, the state also passed an anti-coolie law intended to target Chinese male laborers.[42] Although the Burlingame Treaty provided for labor migration, this state law purported to address the issue of "coolie" labor, the name given to Asian migrants working under oppressive and coercive financial terms that resembled a form of indentured servitude. California then amended its anti-kidnapping law in 1874 to require a bond for immigrating passengers who were convicted criminals or presumed prostitutes.[43] All three enactments were attempts by the state to reassert control over its borders, as a means of addressing what it considered to be the detrimental effects of demographic and cultural change from migration.

Ultimately, the fate of California's foray into the regulation of Chinese immigrants reached the U.S. Supreme Court. The 1874 amendments to the anti-kidnapping law empowered the California State Commissioner on Immigration to exact a $500 bond from ship captains, for any foreign female deemed to be a lewd or debauched woman. Although it did not single out any class of persons, the state law was directed at Chinese female migrants, and ostensibly passed to curb prostitution in emerging Chinese communities in the state.[44] Under authority of the state law, the California Commissioner of Immigration boarded a ship at San Francisco harbor and found that twenty-two Chinese women on board (of the approximately 600 passengers, nearly all of them Chinese) were lewd, thereby barring their entry subject to the payment of the bond by the shipmaster. With the help of the local Chinese community and merchants, the women challenged the validity of the state law on the grounds that it violated the federal constitution. In *Chy Lung v. Freeman*, the Supreme Court agreed with the challengers, and struck down the law.[45]

The *Chy Lung* Court emphatically stated that control over the admission of foreigners into the country was exclusively a federal responsibility. In an oft-quoted passage, the Court declared:

> The passage of laws which concern the admission of citizens and subjects of foreign nationals to our shores belongs to Congress, and not to the states. It has the power to regulate commerce with foreign nations; the responsibility for the character of those regulations and for the manner of their execution

belongs solely to the national government. If it be otherwise, a single state can at her pleasure embroil us in disastrous quarrels with other nations.[46]

This language – emphasizing structural exclusivity, distinct spheres of regulatory authority, and foreign policy consequences – appeared to foreclose the possibility of any non-federal involvement in immigration. Similarly, the Court in *Henderson v. Mayor of the City of New York* struck down a state law that required shipmasters to either post a bond for every landed passenger, or to commute that bond by paying a fee for each passenger, stating "we are of opinion that this whole subject has been confided to Congress by the Constitution." For the most part, one particular aspect of the Court's opinion in both cases has held sway among courts and scholars alike, that the foreign policies of the national government could be jeopardized by the actions of particular states with respect to immigration.[47]

Less well recognized, however, are those aspects of the *Chy Lung* opinion that potentially left the door open for subfederal regulation. First, by its terms, the quoted language from the Court's opinion only referenced "laws which concern the admission" of immigrants; it therefore did not cover all laws that affect noncitizens, while still falling short of expressly barring their entry. On this reading, federal exclusivity governs entry and exit control, but all other aspects of immigrant-related policy remain contested ground between federal and subfederal authorities. The Court in *Chy Lung* never expanded on this possibility, as it resolved the case by determining that California had enacted a law governing admission. Nevertheless, this distinction between entry/exit regulations on the one hand, and other laws that affect immigrants, on the other – now sometimes referred to as the difference between "immigration law" and "alienage law" – remains important in modern judicial appraisals of state and local laws that affect immigrants.[48]

Second, and importantly, the Court followed its key passage on federal exclusivity with an intriguing paragraph that hypothesized conditions under which it may be constitutionally permissible for states to regulate immigration:

> We are not called upon by this statute to decide for or against the right of a state, in the absence of legislation by Congress, to protect herself by necessary and proper laws against paupers and convicted criminals from abroad, nor to lay down the definite limit of such right, if it exist[s]. Such a right can only arise from a vital necessity for its exercise, and cannot be carried beyond the scope of that necessity. When a state statute, limited to provisions necessary and appropriate to that object alone, shall, in proper controversy come before us, it will be time enough to decide that question.[49]

The Court voiced the same idea in *Henderson*, noting that it was not called upon in that case to decide what states could do to protect themselves from paupers, vagrants, and criminals in the absence of Congressional legislation.[50] In these passages, the Court appeared to leave open the possibility of state regulation – even regulation of entry and exit conditions – under the two preconditions: vital necessity and Congressional inaction. As one prominent commentator argued,[51] this possibility for state and local immigration regulation left open by *Chy Lung* has rarely, if ever, been explored because, since 1875, states have avoided enacting regulations that appear to be direct controls over entry and exit. Nevertheless, as we suggest in Chapters 3, 4, and 6, the rhetoric used by states and localities to justify their more recent restrictionist law, which highlights federal legislative failure and a host of public policy concerns occasioned by unauthorized immigrants, implicitly invokes this safe harbor intimated by *Chy Lung*.

Despite the legal ouster of states and localities from direct controls over immigration, as a matter of political reality, states and localities maintained a desire to influence migration, or at the very least, retain control over noncitizens living and working in their jurisdictions. Indeed, California's 1879 Constitution still provided that towns and cities had the right to expel Chinese.[52] Until 1906, state courts naturalized and conferred U.S. citizenship, and until the 1920s, states continued to impose quarantine and health measures, and some allowed noncitizens to vote.[53] Such possibilities, along with the types of regulations that may affect living and working conditions, were not squarely decided in *Chy Lung* or *Henderson*, and thus became contested legal ground in the aftermath of those cases, in the second century of immigration federalism.

### THE SECOND CENTURY OF IMMIGRATION FEDERALISM – FEDERAL PRIMACY AND THE DEVELOPMENT OF ALIENAGE LAW, 1875–1965

Following the first hundred years of the Republic, economic and political pressures created by a series of Supreme Court decisions virtually compelled federal assumption of immigration control. The process began with the Supreme Court striking down state attempts to finance their burgeoning migration control systems and California's attempt to deter Chinese immigration. Eventually, in the early 1880s, Congress adopted both taxes to finance immigration control and Chinese exclusion, mimicking prior state efforts. When the constitutionality of these and other federal enactments were tested, the Supreme Court established the now canonical principle of federal plenary power in immigration regulation.

Despite this transition from state-centric to federal immigration control, states and localities did not remain completely removed from all immigration matters. Instead, this era also witnessed the emergence of "alienage law" – state and local attempts to gain some control over immigration by regulating the everyday lives of immigrants, in areas of employment, property owner- ship, and enforcement. Attempting to decipher this form of state control, the Supreme Court began developing its alienage jurisprudence, a project that would mature in the subsequent era of immigration federalism.

Notably, during this era, the notion of illegal immigration did not conjure the same political and legal consequences that it would after 1965, and con- tinues to do so today. To be sure, several federal and state acts were concerned with the racial composition of immigrants and the exclusion of noncitizens from employment and other opportunities.[54] However, the admissions limi- tations and border policy of this era were largely focused on barring Asiatic migration.[55] The southern border of the United States was not militarized or guarded in the manner it would become in the late twentieth century, and seasonal, uncapped migration from Mexico was an accepted and expected labor reality. Nevertheless, the historical and political dynamics of this second century of immigration federalism, along with the legal doctrines developed in several litigated cases, formed the basis for the subsequent developments of the third era of immigration federalism, when notions of illegality and con- cern with Mexican labor migration became much more pronounced.

*Transitioning to Federal Plenary Authority over Immigration*

While anti-Chinese forces in California suffered a defeat in *Chy Lung*, their restrictionist impulses found expression in national legislation. In the same year *Chy Lung* was decided, Congress passed the Page Act of 1875, regulating the admission of immoral persons, essentially directed at the same Chinese women against whom the California laws were applied.[56] Still unsatisfied with the presence of Chinese, the state of California passed a new constitu- tion in 1879 with an entire Article devoted to Chinese exclusion, including a provision permitting localities to expel Chinese migrants.[57] Soon thereafter, the U.S. State Department renegotiated parts of the Burlingame to moderate Chinese migration in 1881, and Congress passed the Chinese Exclusion Act of 1882, which abrogated key provisions of the Burlingame Treaty. These actions by the federal government were seen as a response to the economic depres- sion of the 1870s, the glut of cheap Chinese labor following the completion of the transcontinental railroad, and political pressure from states (especially California). The Chinese Exclusion Act suspended immigration of Chinese laborers for ten years, and was subsequently amended and extended in 1888, 1892, and 1902, to include provisions allowing for the deportation of Chinese noncitizens and reauthorizing the suspension of Chinese immigration for a longer term of years.[58] These first major federal regulations of immigration substantially resembled California's efforts from 1870 to 1879, thereby achieving, in large measure, the goals of anti-Chinese activists and state laws of that time period, but with an important shift in immigration law to the federal government.

The 1870s and 1880s were also a time during which states with major ports of entry such as New York, Massachusetts, and Louisiana were feeling the financial strain of the U.S. Supreme Court's banning of state taxes and bonds on arriving aliens in its *Henderson* and *Chy Lung* decisions. Thus, along with the Chinese Exclusion Act, the 1882 Congress also enacted a federal tax on immigrants so that the revenues could be used to help maintain existing state systems.[59]

Yet, even as federal immigration regulation emerged in the early 1880s, the national government still borrowed from, and relied on, existing state infrastructure in the actual conduct of immigration enforcement. The 1882 federal immigration laws kept the state systems intact, with Congress relying on state commissioners of immigration to continue their screening and information-collecting duties.[60] It would take almost another decade, with Congress's 1891 Immigration Act, for the federal government to create its own immigration bureaucracy and system for handling immigration.[61] Even as the federal immigration apparatus began to formalize and institutionalize, the federal regulations and those in charge of implementing federal regulations continued to reflect state policies and approaches.[62] Indeed, many of the state officials who created and ran robust state immigration agencies in New York and Massachusetts were recruited into the federal immigration bureaucracy and helped mold the development of federal policy.[63]

Apart from this influence of state actors through participation in federal institutions, the eventual federal assumption of immigration regulation and administration would not mean the complete cessation of state and local policies that affected immigrant lives, and – at least indirectly – influenced migration patterns. What is clear, however, is that in its modified iterations, state-level policy and infrastructure after 1880 would never again reflect the robust and explicit entry and exit controls of the first century of migration regulation. The development of state and local laws to which the remainder of this chapter now turns became much more focused on interventions with indirect, but significant, effects on the movement and residency of noncitizens, such as regulations of employment, property ownership, alien registration, and access to benefits and privileges.

From this formative and transitional period, several key themes and patterns were established that would find echoes in more recent federal and state regulatory systems. First, in the period from 1882 to 1891, federal law governed supreme, but the federal government still relied on state administration and infrastructure for the execution of its policies. Second, in the mid-1800s state laws attempted to utilize private parties (such as steamship companies and shipmasters) to help enforce their regulations, by placing financial burdens on those private parties to defray the costs of inspection and integration, and to cover the costs of immigrants who had the potential to become public charges. Third, state-level policy in the era of transition – either in the form of anti-Chinese laws in California or pauperism concerns and inspections in northeastern states – profoundly affected national policies and the development of federal law. Finally, the subfederal officials were able to influence the development of federal immigration policy through participation in political and institutional structures inherent in our federalist system. We will return to the modern iterations of these themes in detail in the chapters that follow; for now, we simply note that these modes continue to persist in the new immigration federalism, albeit in different forms.

### *The Court Enshrines the Principle of Plenary Federal Immigration Power*

The initial federal forays into immigration regulation in the last decades of the nineteenth century would also make their way into federal court, as immigrants from China began challenging Congress's exclusionary legislation. The constitutionality of various parts of the Chinese Exclusion Act was tested in three seminal immigration law cases: *Chae Chan Ping v. United States* (1889),[64] *Fong Yue Ting v. United States* (1893),[65] and *Wong Wing v. United States* (1896).[66] None of these cases dealt specifically with the relationship between federal and subfederal authority. However, in the wake of the nearly exclusive state control over immigration policy until the 1880s, the Court's thoughts on federal power and its limitations had, and continues to have, a correlative influence on the development of immigration federalism jurisprudence. The first two of these cases firmly established plenary federal control over immigration matters, a principle that continues to animate modern appraisals of both federal and subfederal immigration law. The third case hints at the constitutional limits of both federal and subfederal authority over immigrants in matters beyond entry and exit.

*Chae Chan Ping* challenged Congress's authority to enact a law that barred admission of an entire class of putative immigrants, with the challenger arguing the Constitution did not confer such a power to Congress. The Court disagreed, declaring that the Constitution provided for federal immigration control, describing such control as absolute, exclusive, and beyond judicial review. Using this constitutional power then, the Court found nothing wrong with Congress's decision to bar Chinese immigration, even if it meant excluding individuals who had previously been lawfully admitted. Notably, unlike prior cases, such as *Passenger Cases* or *Henderson*, both of which interpreted the federal power over immigration to stem from the Constitution's grant of authority over foreign commerce to Congress, *Chae Chan Ping* grounded federal immigration authority in the naturalization clause and in what the Court understood as the inherent right of sovereign nations.[67] This shift away from conceptualizing immigration only as a function or subset of commerce, to thinking of it as a federal sovereign function concerned with political sensitivities, foreign relations, and a singular national perspective would significantly influence future state and local interventions to the extent those subfederal enactments could fairly be characterized as undermining those concerns. Further, it allowed for consideration of federal exclusivity or primacy in matters beyond taxation, bonding, or other commercial regulation.

The second case, *Fong Yue Ting*, addressed the deportation provisions of the Chinese Exclusion Act. The provision at issue allowed deportation of Chinese immigrants, even long-term residents, if they could not provide a "credible white witness" to attest to their bona fides as a resident. Similar to *Chae Chan Ping*, the Court approved Congress's authority to provide for the deportation of those it considered unfit to remain, and reified the components of federal immigration power articulated in *Chae*. Put simply, the federal government, as the exclusive and absolute source of immigration power could prescribe virtually any rule for deportation – even expressly racial and retrospective requirements – and such rules were beyond judicial reproach.

In contrast, *Wong Wing* was the only case in this era, and one of only a rare few ever, to reject an exercise of federal immigration power.[68] There, the Court struck down provisions of the Chinese Exclusion Act that permitted federal officials to subject deportable aliens to imprisonment and hard labor prior to their removal. Thus, while *Chae* and *Fong* established that Congress's constitutional power to prescribe rules for entry and exit were beyond judicial reproach, the Court rejected the notion that all exercises of federal power transcended all constitutional limitations. Specifically, the Court ruled that federal officials could not impose penal consequences as part of deportation proceedings, even if Congress could prescribe almost any standard for deportation.[69]

Thus, Wong Wing stands for the proposition that the Constitution can constrain certain types of governmental control over immigrants. Even so, the case's effect should not be overstated. Overall, the jurisprudence of the era chiefly solidified the ascendance and primacy of federal power. Indeed, relying on these foundational cases, Congress has discriminated in immigration policy on the basis of race, gender, marital status and legitimacy, as well as establishing different speech and associational rights for noncitizens, and curtailing their due process rights in immigration matters.[70]

Together, these cases began to establish the scope and limits of the federal plenary power of immigration, and remain the seminal, controlling opinions in immigration cases. They also help us understand why immigration is often perceived or presented as "exceptional" in constitutional jurisprudence, and how that exceptionality sometimes carries over into judicial and political discourse about the proper role of states and localities in immigration enforcement and immigrant regulation.[71] Although plenary federal immigration power, established in *Chae* and *Fong*, and the structural exclusivity, as discussed in *Chy Lung* and *Henderson*, are conceptually distinct concepts, they are borne of the same constitutional logic, and are often described as corollaries to each other.[72] Together then, the suite of cases interprets a federal immigration authority from several provisions of the Constitution and the nature of national sovereignty, and establishes that the political nature of that authority axiomatically excludes individual states from sharing that authority.

Yick Wo, *and the Distinction between Immigration Law and Alienage Law*

Contemporaneous with this rise in federal power to inaugurate the second century of immigration federalism, the Court also began to clarify the limits of states' and localities' authority to continue regulating the lives of noncitizens and local discrimination against noncitizens. In comparison to state laws applied at the moment of admission, the state and local laws finding their way to federal court regulated immigrants already within the jurisdiction, in terms of their residence or their employment. In this then-emerging policymaking, the application of domestic constitutional norms – like the Court applied to the federal government in *Wong Wing* – took on greater significance.

In *Yick Wo v. Hopkins*, the first such case to squarely present the question of discrimination against Chinese, the court struck down a San Francisco ordinance regulating laundry establishments in the city.[73] Interestingly, the ordinance itself was neutrally worded; in other words, it made no mention of race, citizenship status, or national origin. But, prior to its final version, earlier versions of the laundry ordinance had specifically referenced "Chinese" laundries, and it was written in response to angry protests against the growing Chinese presence in the city. The Board of Supervisors struck that reference during deliberations.[74]

Despite the neutral wording of the enacted ordinance, the court found that because the ordinance was created and administered to target Chinese-owned laundries, it violated the equal protection guarantees of the Fourteenth Amendment. As the Court famously wrote:

> Though the law itself be fair on its face and impartial in its appearance, yet, if it is applied and administered by public authority with an evil eye and an unequal hand, so as practically to make unjust and illegal discriminations between persons in similar circumstances, material to their rights, the denial of equal justice is still within the prohibition of the Constitution.

This result and reasoning are significant for several reasons. It was one of the first cases (along with *Chy Lung* and *Wong Wing*) to recognize that under certain conditions, noncitizens can successfully litigate constitutional claims against any level of government. Moreover, the opinion's reliance on the equal protection clause invoked a trope that persists to this day (and that we elaborate on both later in this chapter and in Chapter 6): subfederal immigration laws carry significant risk of unequal treatment along ethnic, racial, and national origin lines, and thus may require application of the Constitution's equal protection guarantee. Finally, the case reveals the substantial gap between federal and subfederal powers vis-à-vis immigrants and provides a striking contrast to *Chae* and *Fong*. Whereas the Court allowed the federal government to expressly discriminate against a specific racial group in its admissions and deportation decisions, it did not permit a city to take action against that same group. This was true even though the city's action was ostensibly undertaken with the same intent and goal as the federal Chinese Exclusion Act itself.

The difference between *Chae* and *Fong*, on the one hand, and *Chy Lung* and *Yick Wo*, on the other, laid the foundation for a distinction that continues to frame immigration federalism analysis. In matters of pure immigration regulation, the federal government enjoys exclusive power, and states may not create their own entry and exit regulations. This principle animated the *Chy Lung* decision. In matters beyond defining the terms and conditions of exit and entry – in the regulation of the everyday lives of noncitizens – the federal government, for the most part, still enjoys broad legislative authority; however, it is not exclusive as it is in the context of pure immigration law. In this other constitutional space known as "alienage law," states and localities are sometimes permitted to legislate in ways that discriminate against noncitizens and regulates their daily lives, provided that such subfederal legislation does not

decided) and 1886 (the year *Yick Wo* was decided), many states attempted several types of restrictions: 1) to curtail the professions that noncitizens could engage in, 2) to limit the accessibility of local and state licenses and permits, 3) to limit access to public benefits, and 4) to bar ownership of real property.[84] Occupational restrictions on noncitizens spanned several fields, including architecture, law, accountancy, dentistry, and medicine, as well as other economic activity such as insurance sales, sanitation work, liquor sales, barbers, taxi and bus drivers, pawn shop ownership, plumbing, and others.[85] The state of New York, for example, consistently added citizenship requirements for several professions, from 1871 to 1976.[86] Importantly, during this time, the concept of "illegal alien" or unlawful presence did not have the same salience it would have after 1965, and clearly not the legal and political significance it has in present day. Thus state and local laws during this era generally were not concerned with the regulation of unauthorized migration and unauthorized work.

In dealing with these several state and local restrictions, the Supreme Court incrementally meandered its way to the immigration federalism doctrines in use today. These cases provide useful historical backdrop but also showcase the variety of claims that had already been tested in courts prior to our current era of immigration federalism. In addition, these cases helped develop the two legal doctrines that have primarily been used to litigate modern immigration federalism cases – equal protection and preemption. And, most importantly, most of the cases intermingled structural power concepts with anti-discrimination concerns, laying the foundation for an equality-based jurisprudence we suggest in Chapter 6.

Characteristic of these decisions are two different doctrinal elisions. First, courts sometimes elided the difference between structural preemption (federal exclusivity) and statutory preemption, often not clearly categorizing state and local efforts as either "immigration" or "alienage" law. Second, even within cases clearly treated as alienage law, courts sometimes elided preemption and equal protection arguments. At times, the Court used both at the same time; in others, the Court purported to use equal protection while relying on structural preemption principles. A prominent example of the latter is *Yick Wo* itself, where the Court, in finding discrimination, cited the paradigmatic structural preemption decision – *Chy Lung* – as its authority for doing so.

The confusion and mingling of these various doctrines uniquely muddles immigration and alienage law, making decisions in the immigration federalism area especially difficult to predict. But, it also suggests that with regard to immigrants, the two conceptually distinct legal doctrines are practically inseparable, and that hard categorical boundaries between federal and state authority are difficult to maintain in practice. As we will argue in Chapter 6, this comingling of doctrines hinted at in these early cases lays the foundation for invoking anti-discrimination norms in contemporary assessments of state and local immigration law, and provides a basis for distinguishing restrictionist laws from integrationist ones.

Equivocation from the Court's decision in *Yick Wo* began soon after that case was decided. This led to a patchwork of judicial decisions on state and local laws that affected noncitizens. In *Patsone v. Pennsylvania* (1914) the Supreme Court upheld a state law barring aliens from hunting wild game against an equal protection challenge by immigrants.[87] And, at that time, state courts were upholding state and local laws that barred noncitizens from economic opportunities and jobs.[88]

Despite this general acquiescence to state discrimination on the basis of citizenship, in *Truax v. Raich* (1915), the Supreme Court struck down an Arizona law that mandated that businesses hire native-born citizens to fill at least 80 percent of their workforce.[89] Ostensibly, the Court did so because it understood the regulation to run afoul of the Fourteenth Amendment's equal protection clause, citing *Yick Wo* as authority. Yet, the Court also suggested that the law was also structurally and statutorily preempted:

> The authority to control immigration – to admit or exclude aliens – is vested solely in the Federal Government. [*citing Fong Yue Ting*] The assertion of an *authority to deny to aliens the opportunity of earning a livelihood when lawfully admitted to the State would be tantamount to the assertion of the right to deny them entrance and abode* for, in ordinary cases, they cannot live where they cannot work. And, if such a policy were permissible, the practical result would be that those lawfully admitted to the country under the authority of the acts of Congress, instead of enjoying in a substantial sense and in their full scope the privileges conferred by the admission, would be segregated in such of the States as chose to offer hospitality.[90]

The same type of mingling between alienage doctrines was also evident between the majority and concurring opinions in *Takahashi v. Fish and Game Commission*, a 1948 case that struck down a state law discriminating against noncitizens. *Takahashi* voided a 1943 California amendment to its fish and game policies that denied commercial fishing licenses to "aliens ineligible for citizenship," a phrase that, at that time, operated as a clinical shorthand for Japanese and Chinese noncitizens.[91] The Court rejected the state's argument that it was preserving scarce natural resources for citizens, invalidating the law because it burdened noncitizens whom the federal government had seen fit to admit. The majority objected to the California law denying lawfully present noncitizens the ability to pursue a livelihood, because, the court understood such a denial as too great an imposition on their ability to work, and therefore to live in the state. Interestingly, the majority also rejected the state's argument that its exclusion of Asian noncitizens from fishing licenses was constitutional because they mirrored federal racial exclusions. As the court stated, "It does not follow … that because the United States regulates immigration and naturalization in part on the basis of race and color classifications, a state can adopt one or more of the same classifications to prevent lawfully admitted aliens within its borders from earning a living in the same way as other state inhabitants." In comparison, the concurring opinion of two justices specifically focused on the racialized nature of the prohibition, opining that the law clearly intended to discriminate against Japanese residents, and was consequently a violation of the equal protection clause.[92]

Between the times *Truax* and *Takahashi* were decided, the Court issued its most significant alienage decision of the mid-twentieth century when it struck down Pennsylvania's alien registration scheme in *Hines v. Davidowitz* (1941) on statutory preemption grounds. That 1939 state law imposed penalties on noncitizens for failing to register with the state and carry documentation in accordance with state regulations.[93] The Court noted in the opinion's footnotes that other jurisdictions, including North and South Carolina as well several municipalities, had enacted similar alien registration laws.[94] Moreover, the Court noted that the California Supreme Court in 1894 and a federal district court in 1931 had previously struck down alien registration laws.[95] Significantly, both of those prior cases were based on the same structural exclusivity reasoning as *Chy Lung*, holding that the state laws had usurped the constitutional authority of the federal government.[96]

Despite favorably citing these prior cases, the *Hines* Court conspicuously avoided both the question whether the state registration law violated the principle of federal structural exclusivity (invalid under *Chy Lung's* reasoning) and the question whether it should be understood as discriminating against a vulnerable group (invalid under *Yick Wo's* equal protection standard).[97] Instead, the Court focused on Congress's enactment in 1940 of a federal alien registration system, a law that came into effect after Pennsylvania's law and the initiation of the lawsuit. Adopting familiar statutory preemption principles, the Court opined that the newly created federal alien registration scheme occupied the entire field of alien registration, and left no room for concurrent state regulation. Like the California Supreme Court fifty years prior in *Ah Cue*, the U.S. Supreme Court curtailed this exercise of state power in spite of the apparent similarities between the goals and methods of federal and state schemes.

Hines stands apart from the other decisions of the era as it is still cited with approval in present day cases – like Arizona v. United States – involving state and local enforcement schemes. But similar to Yick Wo, Truax, and Takahashi, Hines also mingled anti-discrimination ideas into its discussion of federalism. To be sure, the Court conspicuously chose not to decide whether the state statute violated the federal Civil Rights Act, the constitution's equal protection clause, or principles of structural exclusivity from Chy Lung. Yet, despite the Court's purported avoidance of anti-discrimination law, much of the opinion focuses on the potential harm of harassment and personal liberty violations by states applying their own registration systems. Noting that Congress had rejected earlier registration proposals before adopting its 1940 scheme, the Court stated:

> The legislative history of the Act indicates that Congress was trying to steer a middle path, realizing that any registration requirement was a departure from our traditional policy of not treating aliens as a thing apart.... When [Congress provided a standard for alien registration] ... it plainly manifested a purpose to do so in such a way as to protect the personal liberties of law-abiding aliens through one uniform national registrations system, and to leave them free from the possibility of inquisitorial practices and police surveillance that might not only affect our international relations, but might also generate the very disloyalty which the law has intended guarding against.[98]

Thus, again, like its predecessor opinions, Hines evinced a meshing of alienage jurisprudence's dual preoccupations – a concern with the interaction with federal law and policy, on the one hand, and a concern with discriminatory intention and effects, on the other – that continued the doctrinal tension from prior cases and presaged the continued equivocation in the subsequent era of immigration federalism.

Against the trend of immigrant-friendly outcomes in many of the alienage cases of the 1900s, the Court's 1948 decision in Oyama v California allowed states to keep in place their decades-old restrictions on land ownership and use directed at Asian immigrants.[99] Alien land laws in California and Washington, along with eight other states, prevented certain immigrants from property ownership. Such laws were openly nativist and discriminatory, enacted for the express purpose of limiting land ownership by an undesirable group of aliens with the idea that denying them property rights would diminish their desire to immigrate, or, if already admitted, their desire to remain.[100] The California laws prohibition on ownership by "aliens ineligible for American citizenship" was designed specifically to prevent Japanese noncitizen land ownership. At that time, as per the Immigration and Naturalization Act,

Japanese immigrants could not naturalize, and thus were "aliens ineligible for American citizenship."

Although these laws survived constitutional analysis for the first several decades of the twentieth century,[101] in 1948 *Oyama v. California* struck down a portion of the law as violation of the equal protection.[102] The Court's reasoning in the case, however, turned on the specific characteristics of the plaintiff in that case: Oyama was an American-born U.S. citizen of Japanese descent, who was suing to vindicate his rights to inherit property as a citizen. As such, even though *Oyama* mitigated some of the harsh effects of the alien land laws, it did not comment directly on the equal protection rights of noncitizens. It was only later, when state supreme courts struck down the bans on alien land ownership that the alien land laws finally became unenforceable.[103] Nevertheless, the case demonstrated the potential for state and local immigration laws to significantly affect the rights of citizens, a motif that persists through present day: laws ostensibly directed at undocumented immigrants inevitably affect the treatment of lawfully present immigrants and citizens who share the ethnic, racial, or national origin characteristics of undocumented immigrants.

In sum, by the 1950s and 1960s, alienage jurisprudence was beginning to take shape, but the resulting case law provided little clarity as to the scope of state and local authority over the lives of immigrants. Moreover, the cases rarely dealt with the concerns of unauthorized migrants, as the concept and concerns with unlawful migration were not as salient during this era as they would later become. Nevertheless, the cases reveal the Court's struggle to contend with the implications of federal plenary authority over immigration established in the late 1800s against claims to traditional exercises of state police power to regulate the lives of those within their jurisdictions. Mingled with this struggle to deal with the implications of exclusive federal control over the terms of entry and exit from the country, were the Court's initial attempts at applying the equal protection guarantees of the Fourteenth Amendment to noncitizens.

### Bracero Program and the Waning of Federal Exclusivity

Beyond jurisprudential developments, states interacted with the other branches of the federal government in immigration policy matters as well. From 1942 through 1964, the interaction between the states and the federal executive branch were critical in the inception and development of the Bracero Program, a system of seasonal Mexican labor migration operated by the U.S. government. As early as 1940, farming and agricultural interests in California, Texas, and Arizona requested that the federal Immigration Service allow them to bring in Mexican labor.[104] These requests were denied, but by 1942 the urgency of the labor needs and shortages convinced President Truman to negotiate a bilateral agreement with Mexico to provide for seasonal migration of "braceros." The program grew from fewer than a 100,000 workers per year in the 1940s to more than 400,000 per year in the 1950s, before dropping to about 200,000 per year until Congress terminated the program in 1964.[105]

The Bracero program and its demise are significant for immigration federalism because (1) it set networks and processes of migration into motion that continued well beyond its lifespan, and (2) the state-level responses to the program showcased some early efforts by states and localities to promote immigrant integration. Importantly, braceros did not evenly spread through the country; instead, migrant workers concentrated in California, Texas, and Arizona, states that required significant agricultural labor,[106] and continue to be primary players in immigration federalism debates. In total, over the span of twenty-two years, the program processed more than 4 million workers, and in doing so, set the expectations of both the laborers and their putative U.S. employers regarding the availability of this labor stream.

Furthermore, the Program elicited some notable subfederal responses, as some states strove to address several concerns associated with mass, cyclical labor migration, especially one that was racially identifiable. Mexico initially banned the state of Texas as a bracero destination due to the state's history of discrimination against Mexican nationals. The federal government's decision to continue with the Program, despite this condition, forced Texas to adopt more immigrant-friendly and immigrant-protective policies. The state passed resolutions affirming the equal treatment of Mexicans, state officials went on a "good will" tour of Mexico to assure Mexican officials that Texas would address cases of discrimination, and the Texas Governor convened a Good Neighbor Commission to study and remedy those concerns.[107]

Beyond policy changes in Texas during this period, several other states took official action to deal with the increased presence of migrant laborers, both foreign (as through the Bracero Program) and domestic (as domestic workers began seeking work in non-bracero states).[108] States and localities were forced to confront the everyday concerns of laborers such as housing, healthcare, and education. For example, Colorado in 1953 enacted its Migrant Children Education Act, intended "to facilitate the education of migrant children," and Wisconsin enacted a law intended to license and monitor migrant labor camps. Indeed, the U.S. Department of Labor's 1964 publication "*Welcome Stranger! Goodbye Friend!: A Guide to Community Efforts to Improve Conditions for Agricultural Migrants*" listed the various state and local community-based efforts at integrating or at least ameliorating living conditions for this migratory labor supply. Specifically, the guidebook highlights the creation of state committees on migratory labor in twenty-eight states, created for the purpose of coordinating programs such as summer school, health programs, and integration programs.

This negotiation between federal and subfederal power, often mediated by the Supreme Court, and state legislative responses to increased migration, continued after the 1960s. However, the significant judicial and legislative movements that took place by the mid-to-late 1960s, altered the landscape of state and local lawmaking sufficiently to mark a distinct, new era of immigration federalism.

THE THIRD ERA OF IMMIGRATION FEDERALISM 1965–PRESENT

Unlike the dramatic shift between the first and second centuries of immigration federalism, wherein the states quickly receded from primary immigration regulators to secondary players, the shift from the second to the third era of immigration federalism was mainly marked by changes within the federal regulatory structure. Nevertheless, these changes significantly altered the demographics and nature of lawful and unauthorized migration. Combined with evolutions in the judicial doctrines, these shifts in migration policy and population wrought changes in state-level responses, and set the stage for our current phase of the new immigration federalism.

In addition, as we detail later, the Court in this third era continued its evolution of the immigration doctrines developed in the early and mid-twentieth century. But, it was also influenced by important constitutional developments outside of immigration law as well. The Court seemed inclined in the 1970s to apply equal protection jurisprudence to state laws that discriminated against recently arrived immigrants. In reaction to this development, several states began to remove such restrictions on legal immigrants. At the same time, the Court let stand state restrictions on the employment of unauthorized immigrants, signaling the limits to its equal protection approach.

The persistence of state immigration regulations, in turn, prompted Congress to enter more explicitly into the realm of controlling and specifying what states could do with respect to immigrants, authorized and unauthorized alike. Indeed, we start our description of this era with the cases of *Graham v. Richardson* (1971) and *De Canas v. Bica* (1976) because those rulings – the first striking down state welfare restrictions on noncitizens, and the second upholding state penalties for hiring unauthorized workers – led to Congress directly addressing those federalism concerns in federal law. These

**Table 2.2** *Significant Supreme Court immigration federalism cases (1971–1995)*

| Year | Case | Law at issue | Outcome |
|------|------|-------------|---------|
| 1971 | *Graham v. Richardson* | AZ and PA laws denying public benefits to certain noncitizens | State laws struck down |
| 1973 | *Sugarman v. Dougall* | NY law barring noncitizens from civil service positions | NY law struck down |
| 1976 | *De Canas v. Bica* | CA law penalizing employers for hiring unauthorized workers | CA law upheld |
| 1976 | *Mathews v. Diaz* | Federal law denying Medicare benefits to certain noncitizens | Federal law upheld |
| 1978 | *Foley v. Connelie* | NY law barring noncitizens from becoming state troopers | NY law upheld |
| 1982 | *Plyler v. Doe* | TX law allowing state to not fund public education for undocumented children | TX law struck down |
| 1982 | *Toll v. Moreno* | MD University policy denying in-state status to nonimmigrants | MD Univ. policy struck down |
| 1995 | *LULAC v. Wilson*[a] | CA Proposition 187 denying benefits to, and increasing enforcement against, undocumented immigrants | CA law struck down; case settled before appeal to higher federal courts |

Note: [a] LULAC v. Wilson was struck down in Federal District Court, and California opted not to appeal the decision.

interconnected developments – of Court decisions and congressional action – established the possibilities and constraints that states faced with respect to immigration regulation. In Tables 2.2 and 2.3, we provide a summary reference to the significant Court decisions and acts of Congress that shaped the third era of immigration federalism.

### Political Antecedents of the Third Era

Two important events of the 1960s ushered in the third era of immigration federalism. In 1952 and in 1965, Congress comprehensively overhauled federal

**Table 2.3** *Significant federal immigration statutes (1952–2005)*

| Year | Law | Major provisions |
|------|-----|------------------|
| 1952 | Immigration and Nationality Act | Abolished racial bars to immigration and naturalization; token number of Japanese and Chinese immigration allowed. |
| 1965 | Amendments to the Immigration and Nationality Act of 1952 | Abolished national origins quota system established in 1920s; replaced it with visa allocations based on family unity and attracting skilled labor; established first numerical limitation on Western Hemisphere migration, including migration from Mexico. |
| 1986 | Immigration Reform and Control Act | Provided legalization path for many undocumented persons and instituted sanctions for employers hiring unauthorized workers. |
| 1996 | Personal Responsibility and Work Opportunity Reconciliation Act | Determined qualified noncitizens eligible for federal and state public benefits, denied undocumented persons most forms of public assistance, and devolved to states, decisions regarding the provision of state public benefits to nonqualified noncitizens. |
| 1996 | Illegal Immigration Reform and Immigrant Responsibility Act | Significant federal immigration overhaul including provisions to enhance border and interior enforcement, changing procedures for removing noncitizens, instituting new and expanded grounds for removal, and providing new rules on state provision of public benefits and educational assistance; also includes provisions for state and local participation in certain types of immigration enforcement and provisions for starting pilot employee verification program that would become E-Verify. |
| 2005 | REAL ID Act | Created national standards for state-issued licenses and identification cards, including limitations on the immigration statuses for which federally valid licenses and identification cards could be issued. |

immigration statutes, creating the Immigration and Naturalization Act that, in substantial part, still governs immigration law today. Second, the federal government discontinued the Bracero Program that had been in operation from 1942 to 1964, and in a significant turnabout, implemented numerical limitations on migration from the western hemisphere, including Mexico.

Congress enacted major immigration legislation in the 1950s and 1960s, giving courts greater guidance on the scope of federal regulatory interests. These immigration and naturalization changes were part of the broader civil rights revolution of the 1960s, culminating not only in the 1965 amendments to the INA, but also the 1964 Civil Rights and 1965 Voting Rights Acts.[109] The 1952 Immigration and Nationality Act (INA), and its comprehensive retooling in the 1965 amendments to the INA fundamentally overhauled the U.S. immigration system, and eliminated explicit racial barriers to immigration and naturalization.[110] In eliminating those discriminatory aspects of immigration policy, however, Congress instituted per-country limitations on every migrant-sending country. These caps, while "equal" in the sense that they formally treat all immigrants the same, had profoundly disparate effects on countries of high migration to the United States. Most notably, the amendments to the INA imposed, for the first time, limits on legal migration from Mexico. These limitations on Mexican migration were especially drastic as they followed on the heels of the dismantling of the Bracero Program that, in the early 1960s, was still bringing in close to 200,000 Mexican nationals per year.[111] Congress's decision to discontinue the program in anticipation of the 1965 INA amendments disrupted a system on which both U.S. employers and Mexican laborers and their dependents had grown to rely.

In short, these dramatic shifts in federal policy caused a marked change in the demographics, meaning, and political and legal importance of unlawful migration. Practically, these legislative changes also changed the face of immigration discourse and debate, adding a different racial flavor to the state and local enactments that followed. One of the major consequences of the 1965 amendments to federal law was a significant increase in lawful migration from Asia, with a concurrent limitation on lawful migration from Mexico and Central America. This limitation created a new and fast-growing problem of the "illegal immigrant," as employers continued to rely on migrant labor as they had done for the prior two decades, only this time without legal work permits. This, in turn, helped launch the third era of immigration federalism, as several states passed laws on employer sanctions and public benefits in the 1970s, followed by major Court decisions and congressional responses, including the major immigration laws of 1986 and 1996. Importantly, these federal interventions specifically acknowledged the presence and potential of state involvement in alienage regulation and immigration enforcement, thereby setting the stage for the reinvigoration of state and local policies in the early twenty-first century.

*Doctrinal Developments in the Third Era of Immigration Federalism*

By the time federal courts began assessing state and local laws related to immigrants or immigration in the 1970s, the legislative and demographic ground had shifted from the prior eras. Immigration flows and backlogs took on different racialized characteristics, a major legal seasonal worker program was dismantled, and the overarching federal legal overhaul had capped migration from large immigrant sending countries, especially Mexico. The idea and presence of unlawful migrants and unauthorized workers began to take on political and legal salience in ways that were markedly different than before. Courts began hearing cases about long-standing prohibitions on immigrants that were newly challenged given evolving jurisprudence, and were confronted with new state enactments responding to the increasing presence of immigrants generally, the racial characteristics of that immigration, and the increased undocumented migration flows after 1965.

Doctrinally by the 1970s, courts confronted with immigration federalism cases had a more robust equal protection to draw from in determining the constitutionality of state and local immigration regulation. The Court had transformed equal protection jurisprudence with its *Brown v. Board of Education* decision in 1954, holding racial segregation in public schools unconstitutional, and providing the legal interpretation necessary to use the Fourteenth Amendment to challenge state and federal laws that discriminated against particular groups. Following *Brown*, the Court addressed racial and gender discrimination in a variety of contexts, and, in doing so, articulated the concept of "suspect" classifications by states that triggered heightened judicial inquiry.

This rebirth of the equal protection clause appears to have influenced immigration federalism cases as well, as the Court applied the doctrine in a different manner than it did in the prior era. This was evident in *Graham v. Richardson* in 1971, and its progeny, as modern alienage law and appraisals of immigration federalism began to take shape. In a seemingly major victory for immigrants, the *Graham* court invalidated welfare schemes in Pennsylvania and Arizona that barred recently immigrated lawful permanent residents from accessing public benefits. The result signaled a different judicial outlook for these types of restrictions, as compared to the prior era of regulation.

Prior to *Graham*, most state and local restrictions on noncitizen employment and participation in economic activities restrictions survived judicial scrutiny.[112] By 1971, however, the doctrinal ground had shifted, and *Graham* began a trend in the other direction. As other scholars have shown, after

*Graham,* several other decisions and opinions from State Attorneys General led to significant decline in these forms of alienage discrimination.[113]

*Graham,* however, also generated significant doctrinal confusion. Justice Blackmun's opinion forcefully articulated both constitutional bases – preemption and equal protection – for striking down the law. Unlike cases from the prior era like *Truax, Takahashi* and *Hines,* that muddled structural power talk and rhetoric about civil liberties and discrimination, *Graham* was clear in its reliance on both types of claims. On the equal protection claim, the Court treated the legal permanent resident challengers as a discrete and insular minority requiring heightened judicial scrutiny by the Court. On the preemption claim, the Court found that the welfare restrictions tended to influence migration decisions, and therefore impermissibly intruded into a statutory field occupied by the federal government.

While this double-barreled assault on the state welfare restrictions added rhetorical heft to the decision, the opinion failed to reveal how the different provisions worked with each other, or which one should be given priority in judicial analysis of state and local alienage law. Regardless, with its impassioned language in *Graham,* the Supreme Court seemed poised to shut the door on state authority to discriminate against immigrants. However, just a few years after *Graham,* the Supreme Court ruled in ways that limited the case's potential impact.

In *De Canas v. Bica* (1976), the court left in place a 1971 California law that penalized employers for hiring unauthorized workers. California's effort, similar to ten other states and a city,[114] was passed in the context of increasing undocumented migration following Congress's dismantling of the Bracero Program, the institution of severe limits on Mexican migration, and the effects of an economic recession.[115] At that time, lawful migration channels for laborers had been severely proscribed, but by that point, employers in several sectors of the U.S. economy had come to rely on migrant, especially Mexican, labor. Prior to 1965, those employers had relied either on unregulated migratory channels, or the seasonal flows facilitated by the Bracero Program and uncapped western hemisphere admissions. The sudden dismantling of both the Bracero Program and uncapped lawful migration resulted in the increasing unlawful migration that continues to epitomize immigration law. State and local legislative responses to the phenomenon concomitantly increased after 1970. California with the highest undocumented population in the nation responded with its employer sanctions law. At that time, federal law did not contain an equivalent penalty on unauthorized employment.

Although the majority opinion in *De Canas* reaffirmed the primacy of federal regulation in immigration, it concurrently clarified that states maintained the constitutional authority to structure the everyday lives of its residents, which could include, under certain circumstances, regulating on the basis of unlawful immigration status. In a passage still quoted by states and localities seeking to defend the constitutionality of their enactments, the Court wrote:

> Power to regulate immigration is unquestionably a federal power. But the Court has never held that every state enactment which in any way deals with aliens is a regulation of immigration, and thus *per se* pre-empted by this constitutional power, whether latent or exercised.... [S]tanding alone, the fact that aliens are the subject of a state statute does not render it a regulation of immigration, which is essentially a determination of who should or should not be admitted into the country, and the conditions under which a legal entrant may remain.[116]

In contrast to *Graham* then, the court in *De Canas* signaled that preemption analysis would not automatically lead to the striking down of state laws that regulated aspects of immigrants' lives. Further, although the parties in the case both argued about the application (or not) of the equal protection clause, neither the California Supreme Court nor the U.S. Supreme Court addressed the issue in their opinions.

Other post-*Graham* cases involving state and local alienage laws met with varied success, with the Court creating exceptions to the immigrant-friendly position it took in *Graham*. These cases created exceptions to *Graham*'s equal protection guarantee for noncitizens, providing a safe harbor for state and local laws that discriminated against noncitizens, even lawfully present ones. Subsequent decisions protected the authority of states to discriminate on the basis of citizenship for jobs or activities implicating the state's sovereign functions or identity.[117] Based on this "political function" or "political activities" exception, and cases clarifying its application, at present, states may discriminate against noncitizens in voting, elected office, jury service, and other public employment, such as state police officers and public school teachers.[118]

The bright star for undocumented persons specifically, and equal protection claims more generally, was the *Plyler v. Doe* decision in 1982.[119] There, the Court struck down a Texas education law, which allowed public schools to deny enrollment to undocumented children.[120] In doing so, the Court relied on the equal protection clause as the basis for striking down the state law. Further, unlike prior cases, *Plyler* dealt squarely with undocumented persons as the concept is understood today, applying the constitutional guarantee to unlawfully present immigrant children. Notably, the Court insisted on the equal protection ruling, declining to find the state law preempted, despite the fact that federal statutes at that time, as they do now, generally discourage unlawful presence.

*Plyler*, however, proved to be an outlier, high-water mark for immigrants' constitutional rights. The Court's reasoning was elusive, as the opinion focused on the unique characteristics of the primary school-age children at issue, including their diminished culpability for their unlawful states and the policy consequences of a population of uneducated children.[121] In reaching this result, however, the Court declined to label them, or immigrants generally, a suspect class for requiring the strictest judicial oversight. Instead, the court cobbled together its unique concern for children and the consequences of denying them primary education, to reach its result.

Because of this doctrinal uncertainty, since *Plyler*, states and localities have made several brazen attempts to enact legislation intended to provide the Court with an opportunity to overrule the case. Although federal courts have so far declined to do so, they have also declined to extend or extrapolate from *Plyler*, strongly suggesting that the case may be limited to its specific context of undocumented children and access to primary school education. Moreover, *Toll v. Moreno*, a case decided in the same term, undermined *Plyler's* potential instantiation of robust equal protection jurisprudence for all state and local alienage law.[122] The *Toll* Court struck down a state university residency rule that denied in-state tuition benefits to a certain category of temporary, lawfully present immigrants. The Court relied exclusively on a preemption framework, rather than one based on the unequal treatment of those noncitizens, opining that a state could not impose additional restrictions on noncitizens that the federal government had chosen to admit. Indeed, in reviewing its past alienage cases, including *Graham*, the *Toll* Court indicated that the Court's line of alienage jurisprudence was better read as examples of preemption analysis rather than as violations of equal protection.[123]

Indeed, even in *Plyler*, the Court mixed its sympathy for the education of undocumented children with sympathy for the state of Texas. Postulating that in some circumstances the state might have an interest in "mitigating the potentially harsh economic effects" of unchecked unlawful migration, the Court included in a footnote that it "cannot conclude that the States are without any power to deter the influx of persons [unlawfully entering the country], and whose numbers might have a discernable impact on traditional state concerns."[124] Foreshadowing our empirical work that we present in Chapter 3, however, the *Plyler* court noted that "there is not evidence in the record suggesting that illegal entrants impose any significant burden on the State's economy. To the contrary, the available evidence suggests that illegal aliens underutilize public services, while contributing their labor to the local economy and tax money to the state fisc."

Still *Plyler* remains instructive and vital. Federal courts' reaffirmation of *Plyler*, despite several opportunities provided by subsequent state laws to overrule the case (a trend that continues even in the most recent round of immigration federalism decisions by federal courts in 2013), suggests that the Court is not ready to wholly abandon equality guarantees for undocumented persons. More subtly, as we argue in Chapter 6, it allows for the possibility of a resurrected anti-discrimination norm in contemporary immigration federalism jurisprudence.

### Congress Enters the Fray on State Involvement

Just as important as these jurisprudential developments during this third era of immigration federalism, Congress became acutely aware of the complications and possibilities of state and local involvement. Federal statutory enactments in 1986 and 1996 expressly accounted for subfederal policymaking, either attempting to quash state and local activity or trying to unlock their potential for aiding federal efforts and advancing federal aims. This explicit recognition and engagement in federal statutory schemes provided significant opportunities for state and local lawmaking that were utilized in the re-energized period of subfederal immigration regulation after 2004.

Congress's 1986 Immigration Reform and Control Act (IRCA) directly addressed the constitutional leeway provided to states by the Supreme Court's *De Canas* opinion. Ten years after that case, the federal government finally regulated the employment of unauthorized workers by enacting IRCA, which included both a mass legalization provision for millions of then-undocumented persons and provisions instituting a federal system of employer sanctions.[125]

As a corollary to the instantiation of a federal scheme, Congress also seemed to take a cue from *De Canas's* focus on the lack of a specific federal prohibition against state employer sanctions. Thus, alongside the federal enforcement scheme, IRCA expressly forbade "any State or local law imposing civil or criminal sanctions (other than through licensing and similar laws) upon those who employ ... unauthorized persons."[126] With this federal provision, the eleven state and local employer sanctions laws then-in-effect were immediately preempted, in a rare case of express statutory preemption in the alienage field.

As we shall see in Chapter 3, however, the parenthetical exception within that provision also created an opening for savvy activists and receptive states to experiment with new penalties on employers with respect to the hiring of unauthorized workers. Importantly, however, states did not exploit this exception right away it would take them twenty years to do so. States desirous of maintaining their own provisions to discourage the hiring of unauthorized workers utilized this ostensible statutory ambiguity in the late 2000s, starting with the Legal Arizona Workers Act (LAWA) of 2007. LAWA, and the ensuing Supreme Court case that held it constitutional, once again ignited a flurry of state policies intended to penalize the employment of unauthorized workers.[127] This resurrection demonstrates both the constant contest and negotiation between federal and state power in immigration federalism disputes, and the consistent mutation and adaptation of state and local responses to federal constraints. Still, regardless whether the federal preemption of state-imposed employer sanctions were comprehensive or partial, IRCA represented a significant first attempt by Congress in the twentieth century to explicitly engage with state regulations on immigration.

Continuing this trend, the 1996 immigration overhaul – which included some or all provisions of the Illegal Immigration Reform and Immigration Responsibility Act (IIRIRA),[128] the Personal Responsibility and Work Opportunity Reconciliation Act (PRWORA),[129] and the Antiterrorism and Effective Death Penalty Act (AEDPA)[130] – also was keenly sensitive to state and local participation in immigration enforcement and alienage law. While these federal laws comprehensively addressed federal admission and deportation standards and procedures, they also explicitly and left open several possibilities for state involvement in other areas. On the enforcement side, provisions like IIRIRA's section 287(g) allowed states and localities to enter into cooperative agreements with the federal government to help enforce immigration law. Other sections expressly allowed for state participation in enforcing specific immigration crimes.[131] In addition, PRWORA's provisions dealing with noncitizens purported to devolve to states the precise authority the Supreme Court had stripped away two decades earlier in *Graham*: They allowed states to determine whether or not legal permanent residents would be eligible for benefits such as Temporary Assistance for Needy Families (TANF) and Medicaid.[132]

Notably, not all of the 1996 changes were intended to give states the power to be more restrictionist than the federal government or to aid in federal enforcement. Other sections of the 1996 overhaul evinced the awareness that states might choose to take integrative measures to deal with undocumented populations. PRWORA's devolution of welfare decisions to the states meant that states could choose to be more generous than the federal government in providing public assistance to noncitizens. In addition, other provisions of federal law, while generally restricting benefits to undocumented migrants, were drafted in such a way as to permit states, with careful drafting, to offer

not do. At the same time, the court understood other parts of Prop. 187, like its benefits denial provisions, as only indirectly affecting immigration and thus evaluated them under generally applicable preemption and equal protection law. In these instances, the court found that California, in some parts of Prop. 187, had enacted "alienage" law subject to evaluation under preemption and equal protection guarantees. Using this framework, the court found the law's denial of education to undocumented children unconstitutional as a violation of equal protection, but upheld certain other provisions that denied public benefits. Ultimately, the state abandoned its defense of the law, and came to a mediated settlement with those challenging it.[144]

Although Proposition 187 failed in federal court, it nevertheless showcased the possibilities of omnibus state-level restrictionist action. Prior to its demise, and concurrent with efforts to overhaul federal immigration legislation in 1996, activists in other states including Florida, Texas, and Arizona consulted with the proponents of Prop. 187 in hopes of passing their own versions of the law. However, these attempts to spread Prop. 187 did not succeed. While constitutional challenges in federal court might have been a deterrent, proponents of Arizona's copycat measure had learned from California's experience and stripped out the education ban from their initiative efforts.

Perhaps more importantly, such efforts to spread Prop. 187 did not receive the attention or backing of national organizations that were also focused on restricting immigration and deterring unlawful presence. Much of the funding and activist efforts on immigration restriction in 1996 had been geared toward national legislative efforts, as conservative organizations such as Federation for American Immigration Reform (FAIR) and NumbersUSA were focused on passing restrictive legislation and getting President Bill Clinton to sign such legislation.[145] The fact that the proponents of Proposition 187 were relatively disorganized also did not help matters much. For example, the initiative's political consultant in Arizona complained that Ron Prince "did not spend more time in Arizona assisting in a campaign he helped launch."[146] Thus, as the *Los Angeles Times* reported in July 1996, most contemporary observers attributed the failure to proliferate state legislation to a "paucity of funds, lack of organization and a general failure to galvanize voters' interest."[147]

Even though Prop. 187 and its nascent copycats did not survive, their demise presaged a new era of state confrontation of federal policies and state enforcement schemes that avoided the pitfalls of California's ill-fated enactment. Riding the national attention and political momentum from Prop. 187, from 1994 through 1997, six different states – California, Arizona, Texas, Florida, New Jersey, and state officials from New York – filed suits against the federal government, asking to be compensated for the federal government's alleged failure to enforce its immigration laws.[148] Arising from the same political context of Prop. 187, these suits challenged the federal government's enforcement decisions and policies. Eventually, five different U.S. Circuit Courts of Appeal dismissed the claims, but not without engendering some judicial sympathy for the alleged plights of the states.[149]

Moreover, as we discuss in Chapter 4, the initial attempts to spread Proposition 187 to other states laid the blueprint for successful proliferation in the following decade. Future state and local attempts at immigration restriction would have to finesse the main factors contributing to the demise of this early legislation. First, a federal court rejected the legal basis for state immigration laws like 187. Any future attempts would thus have to navigate around and through the several statutory drafting and doctrinal pitfalls into which 187 fell. Second, the state immigration law movement in the mid-1990s was not well positioned to take advantage of partisan dynamics and connections to national organizations. As contemporary reports suggest, the Prop. 187 movement, started in 1993, was beginning to ebb until Governor Pete Wilson made it a critical aspect of his reelection campaign, thereby garnering significant funding from the Republican Party to revitalize momentum for the proposition.[150] There was no national interest or financial support to proliferate state immigration laws, something that proved critical a decade later. Third, Congress passed several laws in 1996, including the Illegal Immigration Reform and Immigration Responsibility Act (IIRIRA), constituting a significant federal overhaul of immigration enforcement. Although Prop. 187 advocates argued that state efforts, which were in some ways harsher toward undocumented immigrants than was federal law, were legally viable despite the new federal laws, neither the federal court nor most immigration commentators agreed.

While the example and lessons of Proposition 187 gained new life in restrictive efforts a decade later, there was one additional legacy, specific to California, that actually hastened the demise of restrictionist legislation in the Golden State. Governor Pete Wilson's tight embrace of the ballot proposition during his reelection campaign helped spur higher voter turnout and a strong backlash against the Republican Party among Latino voters.[151] Hundreds of thousands of Latinos became eligible for naturalization in California during the 1990s, and many of them were beneficiaries of the mass legalization program implemented by IRCA in 1986. As these naturalized voters and a growing wave of second-generation Latino youth entered the electorate, the Democratic Party became dominant in California and the Latino Legislative Caucus grew to be a powerful force in the state legislature. These developments would prove critical in the decade or two following the passage of Proposition 187, as it spawned a new generation of Latino lawmakers in

Sacramento who introduced legislation to improve the lives of unauthorized immigrants, won support from their Democratic colleagues, and ultimately convinced a moderate Democratic governor to sign a string of pro-integration measures in 2013 and 2014. [152]

## SETTING THE STAGE FOR *ARIZONA V. UNITED STATES* AND BEYOND

Starting in the late 1800s, the United States transitioned from a state-centric to federal-centric immigration control system, with the federal government assuming control over entry and exit controls and Congress setting the terms of state participation. Despite this jurisdictional migration, states and localities still remained important actors in the immigration sphere, as several subfederal governments enacted a variety of laws intended to control and deter the presence of noncitizens. These enactments during the second century of immigration regulation, from 1875 to 1965 provided the opportunities for the Supreme Court to develop its immigration federalism jurisprudence. That jurisprudence matured from 1970 onward, settling on a federalism-based preemption framework with erstwhile consideration of the equality concerns inherent in the regulation of noncitizens. And, during this time, Congress began a project of engaging and refining the terms of state and local participation.

That maturation, of course, does not necessarily imply clarity or predictability. Indeed, by the turn of the twenty-first century, and after more than 125 years of development, immigration federalism law – while easy to articulate in theory, has remained muddled in practice. Courts today are still wrestling with notions of federal plenary sovereignty in immigration matters, when pitted against claims of state authority to regulate their jurisdictions in alienage law. Adding to the jurisprudential quandary, the significant federal immigration interventions in 1986 and 1996 both constrained and liberated states in significant ways. Together, these judicial and legislative developments created a platform for the reinvigoration of state and local lawmaking from 2004 through present day, with Arizona playing a particularly prominent role.

Thus, at the turn of the twenty-first century, immigration regulation was still ostensibly a federal matter, although the doctrinal and legislative developments of the prior century had not foreclosed the potential for state and local involvement. To the contrary, these developments revealed the myriad ways that states and localities not only desired to regulate immigrants and immigration, but the legal and political opportunities for them to do so. As we argue in the chapters that follow, the aftermath of the September 11, 2001 attacks and the growth of partisan gridlock in Washington, DC, provided the opportunities for more state and local legislation on immigration.

At the same time, an outbreak of immigration legislation at the state and local level was not inevitable: it would take a set of entrepreneurial activists and opportunistic elected officials to fulfill that potential. These actors, in a relatively short period of time, managed to exploit the opportunities and fissures created by the prior century's jurisprudence. In doing so, they learned from the rise and fall of Prop. 187, and defied conventional legal wisdom about policy options that had heretofore been considered foreclosed. These issue entrepreneurs, first on the restrictive side and then on the pro-integration side, proliferated legislation to such an extent that they captured national attention and started to establish new norms of state and local lawmaking on immigration matters. The chapters that follow tell the story of how exactly the new immigration federalism came to be, focusing on the key political, social, and demographic dynamics that made such a dramatic shift possible, and the legal and political fallout from that transformation.

# 3

# Rise of Restrictive Legislation and Demographic Arguments of "Vital Necessity"

The most notable legislative attempts at immigration restriction prior to 2001 occurred in California. The state had already pioneered modern employer sanctions law for the hiring of unauthorized workers in 1970. Later, not only did voters pass Proposition 187, a 1994 measure that sought to deny public benefits to unauthorized immigrants, the state legislature also passed a slew of other restrictive laws in 1993, including measures barring unauthorized immigrants from obtaining driver's licenses, mandating cooperation between state prisons and federal immigration authorities, and mandating employment agencies to verify the immigration status of applicants before providing them with job placement or training.[1] At the local level, too, controversies had emerged in suburban areas of Los Angeles such as Monterey Park, where local conflicts over the proliferation of Chinese-language business signs grabbed news attention and prompted the city council to consider and enact legislation mandating the addition of English signage in the mid 1980s.[2] Controversy over the visible growth of Asian businesses also emerged in the northeastern suburbs of New Jersey during the 1990s, where voters in cities like Palisades Park pushed their city council to pass ordinances that disproportionately affected Asian immigrant businesses, mandating that karaoke bars close by 9 pm,[3] and requiring the inclusion of English in store signs.[4]

While states such as California and New Jersey had dominated news headlines on immigration restriction in the 1990s, the following decade brought forth another set of venues where immigration restriction was prominent. After a period of relative state and local quietude on immigration following the 1996 federal immigration overhauls, the post-9/11 era once again reignited immigration federalism. Soon after 9/11, localities began using a relatively obscure and dormant part of the 1996 federal immigration overhaul. The so-called 287(g) agreements, named for the section of the INA that provides authority for them, allow local law enforcement and federal authorities to enter into memoranda of understanding with federal officials that empower local officials to be trained in, and enforce, federal immigration law.[5] Notably, despite providing for the possibility of supervised and delegated local enforcement of immigration laws in 1996, localities did not begin entering into such agreements with much frequency until after 2005, with political battles on immigration heating up both nationally and locally. The increase in 287(g) agreements during that time was indicative of a larger trend.

From 2004 through 2012 states and localities aggressively reentered the regulatory field, proposing and passing several high profile laws intended to control immigration and the lives of immigrants. The state of Arizona drew perhaps the greatest attention, starting with the passage of Proposition 200 in 2004, and continuing through the passage of the Legal Arizona Workers Act (LAWA) in 2007 and the Support Our Law Enforcement and Safe Neighborhoods Act of 2010 (often referred to as SB 1070). All of these laws resulted in Supreme Court decisions, and we say more about each of them shortly, as we systematically discuss the types of restrictive laws passed during the last decade. Arizona, however, was not alone in its attempts to pass restrictive laws targeting unauthorized immigrants. Indeed, as early as 2006, Colorado passed an immigration enforcement law that was a precursor to SB 1070,[6] and citizens in San Bernadino, California, began clamoring for a local Illegal Immigration Relief Act that would have regulated day-laborer centers, prohibited day-labor work solicitation, imposed fines and other business penalties on those who employed unauthorized workers, prohibited rental of properties to undocumented immigrants, and mandated English-only for all city business.[7] Although the "Save San Bernadino Initiative" failed to pass, similar ordinances proposed in other places that year and afterwards, did. Restrictive laws began to emerge in other states too, such as Oklahoma, Georgia, Indiana, and North Carolina, states that few Americans would have previously thought of as significant destinations for immigrants. At the local level, too, news stories on immigration restriction began to emerge in places that most Americans had never heard of before: Hazleton, Pennsylvania; Farmers Branch, Texas; Escondido, California; and Fremont, Nebraska.

What accounts for the new geography of these laws? Before we answer that question, it is first instructive to take a more detailed look at the types and varieties of laws that states and localities enacted in this period from 2004 to 2012. After providing this review, the remainder of the chapter returns to this central question of what caused this rapid, and geographically notable, proliferation.

RESTRICTIONIST STATE AND LOCAL LAWS 2004–2012

A significant amount of subfederal policymaking from 2004 to 2012 focused on restrictionist efforts to increase enforcement possibilities. For the most part, these state and local enactments sought to involve local law enforcement officers in enforcement actions against unauthorized immigrants. In addition, states and localities created new state crimes triggered by unauthorized status. And, states instituted employer-sanctions schemes seeking to penalize businesses that employed unauthorized workers. Undoubtedly, during this same general timeframe, some states and localities were also promoting more integrationist legislation as well, a trend that accelerated after 2012. We leave discussion of these integrationist policies to Chapters 5 and 6.

Looking at these restrictive laws in more detail, we can classify them into a set of identifiable categories:[8]

(1) Public benefits laws that restrict eligibility for benefits based on citizenship status;

(2) Employee verification laws regulating the hiring of unauthorized workers by requiring the use of the federal E-Verify database and denying licenses or contracts to employers;

(3) Landlord ordinances that penalize the leasing of property to undocumented persons;

(4) Law enforcement statutes that allow, and in some cases require, that local law authorities verify the immigration status of arrestees and others they come into contact with as part of their law enforcement duties;

(5) Anti-solicitation ordinances, aimed at day laborers and day-labor centers, that regulate the ability of persons to enter into employment contracts in public spaces like streets or commercial corners;

(6) Educational access laws that effectively deny undocumented children the ability to attend public schools, or deny college-age undocumented youth admission or in-state tuition rates at public universities;

(7) Contract laws that void legal obligations in contracts entered into with undocumented persons; and

(8) Identification and driver's license laws that restrict access to licenses and/or penalize vehicle operation by unlawfully present persons.

Before we elaborate on these categories with some notable examples from enacting jurisdictions, a few points to keep in mind. First, the same jurisdictions may have enacted multiple types of these laws, or may have passed an omnibus bill that contains one or more of these elements. Second, many of these legislative areas are not unique to the past several years; as we chronicled in Chapter 2, employer sanctions laws, public benefits restrictions, attempts to dispossess noncitizens from property, and educational access concerns also arose in prior eras, and even in the last few decades, of state and local immigration involvement. What is notable, however, is the volume and method of proliferation of these laws since 2004. State and local immigration policy activity spiked in 2005, with approximately 300 laws proposed across all jurisdictions, and thirty-nine of them passing into law.[9] Since then, proposal and passage of immigration laws – mostly restrictionist from 2004 to 2011, but primarily integrationist from 2012 onward – has continued.

### Public Benefit Restrictions

Of the restrictive state laws passed in the post-9/11 era, the first notable piece of legislation was Arizona's Proposition 200. Passed in 2004, the proposition entitled "Arizona Taxpayer and Citizen Protection Act" sought to accomplish a number of goals related to unauthorized migration and the presence of undocumented immigrants within the state. Notably, the Act begins by listing purportedly empirical truths about undocumented migration, stating that the state "finds" that illegal immigration causes "economic hardship" to the state, and that such migration is driven significantly by the provision of state welfare benefits.

In its operative provisions, Prop. 200 had two main features, relating to voter registration and access to nonfederal public benefits. The first provision sought to change voter registration procedures, requiring residents to prove U.S. citizenship prior to registering to vote. That portion of the law was challenged, and later overturned by the Supreme Court's decision in *Arizona v. Inter Tribal Council of Arizona* (2013), on the grounds that the additional state voter registration procedures were preempted by federal voter registration law, which only required an attestation of citizenship.[10]

With regard to public benefits restrictions (the portion of Prop. 200 that was not challenged and remains in force) the law required that state and local agencies verify eligibility for those benefits by providing strict standards for the type of identification necessary to prove immigration status of the applicants.[11] More importantly, the act mandated that any discovered violations of federal immigration law by state and local authorities in the course of public benefit administration were to be reported, in writing, to federal immigration authorities. It made any such failure to report a misdemeanor under state law. Alabama's HB 56, passed several years after Prop. 200, imposed similar verification and reporting requirements for public benefit agencies, as did the state of Montana.[12]

Although criminalizing the failure to report those who appear ineligible for public assistance was a novel step, more generally, states have varied in their public assistance to noncitizens after Congress passed the Personal Responsibility and Work Opportunity Reconciliation Act (PRWORA) in 1996. Specifically, PRWORA limited federal benefits to only "qualified" noncitizens and prohibited undocumented immigrants from nonemergency relief programs. In an example of federalism-enabling federal law, other PRWORA provisions purported to devolve decision making over noncitizen eligibility for jointly funded federal-state programs and state-only public assistance programs to state governments.[13] And, it specified that states desirous of providing public assistance to unauthorized immigrants would have to do so through enactment of affirmative legislation after 1996.[14]

The provisions empowering state restrictions on public assistance have met with contradictory opinions in state and federal courts, and as of yet, the Supreme Court has not weighed in on their constitutionality. The two most notable cases litigating post-1996 restrictions on immigrant eligibility for public assistance programs yielded mixed results. In *Aliessa v. Novello*, the New York Court of Appeals struck down the state's restrictions on immigrant eligibility, opining that the Supreme Court's prior decision in *Graham v. Richardson* prevented states from adopting divergent requirements for certain welfare programs, despite PWORA's devolution of decision-making authority.[15] In contrast, a federal appeals court reached the opposite result in *Soskin v. Rienertson*, opining that states could use the authority provided by PWORA to limit noncitizen eligibility for certain forms of public assistance.[16]

Not surprisingly, in political and academic spheres, there have been contested claims about the net fiscal impacts of immigration and unauthorized immigration at the state and local levels, both in the short and long terms.[17] In the wake of PRWORA, some states, especially those with high immigrant populations such as California and New York, continued to provide extensive benefits to their immigrant populations, including, at times, for undocumented residents. In general, however, the state situation remains in flux, with some states maintaining programs that are more generous than federal law requires and others choosing to rescind benefits to unqualified immigrants in light of the economic downturn over the past several years.[18] As an example of the latter policy movement, New Jersey's 2010 decision to exclude recently arrived lawful permanent residents (and, of course, other classes of nonimmigrants and undocumented immigrants) from state health care programs was upheld by the state's Supreme Court.[19] For the most part, undocumented immigrants remain outside the protection of federal and most state public assistance programs.

*Employer Sanctions Laws and Restrictions on Unauthorized Workers*

While Proposition 200 was the first major restrictive state law on immigration in the post-9/11 period, other laws would soon follow and spawn imitations elsewhere. In 2007, Arizona passed a law aimed at making it more difficult for unauthorized immigrants to work, and thereby live, in the state by passing the Legal Arizona Worker's Act (LAWA).[20] Although Congress in 1986 had previously invalidated then-existing state prohibitions on the hiring of undocumented workers, Arizona found a way around the federal law. While the Congressional statute – the Immigration Reform and Control Act (IRCA) of 1986 – had displaced all state employer sanctions laws, it nevertheless excepted state licensing laws from federal displacement.[21] Arizona's law fashioned the penalty for hiring unauthorized immigrants as a license revocation, taking advantage of the apparent loophole left open by the Immigration Reform and Control Act.

The key to LAWA is its requirement that businesses within the state check their employees' records against the federal E-Verify database. E-Verify is a federal database initially created in the mid-1990s as a pilot program, and then expanded for general use by the 2000s. It allows employers to submit employee information to federal authorities, who can then check if the employee information matches information in the database.[22] If the information matches, then the employee is ostensibly authorized to work, and the employer is shielded from liability. On the other hand, if the information does not match, the employer is issued a "no-match" letter that is shared with the employee who then has some time to rectify the concern. If the situation is not addressed, the employer must fire the employee, lest the business face sanctions. As constructed under federal law, use of E-Verify is mandatory only for certain federal contractors and those doing business with the federal government, but for private employers it is voluntary; employers may choose to participate in the program to ensure they are shielded from liability under IRCA, but need not do so. LAWA alters that paradigm by mandating E-Verify use within the state for all employers.

After LAWA's enactment, and the Supreme Court case that sustained it (*U.S. Chamber of Commerce v. Whiting* (2011)[23]), several other states followed Arizona's lead. Seven other states – Alabama, Georgia, Mississippi, North Carolina, South Carolina, Tennessee, and Utah – now maintain laws similar to LAWA that mandate E-Verify by most employers in the state, whether private or public.[24] In addition, several other states require E-Verify use by public employers and contractors.

## State Identification Cards and Driver's Licenses

In one area – identification cards and driver's license laws – proliferation of state policies and administrative regulations can be attributed, in significant part, to the emergence of federal law that spurred state action. The REAL ID Act of 2005 created minimum standards for state-issued licenses and identification cards if those cards are to be used for federal purposes, such as access to federal buildings, identification for airline travel, and proof of identity for accessing benefits.[25] Those federal standards list the types of identification and proofs of lawful status that states must request from applicants before issuing licenses or cards to the individual. States could, of course, choose to provide licenses and cards that fail to meet the minimum federal status-verification standards with the consequence that such licenses may not be acceptable for federal purposes once the REAL ID Act becomes fully implemented.

As of now, the Department of Homeland Security has delayed implementation and enforcement of the act.[26] Nevertheless, between 2003 and 2010 seven states – California, Hawaii, Maine, Maryland, Michigan, Oregon, and Tennessee – that previously allowed undocumented persons access to licenses repealed those policies,[27] thereby limiting their licenses and cards to citizens, legal permanent residents, classes of lawfully present nonimmigrants, and, in some cases, immigrants without lawful status, but whose presence is nevertheless made lawful through federal administrative action like deferred action. Although that trend has reversed since 2012 (we discuss this reversal in detail in Chapter 5), the overwhelming majority of states still do not issue licenses or cards to undocumented persons.

## Education Related Laws

As with state identification cards and driver's licenses, the most recent developments in state educational access laws have been integrationist, rather than restrictionist. And, because the Supreme Court's 1982 *Plyler v. Doe* decision (discussed in Chapter 6) held that it was unconstitutional for a state to deny public school education to undocumented children, states and localities have not been able to prevent undocumented primary and secondary school-age children from accessing state schools.[28] Despite *Plyler*, states have nevertheless attempted to bar or discourage undocumented children from attending public schools. A prime example is Alabama's HB 56, which, in one of its provisions, required that the immigration status of enrolled children be provided to, and documented by, public school officials.[29] The clear intent and effect of the information and disclosure provisions was to circumvent *Plyler* and bar undocumented access, as evinced by the state's reason for collecting such information: "Because the costs incurred by school districts for the public elementary and secondary education of children who are aliens not lawfully present in the United States adversely affect the availability of public education resources to students who are United States citizens and aliens lawfully present in the United States, ... ".[30]

In matters of post-secondary education, since 2001 the trend has been toward opening access to higher education for undocumented students through tuition equity legislation (discussed in Chapter 5). In contrast to that trend, however, two states – Alabama and South Carolina with their recent omnibus immigration bills – deny undocumented students admission to their state institutions of higher learning.[31] In addition, five states – Alabama, Arizona, Georgia, Indiana, and South Carolina – buck the move toward tuition equity and deny undocumented students the ability to pay in-state tuition rates for public universities.[32]

### Local Rental and Employment Ordinances

Notable local restrictionist efforts focused on employment and rental restrictions on undocumented immigrants. Like the omnibus state efforts discussed below, the localities' goal with these ordinances was to drive undocumented persons out of their respective jurisdictions and discourage unlawful migration.

The local employment ordinances in Valley Park, Missouri; Fremont, Nebraska; and Hazleton, Pennsylvania, similar to state efforts, penalize the employment of unauthorized workers within the cities' jurisdictions. Like their state counterparts, the city employment laws sanction violating employers by suspending or taking away business permits, and encouraging use of the federal E-Verify database.[33]

In addition, utilizing the zoning and residential control authority traditionally allocated to municipalities, a few jurisdictions – Escondido, California; Farmers Branch, Texas; Hazleton, Pennsylvania; Fremont, Nebraska – enacted ordinances that barred the leasing of property to undocumented immigrants.[34] For example, adopted in 2010, Fremont Ordinance No. 5165 requires prospective renters in the city to obtain an occupancy license from the city; to obtain that license, applicants must disclose identifying information including proof of citizenship or lawful immigration status, which the city then verifies with the federal government. Both the renters and the landlords are penalized for violations of the rental prohibition.

## Omnibus Enforcement Bills

Much media attention over the past several years has been focused on the comprehensive immigration enforcement schemes enacted by several states, which incorporate many of the categories of restrictionist lawmaking outlined above. Of all the subfederal legislative activity over the past several years, the most well known is Arizona's SB 1070, an omnibus immigration enforcement scheme passed in 2010 and officially titled the Support Our Law Enforcement and Safe Neighborhoods Act of 2010. Colorado's SB 90 in 2006 preceded Arizona's efforts by four years and actually included many of the provisions in the Arizona law,[35] but it was the publicity leading up to, and debate surrounding, SB 1070 that truly captured national headlines and fomented heated legal and political debates.

In the wake of Arizona's SB 1070, other states such as Alabama, Georgia, and South Carolina enacted similar multi-subject laws, which were often referred to as copycat legislation.[36] Importantly, while these laws all shared similar characteristics, they also at times contained slight variations, with some states criminalizing or covering a broader range of state legislative concerns. Among the most controversial aspect of these laws, in popular and political discourse, was their empowerment of local law enforcement officials to participate in immigration enforcement. Each of these state laws contained provisions that required state and local police to check immigration status of those whom they stopped or detained, and provided them with the authority, in some cases, to arrest noncitizens on the officer's independent determination that the noncitizen was likely removable from the United States.

Paradigmatic of these omnibus state immigration enforcement schemes, SB 1070 was a wide-ranging statute with several provisions. Often overlooked because it has little operative significance, but conceptually very important, is 1070's section 1, which lays out the intent of the state law. In it, the Arizona legislature unequivocally expressed its immigration control purpose:

> The legislature declares that the intent of this Act is to make *attrition through enforcement* the public policy of [the state]. The provisions of this act are intended to work together to discourage and deter the unlawful entry and presence of aliens and economic activity by persons unlawfully present in the United States.[37]

Recognizing the intent of the law is important because it frames judicial, political, and popular interpretation and understanding of its operative provisions, all of which were created to drive the undocumented population out of the state, and presumably out of the country.

In its operative provisions, SB 1070 covered a range of concerns from state and local law enforcement authority, unauthorized employment, alien registration, local noncooperation ordinances, and providing individuals to sue the state for enforcement of the law. Of these several parts, many survived initial review by the federal trial court, including the section that prevented localities within Arizona from enacting noncooperation or "sanctuary"-type ordinances. In addition, the section creating a right of action against state officials for not complying with the law, another amending parts of Arizona's human smuggling law, another that treated transporting an undocumented person as harboring that individual,[38] and another that created a gang and immigration intelligence task force all survived district court review.

The remaining sections of SB 1070 had their fate determined by the Supreme Court in *Arizona v. United States*, which we address in greater detail in Chapter 6. Two of the contested provisions dealt with the role of state and local law enforcement in immigration enforcement. Section 2(B) required local law enforcement to determine the legal status of those they stop, detain or arrest;[39] section 6 permitted the warrantless arrest, by local officers, of those whom the officer had probable cause to believe were removable from the United States.[40] The third section of the law, its "alien registration" provision, created a state crime for failure to carry registration documents that proved lawful status.[41] Finally, SB 1070 criminalized the solicitation of work by unauthorized workers.[42] Importantly, this penalty directed at unauthorized workers complemented the prior Arizona law (LAWA) that penalized employers for hiring unauthorized workers. And, by creating criminal consequences for the unauthorized *employees* themselves, the state law distinguished itself from federal employment restrictions that only civilly and criminally penalized *employers* who hired unauthorized workers.

The copycat laws in Alabama, Georgia, and South Carolina contained many of the same provisions, a by-product of having used SB 1070 as a template and soliciting advice from SB 1070's authors. As they evolved from SB 1070, however, they contained variations and additional legislative inroads as well. Most notable of the copycats was Alabama's HB 56, passed in 2011, that was even more far-reaching and comprehensive than its predecessor. Similar to 1070, HB 56 began with a statement of intent rife with purportedly empirical truths: "The State of Alabama finds that illegal immigration is causing economic hardship and lawlessness in this state and that illegal immigration is encouraged when public agencies within this state provide public benefits without verifying immigration status."[43] Having laid out several "findings," the bill's opening section then continues with the state's avowedly immigration control purpose, clarifying "the State of Alabama declare[s] that it is a compelling public interest to discourage illegal immigration."

In its operative provisions, Alabama's law mimicked many of 1070's restrictions, including provisions for the participation of local law enforcement in immigration enforcement, a prohibition on sanctuary laws by localities, a right of action to ensure compliance with the law, provisions creating state criminal consequences for harboring or transporting undocumented persons, an alien registration scheme, and employment restrictions. In addition, HB 56 incorporated aspects of Arizona's prior enactments that mandated employers use a federal database to check the status of their employees, and imposed penalties for failing to verify lawful status before the provision of public benefits. Other sections of HB 56, however, went beyond previously enacted policies, innovating restrictionist possibilities not present in its predecessors. The two most notable modifications in that regard were a provision that invalidated all contracts entered into by unlawfully present noncitizens,[44] and education-related provisions that flatly barred state public universities from enrolling undocumented students and another that effectively prohibited undocumented elementary and secondary school students from attending public schools.[45]

## THE ARGUMENT OF DEMOGRAPHIC NECESSITY

As journalists, elected officials, and scholars tried to make sense of the rash of laws being debated and passed in these new places, a consistent narrative – based on demographic change and policy pressures associated with such change – began to crystallize to explain this renewed state and local interest in passing laws to deter the presence of unauthorized immigrants. This demography-based explanation for state and local involvement is appealing. First, economic studies have suggested that the fiscal benefits of immigration are more likely to be concentrated at the national level, while any short-term fiscal costs are more likely to be borne by specific localities, particularly with respect to the provision of public education, social services, and emergency room care.[46] Second, federalism scholars have sometimes assumed the salience of geographic variance. For example, Professor Cristina Rodriguez argued that the demographic shifts caused by globalization and immigration "are felt differently in different parts of the country, and the disruption immigration causes, as well as the viability of different immigration strategies, will vary."[47] Other studies have similarly suggested that punitive measures targeting immigrants are related to the recent arrival of noncitizens,[48] or the growth of immigrant populations.[49] Many media reports have also invoked this same wisdom, of immigration-induced changes leading inexorably to policy pressures and legislative action at the local level.[50] Indeed, even recent press accounts after the beginning of the trend toward integrationist laws, conjure this same logic of demographic change as dictating destiny for restrictionist state and local immigration policies.[51]

This conventional wisdom is largely in line with the complaints of local sponsors of restrictive legislation. These observers of, and advocates for, this new wave of restrictionist policies cast their explanations in the classic federalism-based framework. While acknowledging the late-nineteenth and twentieth century predominance of the national government in immigration matters, they nevertheless argued that in the 2000s, states and localities were facing unprecedented policy challenges caused by increased unauthorized immigration, and that the federal government had failed its constitutional responsibility to regulate and control such migration and its effects. Therefore, they claimed, states and localities not only needed to act, but they were constitutionally authorized to do so.

Notably, by the time of SB 1070 and other contemporary restrictivist enactments, these dual tropes of demographic pressure and federal inaction were familiar themes. First, they resonated with the possibilities left open by the foundational Supreme Court cases on the relationship between state and federal authority on immigration matters. Recall that in *Chy Lung*, while the Court struck down California's imposition of a bond on certain arriving aliens as a violation of exclusive federal immigration authority, it also left open the possibility of lawful state interventions. As the *Chy Lung* court noted, it was not called upon to decide the fate of subfederal immigration policies created in the absence of Congressional legislation at a time when the state faced the vital necessity of protecting itself from paupers and criminals from abroad.

Second, this was not the first time state officials had cast their response through this federalism lens. Governor Pete Wilson had conjured this same rhetoric when framing the need for California's Proposition 187 in 1994. Wilson defended the so-called Save Our State Initiative by depicting California as the victim of federal failure, stating "California has had enough and it's time to stop illegal immigration.... If the federal government were held accountable, they would quickly discover that the cost of ignoring the real and explosively growing problem of illegal immigration is far greater than the cost of fixing it."[52]

Examples of this line of reasoning are replete in the political and legal discourse around immigration over the past ten years. In signing Arizona's E-Verify law, then-Governor Janet Napolitano (and later Secretary of the Department of Homeland Security) declared: "Immigration is a federal responsibility, but I signed [the law] because it is now abundantly clear that Congress finds itself incapable of coping with the comprehensive immigration reforms our country needs."[53] The severity and urgency of problems caused by demographic pressures from immigration were an integral part of the lament from states like Arizona. Unable to wait any longer for the federal government to seal the border and vigorously enforce provisions of the Immigration and Nationality Act,[54] states and localities had to legislate to protect their residents and solve their impending demographic crisis.

This sentiment was also neatly encapsulated by Napolitano's successor, Governor Jan Brewer, in her signing statement accompanying the passage of SB 1070, the law creating a state immigration enforcement scheme and providing state criminal penalties for immigration violations:

> The bill I'm about to sign into law – Senate Bill 1070 – represents another tool for our state to use as we work to solve a crisis we did not create and the federal government has refused to fix.... The crisis caused by illegal immigration and Arizona's porous border.
>
> ...
>
> We in Arizona have been more than patient waiting for Washington to act. But decades of federal inaction and misguided policy have created a dangerous and unacceptable situation.[55]

Indeed, President Obama's remarks after the passage of Arizona's SB 1070 echoed Governor Brewer's signing statement of the law in Arizona: "[T]he politics of who is and who is not allowed to enter this country, and on what terms, has always been contentious. And that remains true today. And it's made worse by a failure of those of us in Washington to fix a broken immigration system."[56]

Local actors made similar claims as well. For example, Lou Barletta, then-mayor of a small city in central Pennsylvania (who subsequently parlayed his notoriety from defending the city's immigration ordinance into becoming a U.S. congressman) who was among the earliest to pass a restrictive ordinance, testified to Congress that "In Hazelton, illegal immigration is not some abstract debate about walls and amnesty, but it is a tangible, very real problem."[57] In this story, state and local immigration laws emerge as compelled solutions to these newfound and intractable policy challenges, such as economic stress, increased language isolation, wage depression, and overcrowding.[58]

This conventional explanation for these various state and local immigration regulations is represented in Figure 3.1.

In sum, many state and local officials from 2004 to 2012 framed justifications of their policies on federal failure to enact comprehensive immigration reform and cited the ostensibly urgent policy challenges they were facing. According to them, their localities were unaccustomed to having many immigrants, and

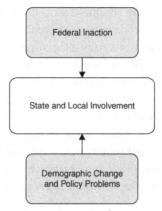

FIGURE 3.1. The vital necessity argument in the contemporary era.

these places now had to grapple with the sudden increase of immigrants and the associated social and policy challenges they were causing, such as overcrowded housing, Spanish being spoken in public spaces, strained social services, and day laborers soliciting work at street corners.[59] As we detail in this chapter, this predominant narrative about restrictive legislation, as a logical response to the sudden growth of low-skilled Latino immigration, took on the aura of unassailable truth as it fell in line with the growing attention that many scholars, demographers and sociologists in particular, were giving to "new immigrant destinations."

The plausibility of this conventional wisdom was bolstered by three key factors. First, Congress had been (and continues to be) deadlocked on comprehensive immigration legislation since 1996. Other than amendments to facilitate federal enforcement, and the Secure Fences Act of 2006, other proposals for either comprehensive or piecemeal federal immigration reform have failed. Next, there was a temporal coincidence of two developments: immigrants, and especially unauthorized immigrants, were moving to places that had not previously had a significant base of foreign-born residents. At the same time, immigration restriction was grabbing news headlines from places that most Americans had never heard of, such as Hazleton, Pennsylvania, and Farmers Branch, Texas. While pairing these two trends together might have been dismissed as simple correlation, there was an emerging body of literature in sociology and demography that drew attention to the particular needs and challenges of immigrants living in "new destinations."

Building on the pioneering work of Audrey Singer at the Brookings Institution, many scholars were beginning to see the value in comparing

other words, what has Congress done lately? Post-2001 Congress has considered comprehensive federal immigration proposals and partial, stand-alone proposals (such as the DREAM Act) several times without passage. Justice Scalia's partial dissent in *Arizona v. United States* noted this recent federal legislative inactivity in response to rising unauthorized immigration, suggesting that federal officials have been "unable to remedy the problem" of unlawful migration affecting Arizona.[68]

As we explain in further detail in Chapter 6, however, the precondition of federal failure depends on how one defines the federal government's actions vis-à-vis immigration policy and enforcement. Certainly, Congress has been beset by partisan divides and plagued by the many vetogates that prevent responsive action. On the other hand, the federal executive has been conspicuously active, setting out memoranda defining the administration's enforcement priorities, allocating enforcement resources in particular ways, and utilizing prosecutorial discretion to address the needs of wide swaths of the immigrant population.

However, we leave a more in-depth exploration of the role of the executive branch in setting immigration policy and the significance of that role in judicial evaluations of state and local lawmaking to later chapters. For our analysis here, it is sufficient to note that the claim of federal dalliance articulated by officials, advocates, and courts is a highly contested one that does not necessarily comport with current budgetary constraints on immigration enforcement or robust executive activity with regard to setting priorities and granting administrative relief. These are forms of federal action taken in the shadow of congressional stalemate on large-scale immigration reform.

Moreover, although the question of federal inaction can be a theoretically and legally contested one, the second part of the conventional justification for state and local restrictivism – that of *demographic necessity* – is subject to empirical evaluation. We now turn to the complaints of state and local officials centered on the policy concerns caused by unauthorized migrants, dispelling those ostensibly empirical claims and revealing more operative factors that spurred state and local restrictionist policy over the past ten years.

## EMPIRICALLY TESTING THE DEMOGRAPHIC NECESSITY RATIONALE

According to the conventional model of immigration federalism (Figure 3.1), the key reason why states and localities moved so strongly toward restrictive legislation was the sudden growth of undocumented immigration in new places, and attendant problems such as overcrowded housing, wage competition, and the growth of Spanish-language speakers. What this dominant narrative ignored, however, was the fact that thousands of cities and towns in the United States had experienced new waves of low-skilled migration, but only a few dozen were making any attempts to pass restrictive legislation.[69] Thus, even in the heyday of this recent round of subfederal restrictive activity on immigration, it did not seem that new patterns of migration were a *sufficient* explanation: Thousands more places were encountering the arrival of Latino immigrants than the hundred or so that attempted to pass restrictive legislation. Another problem with the conventional wisdom of "new immigration as causing new restrictive legislation" was that several places that were considering punitive laws had very few immigrants to speak of. This was particularly true in many localities in central Pennsylvania near the city of Hazleton. Many of these places had considered and passed restrictive laws that were similar to Hazleton's, but immigrants in these localities accounted, on average, for only about 3.5 percent of the resident population.[70] Thus, not only was the influx of migrants unlikely to be a sufficient condition, they were also unlikely to be a *necessary* condition for restrictive legislation.

In this section, we provide a systematic analysis of these demographically driven explanations for policy change, and show that they are empirically wanting. More specifically, we ask: Why did some places in the United States adopt restrictive policies while most did nothing at all? We answer the question as it involves local ordinances and state laws, and we analyze corresponding sets of legislative data: a collection of state legislation and local ordinance information from 2005 to 2011. The National Council of State Legislatures reports nearly 1,200 state immigration laws enacted between 2005 and 2011.[71] In analyzing this data, our goal is to determine the relative importance and weight of several factors that have been proffered by commentators and elected representatives to explain the recent spate of subnational lawmaking.

Our statistical analyses are of restrictive activity at the state and local levels, and we find that factors related to migration play a marginal and inconsistent role. By contrast, the factors that consistently emerge as statistically significant are the political contexts of these states and localities. Specifically, restrictive legislation is significantly more likely in places where Republicans are predominant in the state or county, and they are significantly less likely to be passed in localities where agriculture accounts for a significant share of the labor market. Thus, contrary to what many journalists, and even several social scientists and law professors have believed, the problem of immigration restriction did not arise because of immigrants moving to *new* destinations, but rather from moving to *Republican-heavy* destinations.

During this period some states and localities also enacted "pro-immigrant" or "integrationist" policies, including so-called law enforcement sanctuaries, in-state tuition grants, and municipal identity card schemes. Other studies have noted that partisanship also plays a significant role on the permissive side of subnational legislation, and we leave a fuller examination of the dynamics of such legislation to Chapter 5.[72] Here, in endnotes, we will highlight some relevant data regarding such pro-immigrant actions, particularly to consider the possibility that a particular factor may be insignificant in the case of explaining restrictionist legislation, but nevertheless significant for integrationist policies.

While there was widespread recognition by 2007 that localities were playing a more significant role in regulating the lives of low-skilled immigrant residents, there was little systematic understanding of why some localities may adopt restrictionist policies, while most do not. Part of the difficulty was the fact that many of the places considering restrictionist ordinances were in small municipalities that rarely got coverage in state newspapers and wire stories, let alone national outlets such as the *New York Times* and *Washington Post* or more regional newspapers such as the *Chicago Tribune*. Thus, the dominant understanding of the factors compelling local action on immigration was shaped by heavy coverage of such places as Hazelton, PA; Carpentersville, IL; San Bernardino, CA; and Farmers Branch, TX. Based on those jurisdictions, the likely demographic explanations centered around the size and growth of recent immigrants, the size and growth of the Latino population, and the attendant challenges to this growth, such as overcrowded schools and housing, growth of Spanish-language communities, erosion of wages among native-born workers, and perhaps xenophobia or racial prejudice among native-born populations.[73]

To provide a more systematic test of these demographic factors, we created two datasets – of cities and states – that combines immigration policy measures with a host of other factors that might explain their passage. For our city-level dataset, we started with a baseline of municipalities (defined as "places" in most states, but also including "county subdivisions" in others). Next, we obtained lists of municipalities that have proposed restrictive ordinances and regulations from various sources, including the American Civil Liberties Union, LatinoJustice PRLDEF, the Fair Immigration Reform Movement, the National Immigration Law Center, and the Migration Policy Institute. We then validated these lists by making phone calls to jurisdictions noted as considering or passing ordinances, as well as by monitoring news stories on local ordinances through December 2011. For our state-level dataset, we came up with a measure of legislative activity on immigrant integration based on reports from the National Conference of State Legislatures from 2005 to 2011, and included any measures that bear a significant relationship to illegal immigration. We provide more details on these local and state policy datasets in the Appendixes. In both datasets, we merged information on the passage of legislation with demographic data from the 2000 Census and the 2005–2009 American Community Survey.

### Hypothesized Factors Necessitating State and Local Response

Using our original data set of about 25,000 cities, we tested the relative importance of the following factors:

- *Population of New Immigrants, and Growth of Latino and Foreign-Born Populations*[74]
- *Overcrowded Housing*
- *High Proportions of Households That Are Exclusively Spanish Speaking*
- *Naturalized Share and Latino Share of the Citizen Population*
- *Economic Stress and Relative Group Deprivation*
- *Local Economic Interests*
- *The State-Level Policy Climate toward Immigrants*

**Population of New Immigrants, and Growth of Latino and Foreign-Born Populations** As we noted earlier, the most notable development in immigrant settlement patterns since the 1990s has been the movement of low-skilled immigrants, predominantly from Mexico, to new parts of the country with little recent history of migration. Based on the concerns voiced by elected representatives in many of these areas, we might expect places with high proportions of recent immigrants or places that have experienced a surge in Latino and immigrant populations to face the following public policy challenges:

**Overcrowded Housing** Past research on the politics of immigration at the local level has shown that issues of overcrowding are more common in immigrant destination cities. However, these problems are rarely acknowledged by municipal governments in their planning documents,[75] so we may fail to see a positive association between overcrowded housing conditions and city ordinances related to immigrant tenants.

**High Proportions of Households That Are Exclusively Spanish-Speaking** One of the most prominent concerns about recent migration to new destinations, especially of Latino immigrants, is the fear of linguistic balkanization and the visibility of Spanish in public spaces.[76]

*Naturalized Share and Latino Share of the Citizen Population* There are two ways that we can measure the potential electoral strength of immigrants. The most direct way to do this is to examine the naturalized share of the local citizen population. Still, many surveys of Latinos have shown that native-born Latinos are important allies on immigration reform: even though the foreign born account for only 53 percent of the adult Latino population, and 26 percent of the adult citizen Latino population, surveys have shown consistently high levels of support among Latino voters for legalization programs, and high levels of opposition to restrictive measures at the subnational level.[77] These surveys also show that immigration is one of the highest policy priorities for Latino voters, often trumping even the economy as the "most important problem" facing Latinos.[78]

*Economic Stress and Relative Group Deprivation* We expect the economic stress from wage competition from low-skilled migration to be felt most strongly among those whites and blacks living below the poverty line, where the substitutability of labor is strongest.[79] Alternatively, it may be the relative rates of poverty with Latinos that matter, as Professor Claudine Gay suggests in her study of economic disparity and black attitudes toward Latinos.[80]

*Local Economic Interests* Jurisdictions with industries that are heavily dependent on low-skilled immigrant labor, particularly agriculture, may be less likely to pass restrictive ordinances because of the importance of low-skilled migrants to the local economy.

*The State-Level Policy Climate toward Immigrants* State laws toward immigrants may itself bear a significant relationship to ordinance activity at the local level. For instance, a municipality may, as a form of dissent or opposition, consider a restrictive ordinance in a state where recent policies have been pro-immigrant. Similarly, those seeking to pass such policies may be less likely to do so in places where there have been restrictive measures passed at the statewide level.[81] Alternatively, it is also possible that restrictive legislation at the state level may bear a positive relationship to similar measures at the local level, with either serving as a precursor or model for the other.

While the presence of absence of prior state legislation is a potentially important factor in explaining municipal ordinance activity on immigration, it is also important to explain what factors, if any, explain restrictive laws at the state level. Many of the factors that we hypothesize to predict local legislative activity are also relevant for state activity, albeit at a different scale. Thus, we are able to obtain measures of the population of new immigrants, the growth of Latino and foreign-born populations, and the unemployment rates of whites and blacks at the state level. While it is also possible to generate

**Table 3.1** *Proposal and passage of restrictive ordinances at the municipal level, 2005–2011*

| Status | Number | As share of total |
|---|---|---|
| Pending | 33 | |
| Passed | 79 | |
| Failed/tabled | 13 | |
| *Subtotal* | 92 | 0.5% |
| *Total* | 25,108 | |

*Note:* After 2007, there is a considerable decline in newspaper reports of new municipal ordinances, and a decline in the extent to which advocacy organizations track municipal legislation.

average measures of overcrowding at the state level, there is little theoretical justification to include this factor in explanations of state legislation since land use is generally a local, not state decision.[82]

### Statistical Findings on Local Ordinances

Of the approximately 25,000 cities in our dataset, 125 had proposed restrictive ordinances between 2005 and 2011, and 93 had proposed pro-immigrant ordinances, including measures limiting cooperation with federal authorities on deportations (Table 3.1).[83] On the restrictionist side, approximately 63 percent of proposals had passed, about 10 percent had been voted down or tabled, and a quarter were still pending. On the "pro" side, the vast majority of proposals had passed, with only two pending and one classified as failed or tabled. It is clear from these numbers that the instances of restrictive ordinances go well beyond the well-known cases of Hazleton, PA, and Farmers Branch, TX. However, it is also important to note that these places account for only one-half of 1 percent of all localities in the United States. Also, restrictive activity was not evenly distributed across municipalities in all fifty states. Pennsylvania had by far the highest number of restrictive proposals (twenty-six), followed by California (sixteen), Alabama (nine), Virginia (seven), and Texas (six). Seventeen states had no restrictive municipal ordinance being proposed, while most of the rest had one or two in each.

In order to arrive at systematic answers about the conditions under which cities may consider and pass restrictive legislation, we ran a multivariate regression that can show the contribution of each factor while controlling for all other factors. In addition to our hypothesized factors, we also controlled for

**Table 3.2** *Changes in the predicted probability of restrictive municipal ordinances*

|  | *Proposal* | *Passage* |
|---|---|---|
| Republican majority in county | 2.56 | 4.08 |
| Agriculture jobs (share) | – | 0.66 |
| % of immigrants who are recent (<5 ys) | – | – |
| Growth in immigrant population | – | – |
| Overcrowded households (%) | – | – |
| White poverty | – | – |
| Black poverty | – | – |
| *White poverty (relative to Hispanics)* | – | – |
| *Black poverty (relative to Hispanics)* | – | – |
| *Latino share of citizens* | – | – |
| *Growth in Latino population* | 1.04 | – |
| *Growth in Spanish households* | 1.04 | 1.07 |
| *Restrictive state policy climate* | – | – |
| City population (ln)* | 3.91 | 4.27 |

*Note*: Standardized effects on statistically significant variables are changes in probability of the outcome when the variable is moved from the 25th to 75th percentile and all other variables are kept at their means.

* We have this as a log scale, given the diminishing returns to relative city size at the highest end of the distribution.

city size, and explore its potential relevance after a discussion of our hypothesized factors. Importantly, we remained attuned to issues of multicollinearity, where putting two factors that are closely related into the same explanatory model produces erratic results for those factors. Since some of these factors are highly correlated, we ran alternative model specifications instead of putting every factor in the same regression model. We report our findings from these alternative specifications where relevant. For ease of interpretation, we include a full report on our regression results in **Appendix A** and here provide an abridged illustration of the substantive effects of those factors that are statistically significant in Table 3.2.[84]

***Population of New Immigrants, and Growth of Latino and Foreign-Born Populations*** Having an immigrant population that is composed primarily of recent arrivals (or, having experienced a recent upsurge in Latino or immigrant populations) is not associated with restrictive ordinances. Indeed, it is associated with a greater likelihood of pro-immigrant legislation. Our alternative measure, of the growth of the foreign-born population between 1990 and 2000, or between 2000 and 2007, also has no statistically significant relationship with restrictive ordinance activity, although it is associated with a lower likelihood of pro-immigrant ordinances. Finally, a fast-growing Latino population in the locality, regardless of their citizenship and immigration status, is associated with a marginally greater likelihood of restrictive ordinances being proposed, but not passed.

*Spanish-Speaking Households and Overcrowded Housing* Factors related to recent arrivals, such as the proportion of households that are exclusively Spanish-speaking and the proportion of households that are overcrowded, also bore no relationship to the proposal or passage of restrictive ordinances up until 2007. Since then, however, the growth of Spanish-speaking households has made a marginal difference in the probability of restrictive proposal and passage (increasing by 4 percent and 7 percent, respectively). These effects pale in comparison to those associated with local contexts of political partisanship (discussed below).

*Naturalized Share and Latino Share of the Citizen Population* We included these measures in two separate equations given their high level of collinearity (r=0.47). These factors do not bear any significant relationship to the proposal and passage of local ordinances, whether restrictive or permissive. This further reinforces findings from other studies of local immigrant incorporation that immigrant electoral power may be less important in predicting local government policies toward immigrants today than in the past.[85]

*Economic Stress and Relative Group Deprivation* There is no support for the contention that economic stress or relative deprivation (as measured by absolute or relative poverty rates, respectively) among white residents is related to the proposal or passage of restrictive legislation. Indeed, when relative measures of poverty are used, cities with whites who are relatively better off than Latinos are more likely to propose restrictive policies. However, when it comes to the passage of policies, there is no significant relationship. Finally, black relative deprivation is indeed associated with a higher likelihood of restrictive proposals, but not policy passage. It is unlikely that blacks are driving the proposal of restrictive legislation in most of these cities, since in none of these places are blacks the majority, and they are more than one-third of the population in only one case (Norristown, PA).

*Local Economic Interests* The prevalence of industrial sectors that are heavily dependent on immigrant workers is not significantly related to local ordinances, with one important exception: the likelihood of restrictive policies being passed is much lower in places where agriculture accounts for a sizable number of jobs. It is important to note, however, that the effects are evident in the stage of ordinance passage, but not ordinance proposal. This suggests that immigration restrictionists in agricultural areas may have overreached by pushing for restrictive policies only to find an organized opposition from local businesses to such plans.[86]

**The State-Level Policy Climate toward Immigrants** This factor bears no significant relationship to ordinance activity at the local level. For state-local dynamics, neither the "steam valve" model (localities adversely reacting to state-level policy) nor the "demonstration effect" model (mimicking state-level activity) are at play.

Our analysis also controlled for the size of the city, which turns out to have the strongest effect among all of the variables.[87] While it is tempting to tease out a theoretical explanation for the importance of this factor, we also find in our larger analysis that city size is related to more pro-immigrant legislation. Thus, we cannot rule out the possibility of a finding that is statistically significant but causally suspect: it is unclear why larger cities should propose both permissive and restrictive legislation. Also, the relevance of city size here may be due to the fact that small cities, with populations of fewer than 50,000, are less likely to have local print and television media coverage. This, in turn, could be reflective of the strategies of policy activists (see discussion of issue entrepreneurs in Chapter 4) who are less likely to propose legislation in places that do not stand the chance of media coverage and dissemination, or the limited revenue base of small municipalities that are reluctant or unable to afford legal counsel in the event of a court challenge.[88]

### Statistical Findings on State Legislation

During this same period, legislation at the state level was much more common, with 1,321 laws enacted between 2005 and 2010. Of these, we coded 317 as restrictive, with at least one such law passed in 46 states. These laws ranged in terms of their policy area (e.g., education, law enforcement, public benefits) and in their severity (e.g., ranging from revoking licenses of notaries public who have been denaturalized, to laws denying access to state public benefits to unauthorized immigrants).[89] Taking into consideration only those restrictive laws that we classified as having a significant impact on a state's unauthorized immigrant resident population,[90] the number of laws during this time period drops to 155, with Arizona passing the most laws (15), followed by Virginia (10), and Georgia (9).

Illustrating again that demographic change is not sufficient to produce restrictionist legislation, of the top 25 percent of states where new immigrants make up a sizable portion of the overall population, only 6 of 13 states passed significant restrictive laws during this time. In the multivariate regressions, we tested for several variations of demographic change, including the proportion of new immigrants, the proportional change in the foreign born population, and the absolute level of immigration in the area. On the other end of the demographic spectrum, we found that nine of twelve states at the bottom quartile on this measure passed restrictive laws. Indeed, the passage of restrictive laws is highest for this bottom quartile of states, and lowest among the top quartile. Clearly demographic disruptions caused by recent immigration are also not necessary for state-level restrictive action.

In our multivariate regression analysis that controls for various other factors, the state-level models reveal no support for the hypothesis that restrictive legislation is more likely in states where immigrants have arrived recently, or alternatively, states with the biggest growth in the foreign-born population. Indeed, in some variations of our model, we find less restrictive activity in states with recent immigrant populations (see **Appendix B**). For most of our demographic factors (including poverty rates and growth of the immigrant population), the findings are inconsistent, perhaps due to the small number of cases being analyzed (fifty states).

## AN ALTERNATIVE TO DEMOGRAPHIC NECESSITY: POLITICAL CONTEXT

If demographic factors such as rise in recent immigrants, wage competition, and economic stress fail to predict or explain restrictionist ordinances, what does? Based on our prior work,[91] we proposed that political partisanship[92] may be a salient driver of subnational immigration law.

We hypothesized that Republican-majority areas are more likely to sponsor restrictive ordinances: such contexts provide ripe opportunities for policy entrepreneurs to propose and pass policies, by framing undocumented immigration as one of the most significant problems for local governance. For instance, in 2006 and 2007, six cities in California (Apple Valley, Costa Mesa, Escondido, Lancaster, Santa Clarita, and Vista) passed restrictive ordinances on matters ranging from day laborers, employers, and landlords.[93] These various municipalities shared little in the way of large-scale recent immigration or rapid changes in local unemployment, but did share one common characteristic: electorates that leaned heavily Republican (with a party registration advantage ranging from sixteen percentage points to thirty percentage points in these cities) in a state where registered Democrats had an eight percentage-point advantage over Republicans.[94]

The political opportunities that Republican-heavy municipalities presented to policy entrepreneurs on immigration restriction continued through 2010, as the *Los Angeles Times* reported on the successful attempts of a local tea party activist in getting Republican-heavy cities in Southern California such as Temecula and Murrieta to pass restrictive measures, after failing to do the same in larger, more politically diverse cities such as Riverside and Ontario.[95] Finally, in cases where policy entrepreneurs are not involved in local efforts, political ambition may be a critical factor, as Republican-heavy districts offer the chance for primary challengers to mobilize party activists who care intensely about the issue of illegal immigration.[96]

Among our hypothesized factors, partisanship has the strongest and most consistent effects. *After controlling for all other factors,* municipalities in Republican-majority areas are 2.5 times more likely to <u>propose</u> restrictive ordinances (see Table 3.2). And they are 4 times as likely to have <u>passed</u> such ordinances compared to Democratic areas.

The role of partisanship is also striking at the state level. As we noted earlier, there is no significant or consistent relationship between various immigration-related factors and state-level legislation. In the case of partisanship, however, the results are consistently significant: After controlling for various demographic factors, states with a majority of Republican voters have passed more than twice as many significant pieces of restrictive legislation (four, on average, during this period) as did those states with a high proportion of Democratic voters (1.6, on average). Another way to look at the state results is to differentiate between those states with multiple pieces of significant restrictive legislation (three or more) versus the rest. Republican-majority states are nearly 300 percent more likely to be in this group than are Democratic-majority states.[97] Finally, we also updated the analysis to account for laws enacted outside of the 2005–2010 period, by analyzing all current state laws on enforcement and work verification.[98] Here, too, we find that partisanship has the strongest effect on the existence of restrictive state-level policies, and that factors such as the growth of the foreign-born population or the recency of the immigrant population do not matter (see **Appendix B**).

### Conclusions from the Empirical Data

Our analysis shows that the restrictive responses of local governments to undocumented immigration are largely unrelated to the objectively measurable demographic pressures credited in the conventional model of subnational immigration regulation. Our evidence discounts the saliency of recent immigrant population growth, the proportion of Spanish-dominant households, and local economic and wage stress in proposal and passage of such laws. These ordinances are also largely unrelated to the electoral empowerment of Latinos, given that places with large proportions of Latino residents and citizens are no more or no less likely to propose legislation, whether restrictive or pro-immigrant.

Instead, we find that political factors not commonly cited by proponents of state and local immigration laws are more important. The partisan composition of the area plays an important role, second only to city size. However, because city size is positively associated with both pro and restrictive ordinances, party composition is the only factor that displays statistically significant and theoretically consistent effects (negative on the restrictive side and positive on the pro side). Finally, partisanship has, by far, the strongest relationship at the state level.

Generally, we learn that several hundred jurisdictions have experienced demographic change identical to, or more severe than, ordinance-enacting jurisdictions like Hazelton, and yet an exceedingly minute number legislate in response. This ten-thousand foot perspective shows that the purported inevitability – of large numbers of recent immigrants prompting demographic disruptions and policy challenges, which then push legislators to action – is not evident in a comprehensive examination of the data based on statistical analyses that control for various other factors.

How does the argument for demographically driven legislative change hold up using considerations of necessary and sufficient conditions? Among municipalities that passed restrictive ordinances, new immigrants averaged about 3 percent of the total resident population, only slightly higher than the 1 percent average for municipalities across the country.[99] Even taking the case of a restrictionist city with the highest proportion of recent immigrants – Herndon, Virginia, where recent immigrants accounted for 14.5 percent of the town's residents in 2000 – we find that 129 other municipalities took no action, despite having even higher proportions of recent immigrants, including 23 with recent immigrants accounting for over 25 percent of the town's residents. Indeed, the majority of jurisdictions that can claim to share the necessary demographic factors – such as growth in immigrant populations, having a recently arrived immigrant population, or a high proportion of Spanish-speakers among immigrants – do not propose or pass immigrant-related laws. Therefore, demographic change from recent immigration is *not a sufficient condition* for restrictive action. Factors other than the increased presence of recent immigrants – mainly, partisanship – generally must manifest prior to policy expression.

Even if immigration-induced change within a jurisdiction is insufficient, by itself, to provoke legislative response, might such change be necessary? We find that twenty-one out of the fifty-one municipalities that have passed restrictive ordinances (or 42 percent of the cases) have recent immigrant populations that are below the national average for cities. Indeed, in a quarter of the cases (thirteen out of fifty-one), recent immigrants accounted for fewer than 0.5 percent of the city's residents, and where the proportion of Spanish-dominant households were less than 1 percent of all households in the city. Thus, we draw the critical conclusion that *demographic change is not only an insufficient condition; it is an unnecessary one as well.* Partisanship, by itself, can result in local policy expression without underlying demographic upheaval.

These illustrations are even more dramatic at the state level. Of the top 25 percent of states where new immigrants make up a sizable portion of the overall population, only six of thirteen states passed significant restrictive laws during this time, thereby illustrating that demographic change is not sufficient. On the other end of the demographic spectrum, we find that nine of twelve states at the bottom quartile on this measure passed restrictive laws. Indeed, the passage of restrictive laws is highest for this bottom quartile of states, and lowest among the top quartile. Clearly demographic disruptions caused by recent immigration are also not necessary for state-level restrictive action.

The catalytic characteristic common to most enacting jurisdictions is not demographic upheaval; rather, they share a partisan mix highly receptive to restrictionist legislation. We saw this in our regression findings, but it is also apparent in the raw data, where 71 percent of municipalities with restrictive ordinances are in Republican-majority counties. Although we do not have finer-grain data on partisanship for all municipalities in the United States, we were able to obtain such data on places with restrictive ordinances.[100] Here, too, we find that a high proportion of restrictive ordinances (77 percent) have passed in Republican-majority municipalities. At the state level, nearly three-quarter of restrictive states had a Republican majority of voters during this time period, and for those who passed two or more pieces of legislation, the proportion is even higher (81 percent).[101]

To sum up, we find severe limitations to the conventional explanation of immigration restriction as the result of demographic pressures from new migration. Instead, the statistical evidence point to political factors as potentially being more important: states and localities with higher levels of Republican voters are more likely to pass restrictive legislation, regardless of underlying demographic realities. Why might this be the case?

We turn now to explore the relevance of this factor in more detail, explicating our counterargument to the conventional model of immigration federalism, a framework that we term the Polarized Change model. The importance of partisanship and political contexts that define the Polarized Change model underlie the novelty of the new immigration federalism. As we shall see, this recent spate of state and local laws uses the language and scaffolding of federalism as the terrain on which to instantiate a preferred national policy vision on immigration. This national policy vision, however, is one accomplished through the use of receptive state and local jurisdictions, and not through the traditional channel of Congress in making immigration law.

# 4

## A Political Theory of Immigration Federalism: The Polarized Change Model and Restrictive Issue Entrepreneurs

In the immigration sphere, claims of demographic necessity and public policy imperatives can sometimes shield other practical and political realities. In Chapter 3, we took a hard look at the recent resurgence of state and local immigration lawmaking, describing the types of restrictionist policies that captured the national agenda from 2004 to 2011, and assessed the merits of the "necessity" narrative as found in many journalistic and scholarly accounts – that the combination of demographic pressures from new patterns of migration, combined with federal inaction, created irresistible pressure for states and localities to act. Our analysis suggests that those justifications do not hold much water, either theoretically or empirically. Here, we turn to the other surprising finding from our quantitative investigation – that political contexts and partisanship matter in immigration federalism, and are salient regardless of the underlying demographic or policy realities facing a state or locality.

While we show that partisanship has a statistically stronger relationship than do various demographic factors in explaining legislative change, perhaps a more interesting question is how these political factors actually function to produce such policy expressions. After all, on almost every hot-button legislative topic it is often easy to blame outcomes on politics or political factors. As such, the kinds of robust political explanations we offer here seek to go beyond ad hoc pronouncements on the importance of politics, which have pointed to disparate factors such as political interest groups,[1] legacies of Jim Crow,[2] and racial gaps between voters and residents.[3]

Instead, we use the conclusions drawn in Chapter 3 to develop an overarching model to replace conventional explanations, accounting for the specific context of immigration discourse. This "polarized change" model of subnational immigration regulation proffers our theory on why partisan debates specifically influence immigration policy, and how the political process has shaped both federal and state legislative efforts during this new surge in immigration federalism. This new model, grounded in theoretical frameworks provided by legal and political science scholarship, accounts for our empirical findings on partisanship and demography. It also incorporates qualitative evidence gathered from news reports, interviews, and congressional dynamics, which highlight the work of selected policy activists in immigration law.

The glaring theoretical defect with the conventional account of state and local immigration action is that it conceptually separates the precondition of federal inaction from the consequence of state and local action that fills the federal legislative void. In other words, it conveniently reduces the phenomena of immigration federalism to the combination of *policy pressures from below* that confronts *legislative inaction from above*. But, this conceptual simplicity fails to capture important nuances and complexities that actually inform immigration policy dynamics at both levels simultaneously.

First, the current status quo of federal legislative inaction on immigration is not the same as having a blank policy slate. As Chapter 2 details, since 1952, the federal government has relied on the Immigration Nationality Act, with many statutory provisions that have been added or amended over the years. In addition to statutory provisions on the matter, immigration is also subject to the various regulatory provisions and enforcement priorities of the Executive branch and subject to congressional oversight and budgetary authority. Thus, the precondition of federal inaction itself is a highly dubious starting point from which to explain why states and localities have sought to regulate immigrants and immigration. Various elected officials, and portions of the voting public may disagree with or oppose the federal laws and the manner of their execution, or believe that the legislative environment needs to be updated or otherwise modified, but that disagreement does not nullify the existence of the background scheme.

Undoubtedly, even with the concession that there is no policy vacuum on immigration at the national level, one might still argue that those existing federal laws and regulations, many enacted decades ago, are ill-equipped to solve the policy challenges posed by recent immigrants, particularly low-skilled unauthorized immigrants from Mexico. However, as we have already seen, the empirical evidence offers little to support the contention that restrictive legislation was more common in places with recent arrivals, or with more Mexican immigrants, or with more Spanish-dominant households, or with more objective conditions for labor competition between immigrants and the native born. In other words, even if recent immigrants were causing new and unanticipated problems, restrictive laws were not necessarily popping up in places where those problems (if any) would be presenting themselves.

Second, policy problems caused by demographic changes at the state and local level are not self-evident; that is, simply because demographic change may have occurred does not mean that policy problems automatically arise or require legislative response. Rather, as many established scholarly models in the literature on public policy and public opinion have shown, *they depend on problem definition, attribution of blame, and political mobilization.*[4] But, as we demonstrated, policy challenges related to increased immigration constitute neither a necessary nor a sufficient cause for restrictive legislative action at the subnational level. Furthermore, economic rationales that stress the importance of wage competition and local fiscal pressures are unable to account for the timing of restrictive efforts at the state and local level. These efforts rose dramatically in 2005 and 2006, during a time of low unemployment and booming economic growth, undercutting wage competition and local fiscal pressures as plausible explanations.

Finally, the conventional explanation assumes the existence of federal failure, but provides no empirical or theoretical explanation for federal legislative inaction. If the factors that explain federal inaction on new immigration legislation are wholly unrelated to the factors that can explain local action, then having a two-tiered explanation may be sufficient – with partisan gridlock explaining the former, and demographic factors explaining the latter. However, we find that this is not the case. Indeed, as we argue in this chapter, two sets of factors – what we characterize as *party polarization* and *ethnic nationalism* – when mobilized by *issue entrepreneurs*, account for both federal inaction and the rise in subnational legislation, and thus have greater explanatory value than attempts to describe the two sets of phenomena in a piecemeal manner. Fundamentally, we argue that both the precondition of federal legislative inaction and the consequence of state and local restrictionist action to fill that legislative void are related phenomenon, and any viable theory of the new immigration federalism must account for both aspects.

In response, our model of polarized change incorporates our findings on the saliency of partisanship and allows for the possibility that a single mechanism influences both national and subnational dynamics. The Polarized Change model draws on major theoretical traditions in the public policy scholarship on legislative change, such as the multiple streams tradition and the punctuated equilibrium framework of policy change,[5] and relates it to existing work in legal scholarship on legislative cascades,[6] private lawmaking,[7] and the influence of political parties on federalism dynamics.[8] Much like in these other frameworks, we argue in our Polarized Change model that the entire process of policy change on immigration – from opinion formation among voters to agenda setting and legislation at the national and subnational levels – was shaped powerfully by the work of political parties and issue entrepreneurs (those who do the work of promoting the salience of a particular issue, offering particular frames for understanding those issues, providing particular solutions, and identifying opportunities and venues for policy change). In our theoretical exposition, it is worth saying a bit more about party institutions and their potential relationship to immigration federalism. (We will reserve our theoretical discussion of issue entrepreneurs later in this chapter, as we discuss the concept in specific relation to the model we propose).

Party dynamics and structures of federalism can, under the right circumstances, help breed policy proliferation across jurisdictions. Partisanship as filtered through intra– and inter–political party contests, and institutions of federalism, like Congress and state elected positions, allows for affiliations across levels of government that can help achieve an overall strategy of policy proliferation. Thus, our polarized change model posits a dynamic feedback loop between subfederal and federal lawmaking cemented through the structural connectedness baked into our federalist structure. Specifically, the dominant presence of two rival political parties at all levels of government facilitates the tendency for subfederal enactments to anchor the political positions by national party members. The parties themselves, as institutions of ideological affiliation that transcend geographic boundaries, provide the connective tissue between federal and subfederal actors, and provide opportunities for factional contests within party electoral contests (including, most notably, primary elections).

As Dean Larry Kramer has long argued, national lawmakers of a particular party are, to some extent, dependent on state and local officials from the same party for endorsement and political support.[9] As he noted, political parties have created "a political climate in which members of local, state, and national chapters are encouraged, indeed expected, to work for the election of party candidates at every level – creating relationships and establishing obligations among officials that cut across governmental planes."[10] While Kramer primarily understood this connectedness as a way of preserving state power,[11] we instead use his observation to advance the claim that this politically interdependent structure is effective at advancing partisan goals, perhaps especially by helping to create appropriate conditions for horizontal policy proliferation across state and local jurisdictions.

The federated nature of political parties forces national lawmakers to take heed of the immigration positions taken by subfederal officials affiliated within their political party. When state and local politicians – at the behest of issue entrepreneurs – promote restrictionist policies in their jurisdictions to gain notoriety or to challenge incumbents by exploiting intraparty schisms, party members at the federal level must account for these positions lest they harm their own chances for reelection.[12] In 2006, for example, incumbent Congressman Jim Kolbe from Arizona faced a serious challenge in GOP primary contests from Republican candidates who took much harder-line stances on immigration and border security issues.[13]

State and local officials' policy preferences are able to anchor the positions of national lawmakers because national party members are in part beholden to the endorsements and support of those state and local members. After a state or locality enacted a restrictionist law, national lawmakers from that jurisdiction had to take care not to oppose such efforts lest they provide fodder for a restrictionist challenger in the next intraparty primary election. Accordingly, subfederal immigration policies like Arizona's LAWA or SB 1070 encouraged stalemate at the national level by ensuring that congresspersons, especially House members from racially homogenous, heavily conservative districts, resist comprehensive federal reform proposals that water down enforcement methods or include legalization programs in addition to enforcement programs. As we discuss below, Senator John McCain's move from a moderate on immigration matters and a supporter of DREAM Act and comprehensive immigration reform, to rejecting congressional compromise and ideologically aligning with SB 1070, showcases the power of this federated party dynamic in action.

The bottom line is that subfederal policy proliferation and federal legislative silence (or action) are not independent phenomena; they are inextricably linked by the structure of our federalist system and correspondingly federated party structures. In our model, restrictionist positions that find traction in particular subfederal jurisdictions will necessarily tie the hands of national lawmakers of the same party. Completing the feedback loop, state and local officials can, and as we shall see, did, argue that this federal stalemate creates the appropriate precondition of federal inaction and ineptitude that justifies further subfederal proliferation.[14]

In addition, our framework highlights the influence of immigration issue entrepreneurs in creating the conditions necessary for subnational immigration regulation, framing the narrative necessary for judicial and political acceptance of restrictionist legislation, and the targeting of specific jurisdictions with partisan conditions that are ripe for enacting such regulation, with an eye to more widespread adoption. The key insight with this model is the connectedness – the unitary nature – of both the dynamics at the federal and subfederal levels. Instead of conceiving of these two aspects as independently moving parts, we suggest that both are influenced concurrently, by the same actors or by actors working in a connected network with each other. The stalling of the one (federal legislation) provides the constitutional and political leverage for activity at the other (activity at the state and local level). Additionally, in our view, subfederal-level proliferation becomes a goal in itself, without the contingency of awaiting federal action. Further, our alternative model showcases how issue entrepreneurs have been able to intensify interparty polarization and post-9/11 ethnic nationalism, to effectively promote their causes. To be clear, our description of this process is not intended, by itself, as a negative judgment on the work of these entrepreneurs: rather, we seek to present a more realistic appraisal of the mechanism producing subnational immigration regulation.

We start with, and focus on, the work of restrictionist issue entrepreneurs because they acted first. In this new surge of immigration federalism, restrictionists were the first to exploit the power of state and local action to create a new de facto national policy. Until 2011, integrationists were still, by and large, focused on national legislation and the few organizations that were state-focused were largely playing defense, attempting to stall restrictionist laws in state legislatures or fighting them in federal courts. It was only after 2011 that national and state-level integrationists began to adopt a more concerted and organized strategy of state-level proliferation that had previously been the hallmark of immigration restrictionists. We turn to the integrationists' adoption of this strategy in Chapter 5, but in the rest of this chapter we describe the Polarized Change model as it applies to restrictionist issue entrepreneurs, and show how they managed to proliferate state and local legislation from 2004 through 2011.

## DESCRIPTION OF THE POLARIZED CHANGE MODEL

The underlying premise of the Polarized Change model is that policy challenges resulting from demographic change do not inexorably produce legislative efforts at policy change. Calls for policy change emerge even without underlying objective conditions such as rapidly growing immigrant populations (not necessary); further, objective conditions often do not lead to efforts at local legislation (not sufficient). What is more important than the objective basis for a policy problem is its *perceived existence and importance* among those who are critical to the legislative process.[15]

In Figure 4.1, we situate the role of issue entrepreneurs in the larger process of immigration policy change. One may typically think of elected representatives as key actors on legislation. And, in recent years, state and local officials like Lou Barletta from Hazleton, Pennsylvania, Governor Jan Brewer of

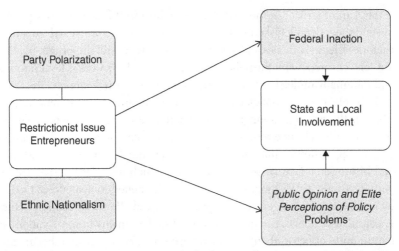

FIGURE 4.1. Polarized change model of subnational immigration legislation.

Arizona, and Sheriff Joe Arpaio (self-dubbed "America's Sheriff") of Maricopa County have become nationally known, the household names and faces connected with the subfederal restrictionist movement of 2004–2011.

Although these, and other, elected officials have gained significant notoriety, we show that in the case of state and local legislation on immigration, issue entrepreneurs play an outsized role relative to elected representatives. These key activists coordinate action across local jurisdictions, and between levels of government. In various jurisdictions, restrictionist issue entrepreneurs also create model legislation that can be easily mimicked, and they craft such legislation to test the limits of constitutional constraints at the subfederal level. Critically, based on our empirical analysis and theoretical reasoning, we eliminate the "demographic change and public policy problems" found in **Chapter 3** (see Figure 3.1 on the conventional model), and replace it with the "perceived existence of policy problem," underscoring the subjective nature of such claims and their production through a process of politicization.[16]

According to some theoretical accounts, the idea of federalism and the presence of such entrepreneurs go hand in hand. The fundamental idea behind federalism is that it allows for multiple instances and places to deliberate and instantiate law and policy. In the United States, there are fifty states and the District of Colombia, and over 25,000 local jurisdictions. These myriad "points of law production," as Professor Judith Resnik notes, provide innumerable opportunities for (in her terminology) "norm entrepreneurs" to shop their policies and attempt to persuade elected officials and other governmental actors.[17] In other words, the "who" of federalism in this account is expanded beyond the federal legislature–state legislature narrative of stylized federalism rhetoric. Elected officials and governmental units are still important, but they are "co-venturers" with the policy entrepreneurs, whose work is less examined and minimally understood in most studies of federalism dynamics.

To be clear, we are not claiming that issue entrepreneurs are solely responsible for the way that immigration policy has developed at the national and subnational level since 2001. Instead, they play a central role in taking advantage of opportunities that are themselves generated by two other historical and institutional factors: *party polarization* (which includes the rise of interparty divisions in Washington DC after 2000, abetted to a significant extent by ideological challengers in party primaries), and *ethnic nationalism* (which encapsulates the twin rise in racial and cultural antipathy in immigration discourse and concerns about homeland security after the September 11, 2001 attacks). Party polarization presented the opportunity to shift immigration policy away from a bargaining dynamic among varied interest groups and legislators where compromise is possible, to a pattern of retrenchment where interparty divisions engender gridlock through the use of filibusters.[18] And the rise of national security concerns presented opportunities to expand the rhetorical scope of ethnic nationalism and its salience to a wider population, and to a broader set of issues – that is, to concerns about unlawful labor migration through the southern border.

Even when party polarization and ethnic nationalism rise, however, there must still exist actors and institutions through which they can be filtered and utilized. In most cases of state and local restrictionism from 2004 to 2011, immigration issue entrepreneurs played this critical role of policy catalyst: they challenged moderate Republicans well before the tea party's rise in 2009, they helped to shift immigration policy from an interest group bargain to a partisan stalemate, and they were early champions of this "border security" variant of ethnic nationalism, mobilizing constituents and pressuring legislators to resist the existential threat represented by immigrants. In addition to capitalizing on these factors to block bipartisan legislation at the national level, these issue entrepreneurs also played an important role at the subnational level: identifying the places where opportunities are greatest, offering model legislation and political counsel to ensure legislative passage, and lending legal expertise to ensure that the provisions have a colorable constitutional basis.

Thus, in important ways, our notion of restrictive issue entrepreneurs borrows significantly from John Kingdon's concept of policy entrepreneurs who hold a deep and longstanding commitment to particular policy solutions and who wait for the right windows of opportunity to promote their preferred solutions.[19] We find this formulation to be far too broad, incorporating a large multitude of actors in various states and localities, and unhelpful in differentiating the post-2001 period from the Prop. 187 period. Unlike in Kingdon's framework, moreover, the restrictionist issue entrepreneurs who pioneered and proliferated state and local legislation did not simply wait for the right circumstances where the multiple streams of policies, problems, and politics would converge. Instead, they created these very opportunities in a federated framework by working in a coordinated fashion, helping to engender policy gridlock in Congress as a necessary condition and justification for state-level proliferation.

## THE POLARIZED CHANGE MODEL IN THEORY AND PRACTICE, 2001–2012

Here, we flesh out the details of the Polarized Change model as it applies to immigration legislation at the national and subnational levels from 2001 to 2012. First, we use existing theoretical frameworks on policy proliferation and federalism dynamics to identify and describe the class of key policy actors we call issue entrepreneurs. Then, we provide a few examples from the past decade of issue entrepreneurs in action, noting the two contextual factors that have structured the opportunities for legislative change on immigration since 2001: the rise of party polarization and ethnic nationalism.

To develop this narrative, we take a close look at key instances of congressional and subnational immigration action from 2001 onward. Thus, complementing the quantitative data presented in Chapter 3, here we analyze qualitative data from news reports and in-depth interviews with key policy actors to show how issue entrepreneurs work in the immigration legislative landscape.[20] Our analysis here gets into the details of the policy and political work of key actors and events in immigration lawmaking during the period from 2001 to 2012. This rich description of the political capture and mechanism of policy change is vital to understanding the deficits of the conventional model and evaluating the difference the polarized change model makes for the way in which federalism interactions are typically understood, and the value of that jurisdictional variegation in conventional federalism models.

### The Agents of Polarized Change – Restrictionist Issue Entrepreneurs

Who are these issue entrepreneurs on immigration, and how did they mobilize and coordinate action at the national and local levels? One way to think of these actors would be to include those whose activism has generated national news, and who seek to influence policy on immigration beyond their immediate jurisdiction. Such a definition, however, would produce a list that is extremely long, including *local representatives* such as Lou Barletta (former mayor of Hazelton, PA, now U.S. representative from Pennsylvania's 11th congressional district), *law enforcement officials* such as Joe Arpaio of Maricopa County, AZ, *state legislators* such as Russell Pearce (R-AZ) and Virgil Peck (R-KS), *governors* such as Jan Brewer (R-AZ) and Robert Bentley (R-AL), *U.S. representatives* such as Tom Tancredo (R-CO), Jim Sensenbrenner (R-WI), and Steve King (R-IA), *advocacy groups* such as the Federation for American Immigration Reform and NumbersUSA, *research organizations* such as the Center for Immigration Studies, national *radio personalities* such as Glenn Beck, John Kobylt, and Kenneth Chiampou, *television personalities* such as Lou Dobbs (formerly of CNN) and Bill O'Reilly (Fox News), *legal advocates* such as Kris Kobach, the Immigration Reform Law Institute, and other organizations such as the American Legislative Exchange Council whose concerns lie well beyond immigration, but who have nonetheless played a role in coordinating restrictive legislative efforts across states on the issue.

Such a broad definition is not only unwieldy from an empirical perspective, it is also unhelpful for our theoretical model of polarized change, which reserves the label of issue entrepreneur for those actors who wield influence at both federal and subfederal levels, and have been central to a strategy of state and local proliferation. While we acknowledge that many players influence immigration policy, we focus on this narrower set because of their multi-level reach and forward-thinking legislative strategy. Moreover, the activities of this narrower group of actors is much more consequential for considerations of federalism because they challenge standard assumptions that undergird federalism analysis generally, and immigration federalism analysis specifically.

We arrive at a theoretically cogent set of actors in the restrictionst arena by applying and modifying existing legal frameworks for policy instantiation. Using the background theoretical literature, we establish the following key criteria for identifying restrictionist issue entrepreneurs for our model. First, the issue entrepreneurs we identify took advantage of limited public knowledge about immigration policy and problems. Relatedly, they linked restrictionist policy goals with the rhetoric of state and local autonomy. Third, they were able to recruit the wider set of actors described above to their cause. Finally, these actors worked in a network, each specializing a set of tasks that, when coordinated with other entrepreneurs, led to policy proliferation at the local level and timely legislative gridlock at the national level.

Applying this framework, the identities and achievements of restrictioin-ist issue entrepreneurs comes into clearer focus. Based on their influential work during the rise of state and local restrictionism from 2004 to 2011, we identify five key entrepreneurial individuals and organizations. Individuals included *Tom Tancredo* (U.S. representative from Colorado from 1999 to 2008, and a 2008 presidential candidate), *Kris Kobach* (legal counsel to restric-tionist organizations and jurisdictions and coauthor of Arizona's SB 1070 law), and *Lou Dobbs* (host of a prime-time CNN program, *Lou Dobbs Tonight*, from 2003 to 2009). In addition, national organizations acting as issue entre-preneurs included the *Federation for American Immigration Reform (FAIR)* and *NumbersUSA*. Below, we first amplify the theoretical foundation of our selection of these particular entrepreneurs. Second, to familiarize readers, we provide a brief description of each of these key figures and the roles they've played in national and subnational immigration policy during the period of restrictionist state and local resurgence.

The idea of interested private parties and organizations that coalesce around an issue or cause, and then employ various methods to influence public policy related to that cause is well studied.[21] These descriptions distinguish a distinct species of policy actors who seek policy change by helping frame challenges, disseminating information (or misinformation), networking across jurisdic-tional lines, and raising money for such activities.[22] Other scholars have even noted immigration entrepreneurs (Kris Kobach) by name.[23]

The "issue entrepreneurs" we identify in the Polarized Change model are the evolved descendants of these political actors. The descriptor "issue" emphasizes that these actors appear to truly care about, and believe in, the substantive restrictionist position they attempt to achieve. Immigration issue entrepreneurs do not seem to be using a restrictionist agenda as a convenient vehicle to activate a broader states or local rights platform.[24] Indeed the juris-dictional notion of states' rights or localism is coincidental and convenient to their cause, as a broader promotion of subfederal power does not appear to be a primary goal. As such, they not only promote their policy vision at the sub-federal level, they concurrently undermine other state and local efforts aimed at integrating or ameliorating conditions for unauthorized immigrants.[25] In other words, they care about state and local power only to the extent it serves their substantive policy goals.[26] It is, as with much contemporary federalism, a federalism of convenience and opportunism.

The issue entrepreneurs' key intuition – connecting these substantive misperceptions and subnational policy proliferation – is exploitation of the discourse of state and local rights for their particular policy ends. For a period of time, restrictionist issue entrepreneurs were able to effectively deploy federalism tropes to rally local majorities and elected officials to their cause. Recent political science research suggests that federalism-based framing of policy issues by political elites are consequential to citizens' beliefs and voting.[27] As such, the ability of restrictionist issue entrepreneurs to target willing elected officials, and supply those officials with federalism-based rhetoric to defend substantive immigration enforcement positions, measurably influences the failure of federal proposals.[28] Even if national majorities favor certain aspects of federal immigration reform,[29] significant constituencies within that diffuse majority may be convinced to oppose specific national reforms to preserve state involvement in enforcement schemes. This may be especially true after enactment of a state or local policy, as citizens who previously were agnostic toward restrictionist legislation, may now support the restrictionist laws, not because of the substantive policy position, but to protect state and local authority.

In the restrictionist context, entrepreneurs promoted a series of ostensibly empirical and factual claims regarding the public policy challenges caused by recent unauthorized migration. These statements of demographic necessity would eventually make their way into the purpose statements of state legislation like Arizona's SB 1070 and Alabama's HB 56, and were key talking points in elected officials' campaigns to justify those laws. These perceptions persisted despite the experience of jurisdictions passing immigration legislation – from Riverside, New Jersey, and the states of Oklahoma and Alabama – which have all suffered greater economic distress *after* the legislation passed, and *subsequently* drove out labor and consumer sources.[30] Similarly, the idea of immigrant criminality motivating laws like SB 1070 and HB 56 has been proven to be a "myth."[31] Despite a marked drop in violent crime in Arizona, issue entrepreneurs, as purveyors and disseminators of immigration "facts" have consistently galvanized receptive constituencies with their message of the danger posed by migrants.[32] Thus, similar to the policy actors described by other scholars, restrictionist issue entrepreneurs are able to succeed and endure, despite championing empirically dubious claims.[33]

In addition, a few intensely interested actors are sufficient to trigger a legislative epidemic, if those actors are properly credentialed and positioned.[34] A key characteristic of this small group is the ability to recruit other credentialed and influential actors, such as the larger group of officials, organizations, and media personalities listed above. Because of the opportunities presented by party polarization, this broader set of elected actors is easy to discover for immigration policy purposes. State and local officials naturally fit into the entrepreneurial framework as they are key facilitators and molders of public perception.[35] They effectively frame and promote the issue entrepreneurs' message that demographic "facts" cause urgent policy problems, and are experts at manipulating the perception of public policy crisis for political gain.[36]

Finally, restrictionist issue entrepreneurs are appropriately networked, showcasing the ability – as a collective whole – to work across multiple jurisdictions, both among the many states and localities, and between federal and subfederal levels.[37] Each of these actors also performed a specialized set of critical roles: lobbying federal legislators to block legislative efforts, designing model legislation for the state and local level, offering legal counsel and expertise, framing and making immigration issues salient to the general public, mobilizing and informing issue activists, and keeping unseemly, race-specific immigration discourse out of the mainstream.

As we describe in detail later, the five issue entrepreneurs we select based on this framework may fill many of these roles within a networked system. Further, they, as a group, evinced the ability to fulfill the prerequisites for policy proliferation and legislative cascades described in the literature, using a combination of demographic concerns and federalism rhetoric uniquely available in the immigration context.

(1) Tom Tancredo played a sustained and crucial role in organizing the legislative opposition to bipartisan federalism solutions that included a path to citizenship for the unauthorized immigrant population in the United States. As early as 2001, he publicly countered White House attempts to gather support for a legalization program after the state visit of Vicente Fox to Washington, DC.[38] Subsequently, Tancredo recruited new members into the Immigration Reform Caucus, a group that successfully prevented or delayed bipartisan attempts at federal immigration reform by the White House and Senators Sam Brownback (R-KS) and Ted Kennedy (D-MA). Tancredo's success in blocking bipartisan legislation on immigration continued through the 2006 and 2007 efforts at comprehensive immigration reform, as he rallied conservatives in the House and Senate to oppose provisions in the bill that would lead to an eventual path to citizenship.[39] During his time in Congress he commanded a sizable group of legislatures in the Immigration Reform Caucus, providing him the power to access party leadership and influence House votes.[40] He also entered the presidential race in 2007, seeking to force other candidates to address the topic of illegal immigration.[41]

Finally, Tancredo has also been heavily involved in promoting the salience of immigration across various states and localities. He did so by introducing bills and amendments to withdraw federal funding from so-called sanctuary cities,[42] proposing that legislators and mayors who championed such legislation face criminal charges,[43] urging the Department of Homeland Security not to undermine the enforcement efforts of groups such as the Minuteman Project,[44] and lending support to legislative efforts against illegal immigration in states such as Pennsylvania[45] and Arizona.[46]

(2) While Tancredo is an example of an issue entrepreneur whose involvement tended to a greater focus on the national level, Kris Kobach is an individual whose dual involvement has generally favored the state and local level. Kobach's first major involvement in immigration control was his authorship of the National Security Entry-Exit Registration System (NSEERS) in his role as chief adviser to Attorney General John Ashcroft on immigration and border enforcement.[47] However, most of his subsequent involvement on immigration has been at the state and local levels. As early as 2002, Kobach authored a memo while working at the Department of Justice that called for "allow[ing] local police officers to make arrests for civil violations of immigration law," a move that was initially opposed by the White House, but subsequently adopted by the Office of Legal Counsel.[48]

After moving to Kansas, he worked first as a law professor, publishing academic articles building the legal and theoretical case for state enforcement authority, and opposing aspects of comprehensive federal immigration reform, including the DREAM Act.[49] His legal work relies on the fundamental, but unsupported, empirical claims of the conventional model of "vital necessity," including the notion of insurmountable fiscal and policy pressures created by unauthorized migration: "Without question, the most significant force driving action at the state and local level is a fiscal one. In city after city, and state after state, governments have acted for one overriding reason: They can't afford to. Illegal immigration is expensive."[50] Demographic change is critical to his defense of state and local action, as he contends, "Arizona's fiscal burden may not come as a great surprise, given its location on the border. However ... every state is a border state now. Numerous other states have experienced a recent influx of illegal immigration."[51] In helping advance the conventional model, his work also lays the doctrinal and theoretical foundation for greater state and local immigration enforcement authority, premising his defense both on a claim of the inherent sovereign authority of states to control enforcement within their borders (an argument later championed by Justice Scalia in his *Arizona* dissent), and on the practical utility of enhanced enforcement as an effective incentive for self-deportation and deterrence of future unauthorized migration.[52]

Both as a law professor, and then later as Secretary of State for Kansas, Kobach has served as legal counsel for many states and localities that have passed restrictive legislation, including the city of Hazleton, PA's rental ordinance which was passed in 2007, and eventually struck down in 2013,[53] and other similar cases such as *Vasquez v. City of Farmers Branch, Texas*, and *Gray v. City of Valley Park, Missouri*. Kobach also provided legal counsel on constitutional challenges involving state legislation in Arizona and Alabama. Both the underlying state and local laws, and the resulting federal court litigation, provided Kobach with important opportunities to operationalize and test his doctrinal arguments and academic theories for state and local immigration control.

Perhaps more centrally to our model of issue entrepreneurship, Kobach authored much of the subnational legislation that wended its way through federal courts, with each subsequent effort purporting to expand the scope of subnational participation in immigration enforcement.[54] Kobach's entrepreneurship was perhaps most evident in Alabama's HB 56 in 2011, as reported in the Mobile Press-Register:

> Kobach got his introduction to Alabama politics in 2007, through a conference hosted in Birmingham by the Eagle Forum of Alabama, a conservative think tank. There, he met state Sen. Scott Beason, R-Gardendale, who said the two developed a relationship that centered on their shared concerns about the nation's immigration policy.
>
> Beason, who carried the immigration bill in the Alabama Senate, said he leaned heavily on Kobach to help write it.[55]

As Kobach's entrepreneurial work in Alabama reveals, restrictive state legislation on immigration is not a simple matter of homegrown solutions to persistent and thorny local problems, as legislators often portray the issue.[56] Instead, it often involves sponsorship and expertise from outside actors who make critical choices on venues based on political opportunities (large Republican majorities in the legislature and a Republican governor), to build a case for the necessity and constitutionality of subfederal action. We will explain the strategic benefits of this particular method of policy proliferation in greater detail later.

Kobach's coordinated efforts at the subnational level eventually brought him into the spotlight of national politics, as Mitt Romney trumpeted the Kansan's endorsement prior to the South Carolina presidential primary[57] and enlisted Kobach as a campaign surrogate to discuss the need for immigration restriction.[58] Indeed, Kobach's apparent goal of developing *de facto national policy on immigration through a proliferation of state laws* was evident in his remarks while endorsing Romney: "Illegal immigration is a nightmare for America's economy and America's national security. Mitt Romney is the candidate who will finally secure the borders and put a stop to the magnets, like in-state tuition, that encourage illegal aliens to remain in our country unlaw-fully. He is also the candidate who will stand shoulder to shoulder with the states that are fighting to restore the rule of law."[59] In many ways, his vision recalled the role of states prior to 1875 when they independently exercised immigration authority, or perhaps from 1875 through 1891, when the federal government provided substantive restrictions, but recruited and used the enforcement infrastructure of states to help effectuate those federal goals.

Issue entrepreneurship is not, and was not during this past resurgence of state and local immigration lawmaking, merely the handiwork of a few indi-viduals. Indeed, the most intensive and sustained involvement in this issue has been provided by the organizations Federation for American Immigration Reform (FAIR) and NumbersUSA. These organizations have devoted consid-erable resources, both to defeat moderate legislation at the national level and promote restriction at the subnational level. They have large national mem-berships and can mobilize public phone and email campaigns to national lawmakers that produce tangible results.[60] Importantly, these organizations bring a considerable measure of institutional investment and continuity that individuals like Tancredo and Kobach lack. Thus, while Tancredo's leader-ship on the issue declined after his departure from the U.S. Congress, and Kobach's centrality rose only after 2005, FAIR has been a tireless advocate for immigration restriction since 1979, and NumbersUSA has been doing so since 1997. Both organizations have had their greatest impact after 2001.

(3) FAIR boasts a national membership of more than 250,000 individuals and, since its founding, has advocated for sharp reductions in legal and illegal immigration, including "a temporary moratorium on all immigration except spouses and minor children of U.S. citizens and a limited number of refu-gees."[61] In its first two decades, the organization focused its advocacy on legisla-tion and enforcement at the national level, but it has also broadened its efforts with state lobbyists and regional field offices. While the organization does not have local chapters, it works in partnership with other organizations, often providing legal and political expertise, as well as resources and personnel to local legislative campaigns. Indeed, as the Los Angeles Times reported in 1994, FAIR's lobbyist in Sacramento, Alan Nelson, helped write the state's restrictive ballot measure, Proposition 187.[62] It is important to note, however, the national organization was not directly involved in California's proposition campaign, a claim that is supported by proponents and opponents alike of Proposition 187.[63] Getting involved in state legislation was not in keeping with the vision of FAIR in the 1990s, as the organization was focused exclusively on national legisla-tion. Indeed, the organization played a critical role in the design of immigra-tion restriction in the various bills that Congress passed in 1996.[64]

By 2004, however, FAIR saw more strategic value in getting involved in state legislation as a way to influence the national agenda on immigration policy. It got involved in Arizona in 2004 primarily as a means to derail the political momentum behind national immigration reform efforts by Republican moderates from Arizona such as John McCain and Representatives Kolbe and Flake.[65] The organization gathered signatures for Proposition 200 in 2004 and filed lawsuits after the measure's passage to ensure its broadest application. Since 2004, FAIR has institutionalized its support of state and local ordinances through its legal affiliate, the Immigration Reform Law Institute (IRLI). This group, with Michael Hethmon and Kris Kobach as lead advisers, offers legal counsel and model legislation to states and localities contemplating restrictive action, and challenges state and local laws when they expand the rights of unauthorized immigrant residents in cases such as the California provision allowing in-state college tuition for unauthorized immigrants who graduate from the state's high schools[66] and San Francisco's issuance of municipal identification cards.[67]

(4) Along with FAIR (and its legal arm, IRLI), NumbersUSA is the other major organizational force in immigration politics, fulfilling the vital role of derailing attempts at national, comprehensive immigration legislation through its work with specific legislators. The national organization was founded in 1997 by Roy Beck, advocate for immigration reduction and author of a best-selling book on the topic in 1996.[68] Critical to the group's founding was Dr. John Tanton, a one-time environmentalist turned immigration crusader who spawned a number of prominent organizations like FAIR, NumbersUSA, and the Center for Immigration Studies.[69] Groups such as the Southern Poverty Law Center have long contended that Tanton's network is a multi-pronged effort at mobilizing racial antipathy toward Latinos,[70] and recently archived correspondence from Tanton at the University of Michigan indicate that he often invoked race and the threat of Mexican immigration to white racial dominance.[71]

As worries over Dr. Tanton's explicitly white nationalistic rhetoric grew,[72] Beck attempted to distance NumbersUSA from Tanton by 2002. However, reports show continued contact and relationship between NumbersUSA and other organizations directed by Tanton, and arm's-length coordination on state legislative efforts between more mainstream groups and racial hate groups.[73] This ostensible distancing helps NumbersUSA serve its specific role in the entrepreneurial landscape. The organization provides the critical legitimating mechanism for the restrictionists in immigration discourse, channeling the racial and ethnic hostility of many of its supporters into race-neutral policy positions palatable to national lawmakers.[74]

Although NumbersUSA had only 4,000 members in 2001,[75] it swelled to nearly 500,000 members by mid-2007, as bipartisan comprehensive immigration reform efforts looked increasingly likely. Beck credited the growth in membership to a few primary factors, including the events of 9/11 and the immigration stance of President Bush.[76] The organization works to stall moderate bipartisan efforts on immigration issues, even when those proposals comport with national majoritarian preferences.

Indeed, NumbersUSA's work was critical to derailing the 2007 comprehensive federal immigration bill, which had, at that point, received the support of President Bush, the U.S. Chamber of Commerce, the high-tech industry, the Catholic Church, immigrant-advocacy organizations, and several industries reliant on immigrant labor, including farming, food services, and construction.[77] During the weeks leading up to the floor vote on the bill, NumbersUSA coordinated weekly phone calls with the Congressional Immigration Reform Caucus, mobilized its members to engage key senators, and provided those senators with the information and arguments necessary to oppose the bill.[78] Several actors, including pro-immigrant advocates, restrictionists, and members of Congress, have credited NumbersUSA with causing the collapse of the bill in the Senate.

(5) Finally, media actors have played a significant role in facilitating the work of issue entrepreneurs on immigration restriction at the national and subnational levels. Indeed, one media personality in particular, Lou Dobbs, played such a key role in both levels that he merits the designation as an issue entrepreneur. *Lou Dobbs Tonight* on CNN promoted the cause of immigration restriction in several ways: (1) providing sustained attention to national and subnational manifestations between 2003 and 2009, (2) raising the issue's salience among activists and non-activists alike, (3) providing a platform for restrictionists to express their views with little critical analysis or challenge, and (4) occasionally making fundraising appeals for the legal defense of subnational legislation.

Immigration was Dobbs's signature issue from the very founding of *Lou Dobbs Tonight* in June 2003. In the inaugural year of the show, Dobbs covered the topic of illegal immigration in 151 of 257 shows (59 percent).[79] During this time, he devoted about as much time to his other signature topic: outsourcing, an issue championed more by Democrats than by Republicans (160 shows). Since then, however, immigration reigned supreme in his program, as he covered the topic in 1,189 of 1,413 shows (84 percent), while the issue of outsourcing dipped to 565 (or 49 percent). Little surprise, then, that a Media Matters Report noted in 2008 that, "instead of *Lou Dobbs Tonight* his program might be more properly called *Lou Dobbs Crusades Against Illegal Immigration Tonight.*[80]

His coverage of illegal immigration focused both on national legislation and personalities such as Jim Sensenbrenner, who introduced legislation in 2005 that would make illegal immigration and assisting illegal immigrants a felony, but also local groups like the Minuteman Project, which recruited volunteers to patrol the U.S.-Mexico border.[81] Dobbs also provided a national platform for Hazleton, Pennsylvania, and its then-mayor Lou Barletta, including devoting an entire show to a town hall meeting on immigration hosted by the city.[82]

Dobbs also often took on the role of an advocate; even going so far as making fundraising appeals for the city's attempts to defend itself against legal challenges by the ACLU and MALDEF.[83] The extent of Dobbs's advocacy on subnational policy was perhaps most evident in the case of Governor Eliot Spitzer's decision to make driver's licenses available to unauthorized immigrants in New York in 2007. He devoted more than thirty shows to the topic, criticizing Spitzer's proposal, inviting his guests to do the same, and mobilizing public opposition. The level of mobilization was intense and sustained, and was largely credited in forcing Spitzer to drop his proposal, who declared, "It does not take a stethoscope to hear the pulse of New Yorkers on this topic."[84]

### Issue Entrepreneurs in Context

These issue entrepreneurs are notable in our Polarized Change model for the multifarious work that they have done: they have engaged in both federal and subfederal levels, sharpening prior conditions of party polarization and shaping the rise of ethnic nationalism – all to advance a restrictionist agenda that has depended both on preventing bipartisan, moderate legislation at the national level and proliferating restrictive legislation at the subnational level. Here, we provide an illustration of these dynamics from 2001 to 2012, breaking the period into the three presidential terms it covers. This division by presidential terms is useful because of the ways in which the restrictionist entrepreneurial activity affected key political constituencies and influenced electoral politics. We stop our story of subnational restrictionist fervor at 2012 because that year marked a political and legal turning point in immigration federalism. We continue our narrative of developments post-2012 – that is, after the Supreme Court's *Arizona v. United States* opinion, President Obama's Deferred Action for Childhood Arrivals Program, and his subsequent reelection – in the chapter that follows.

<u>Bush's First Term (2001 to 2004)</u> The scholarship on partisanship has noted a marked increase in polarization since 2000, after a protracted and contentious debate over the legitimacy of the presidential election and sharp disagreements over tax cuts in 2001 and the prosecution of the Iraq war in 2003.[85] The growth in polarization has taken several forms: in the increasing number of party line votes on legislation, increased use of the filibuster to protect the minority party's interests, contentious debates over the confirmation of presidential nominees, a greater divergence between Democrats, Republicans, and Independents in the electorate, and increasing factionalism within the Republican Party.[86]

Despite the general rise in party polarization, it was not inevitable that legislative attempts on immigration policy since 2001 would divide sharply along party lines and fail to pass the U.S. Congress. Indeed, Bush was able to centralize in several areas of domestic policy that his own party had, for many years, left to states.[87] For instance, the No Child Left Behind Act passed by overwhelming majorities in the House and Senate in 2001,[88] and even contentious measures such as the 2001 tax cuts and the 2002 Iraq War Resolution managed to draw enough bipartisan support to reach the president.[89] In the immigration context specifically, prior votes on landmark legislation also garnered sufficient bipartisan support to pass: the 1986 Immigration Reform and Control Act, won nearly 43 percent of Republican support in the U.S. House in addition to 65 percent of Democrat support in the chamber.[90] Similarly, in 1996, 94 percent of Democrats joined 100 percent of Republicans in the U.S. Senate in favor of the Illegal Immigration Reform and Immigrant Responsibility Act.[91]

With the strong backing of President Bush and Senators such as Sam Brownback (R-KS) and Ted Kennedy (D-MA), it seemed that immigration reform might once again pass the U.S. Congress after 2000. Immigration reform was high on the Bush administration's legislative agenda in the summer of 2001. Having passed a contentious and ambitious ten-year tax reduction plan, the administration was gearing up to work on a way to regularize the flow of migrants from Mexico and provide a path to legalization for those already residing in the United States. The administration was especially eager to show progress on this issue in advance of the state visit of President Vicente Fox, a personal friend of the president, in early September.[92] Even though the September 11 attacks delayed any attempt at comprehensive immigration reform, a bipartisan group of legislators still tried to pass smaller measures.

One such attempt was in 2002, as legislative leaders in Congress tried to pass a seemingly obscure and relatively uncontroversial provision allowing eligible noncitizens to apply for immigrant visas while still in the United States. Section 245(i) of the Immigration and Nationality Act had passed in 1994, and renewed in 1997 and 2000. The Bush administration pushed vigorously for the measure with the hope of having a signed bill prior to the president's visit to Mexico in March 2002. The Democrats hoped to make the extension permanent. Tancredo mounted a vigorous opposition, claiming that the bill would "invite future terrorists to exploit lax enforcement of the immigration laws."[93] He succeeded in pushing for a two-thirds supermajority rule on the legislation, FAIR lobbied wavering legislators, and NumbersUSA mobilized its grassroots supporters to maximize Republican opposition to the measure in Congress.[94] The resistance emboldened opposition in the U.S. Senate where it subsequently stalled. Thus, even though the bill had the backing of the Bush administration, the insurgent activities of issue entrepreneurs derailed bipartisan attempts to allow for limited adjustment of status by pushing many moderate Republicans into the restrictionist camp.[95]

Accordingly, our theory emphasizes that national legislative gridlock on immigration matters is specifically influenced by party polarization, not just heterogeneity and interest diffusion as it may be in other regulatory areas.[96] Undoubtedly, such heterogeneity and diffusion does exist in immigration law as well; those clamoring for federal immigration laws are sometimes a strange amalgam of interests, from immigrants' advocacy groups to private business interests, who either need a labor source or are trying to avoid state-by-state regulations.[97] Additionally, the platform for national legislation is broad, ranging from providing pathways to legalization, to creating uniform employment regulations, to reconsidering admissions limitations and enforcement priorities.

In the past decade, disparate groups have demonstrated the capacity to coalesce to advance federal immigration reforms. Many of these proposals enjoyed the support of national majorities and bipartisan congressional support. So, despite the frailties described earlier, pro-immigrant (or anti-regulation/ anti-enforcement) forces are capable of joining together for sufficient periods of time to place legislation on the national agenda, and to force floor debate and votes. Yet, because of the number of vetogates inherent in the federal legislative process, it is much easier to defeat federal legislation than to shepherd it to passage;[98] capitalizing on these difficulties, focused minority interests represented by restrictionist issue entrepreneurs have been able to defeat those clamoring for national immigration legislation. National proposals moderate and compromise the restrictionist agenda in significant ways, and the federal legislature provides far less opportunities for envelope-pushing and productive entrepreneurial activity than do subfederal forums.[99]

Thus, the Polarized Change model helps explain why, in the immigration field, congressional gridlock may be even more difficult to overcome than the other regulatory areas. While subject to some of the same concerns about heterogeneity of interests and the difficulty of maintaining coalitions, it also features activists and insiders, like Tancredo, capable of polarizing immigration politics and stagnating federal reform, even when majority interests coalesce.

In addition to exacerbating party polarization, issue entrepreneurs also took advantage of the rhetorical opportunities offered by the September 11 attacks, which birthed a new form of ethnic nationalism. The post-9/11 version of ethnic nationalism championed by issue entrepreneurs moved beyond the "culture threat" concerns articulated famously in 1991 by conservative commentator and then-Republican presidential candidate Pat Buchanan, who infamously argued "if we had to take a million immigrants in, say, Zulus, next year, or Englishmen, and put them in Virginia, what group would be easier to assimilate and would cause less problems for the people of Virginia?"[100] Although the fear of cultural balkanization was still prominent among immigration restrictionists after 9/11,[101] the attacks introduced a new dimension of national security to the public discourse on immigration restriction.

Viewing migration from Mexico as a security threat to the United States was not an inevitable result of 9/11; instead, it was the long-standing work of restrictive issue entrepreneurs that made the conflation take hold. With national security considerations adding a level of legitimacy and plausible deniability to the role of racial antipathy in nativist sentiment, issue entrepreneurs made sure to invoke this dimension frequently in their opposition to immigration. They frequently lumped illegal immigrants together with terrorists in discussions ranging from the U.S.-Mexico border crossing[102] to the attempt by states to grant driver's licenses to unauthorized immigrants.[103] Indeed, as Professor Jennifer Chacón has noted, the term "border security" emerged only after 9/11, as prior discussions of "border control" took on military metaphors as they subsumed concerns about homeland security and terrorism.[104] The conflation of terrorism and illegal immigration, in turn, had a chilling effect on legislative attempts at the national or subnational levels that were perceived as being "soft" on illegal immigrants. As James Carafano, a homeland security expert at the conservative Heritage Foundation noted: "the connection between immigration and terrorism in policy discussions did make it more difficult to have a rational debate with some people, who could just throw in terrorism and halt the conversation."[105]

This invocation of security tropes, combined with an almost exclusive focus on unwanted migration from the southern border, situates the proliferation of subnational immigration regulation within the dominant American historical narrative of the past fifteen years, and illustrates how 9/11 changed the discourse of immigration. Kris Kobach, for example, argued in a widely cited law review article that local law enforcement officers possess the inherent power to enforce federal immigration laws.[106] While his reasoning applied to the use of local law enforcement to address all unauthorized migration (which overwhelmingly occurs across the southern border for labor-related reasons) – and not just national security threats – his argumentation and rhetoric was almost exclusively premised on the danger of terrorists and 9/11. Indeed, the entire article reads as if state and local control of unauthorized migration and anti-terrorism regulation are one and the same: "The terrorist attacks of September 11, 2001 underscored for all Americans the link between immigration law enforcement and terrorism."[107] Fundamentally, he makes his case for greater state and local enforcement latitude by suggesting that such authority might have prevented 9/11.

In addition to cloaking the issue of unauthorized migration through the southern border with an anti-terrorism veil, the invocation of security tropes provided issue entrepreneurs with the necessary language to covertly indulge the racial and cultural prejudices of a portion of the citizenry. Racial profiling and disparate enforcement seem to inevitably *result* when states and localities attempt to enforce immigration (although, one might worry about the racial disparity in immigration enforcement generally, regardless whether federal or subfederal entities engage in it[108]). Indeed, scholars like Michael Wishnie have long maintained that devolved immigration decision making will lead to increased bigotry.[109] Findings by the Department of Justice regarding local immigration enforcement in Arizona support his contention.[110] But, missing from these important explorations of the effects of subnational immigration regulation is an account of how ethnic nationalism and racial prejudice work to *produce* state and local regulation in the first instance.

To fill that void, the Polarized Change model accounts for restrictionist issue entrepreneurs' effective exploitation of latent racial prejudice to build party and local majority support for immigration legislation. A deeper look at the way in which entrepreneurs galvanized local electorates or portions of the Republican party reveal the precise mechanism by which nebulous racial and cultural concerns can be exploited within political factions to produce immigration policy. Through the prism of national security and homeland sanctity, entrepreneurs successfully moved explicit racial and cultural reasons for restriction from the fringe of political discussion to the mainstream. The racialized component of homeland security discourse is evidenced by the focus on Mexican migrants and the southern border, and the use of explicitly racialized rhetoric to drum up support for restrictionist policies. Indeed, this rhetoric would grow even more heated in Bush's second term, as media personalities like Lou Dobbs began referencing threats of criminal gangs and infectious diseases emanating from Mexico and other Latin-American countries.[111]

This is not to say that racial anxiety was always invoked explicitly in arguments tying the need for immigration restriction to national security. Indeed, Kobach's references to the national security threats from unchecked migration make no mention of the kinds of arguments made by Lou Dobbs and other conservative media commentators. At the same time, there is ample research from the post-9/11 period that indicates that evocations of terrorism often produced increases in racial anxiety.[112] In sum, our Polarized Change model elucidates the ways in which restrictive issue entrepreneurs harnessed, and sometimes exacerbated, racial anxiety in the context of national security to shift public sentiment toward viewing Mexican migration as a security threat to the United States.

Finally, as per our model in Figure 4.1, issue entrepreneurs in Bush's first term began working at both federal and subfederal levels. Even before state legislative efforts at immigration restriction were making national headlines in 2006, groups such as FAIR were getting involved in subnational efforts to restrict immigration. For example, during the summer of 2001, the organization played a supportive role in advising local activists in Iowa who were mobilizing against Governor Tom Vilsack's Model Cities program to create "immigration enterprise zones" to address the state's chronic labor shortages.[113] In 2004, however, the organization deepened its involvement with state legislative efforts, devoting considerable staff and financial resources to pass Proposition 200 in Arizona.

FAIR's direct involvement in Arizona in 2004 was a significant shift from its arm's-length approach to Proposition 187 in 1994, and it exemplifies the two-level nature of the work of restrictive issue entrepreneurs during this period. The organization got involved in Arizona's law, not because of a deep interest or belief in the value of state legislation. Indeed, as we shall see later, a minor dispute emerged between FAIR and Kris Kobach in 2011 over whether a national E-Verify law was preferable to stronger E-Verify laws in particular states. Instead, FAIR saw the importance of making a strong show of political force in Arizona, to counter the moves by President George W. Bush and Senator John McCain to push for immigrant legalization.

In January 2004, the organization viewed with alarm as George W. Bush announced immigration reform as a top legislative priority. On the same day that President Bush announced his intention to push for comprehensive immigration reform, Dan Stein, the President of FAIR appeared on CNN News and said "When we look at the president's proposal, what we see are low wages and desperate workers, a program that rewards cheaters, people who jump the line, basically ripping off the taxpayers, stealing residency, and working illegally."[114] Furthermore, John McCain, a strong presidential contender in the 2000 presidential primary and presumed front-runner for the 2008 election, had teamed with two House members from Arizona to push for legislation that would create a pathway to citizenship for unauthorized immigrants. McCain argued that such a move was not only morally imperative, given the number of border crossers dying in the Arizona desert, but also politically shrewd, given the growing importance of Latino voters in presidential elections.[115] Thus, FAIR's entry into Arizona was a significant departure from the organization's past focus on lobbying within the Beltway. And, importantly, the organization's support for Proposition 200 was more than merely rhetorical; it donated $400,000 to the signature-gathering effort on behalf of the proposition,[116] and it subsequently filed a lawsuit in Arizona to make sure that the benefit provisions in the law would be interpreted broadly.[117]

Bush Second Term (2005 to 2008) Soon after the 2004 election, the Bush administration again made comprehensive immigration reform a policy priority, encouraging renewed efforts at bipartisan legislation. At the same time, the president's standing within the Republican Party was diminished considerably. Not only was Bush a lame-duck party leader whose vice-president had forsworn any plans to run in 2008, he also lost considerable standing among conservative activists who were frustrated with the administration's failure to rein in government spending[118] and its inability to privatize aspects of Social Security in early 2005.[119]

Thus, issue entrepreneurs such as Tom Tancredo (R-CO) and NumbersUSA found it much easier to mobilize Republican Party activists and elected officials toward a more restrictive position. Making effective use of conservative talk radio and constituent pressure, they thinned the ranks of Republican moderates on immigration, making the parties more polarized on the issue than they would have been otherwise.[120] This was perhaps most evident in the case of Jim Sensenbrenner (R-WI), who spearheaded an enforcement-only measure in 2005, although he previously supported legislation such as the § 245(i) provision Tancredo opposed in 2001 and 2002.[121]

The exacerbation of party polarization by issue entrepreneurs continued through 2007, when comprehensive immigration reform legislation had majority support in both chambers of Congress but failed to overcome the Senate filibuster, as restrictionist organizations put enormous pressure on moderate Republicans to prevent cloture. As the New York Times reported:

> The big war broke out in 2007, after Mr. Bush proposed a systemic overhaul including a path to citizenship for most illegal immigrants ...

FAIR rallied talk show hosts. The Center for Immigration Studies churned out studies of the bill's perceived flaws. Numbers USA jammed the Capitol's phones.

Their success became the stuff of lore. They "lit up the switchboard for weeks," said Senator Mitch McConnell of Kentucky, the Republican leader, explaining his decision to oppose the bill. "And to every one of them, I say today: 'Your voice was heard.'"[122]

This covert and overt multi-level work in derailing federal immigration law has largely gone unexamined because restrictionist issue entrepreneurs have not concurrently advanced an alternate comprehensive legislative solution at the federal level.[123] Indeed, groups such as FAIR consider "comprehensive immigration reform" simply a code for amnesty, and see maximal enforcement as the only acceptable solution.[124] Thus, restrictionist issue entrepreneurs are focused mainly on forestalling bipartisan congressional action that would moderate hard-line restrictionist goals. Relatedly, they do not attract the attention that a special interest group garners when it seeks concentrated fiscal gains or private benefits.[125] Because they work at multiple levels, they utilized congressional delay to build subnational momentum toward a more restrictionist national stance.[126] Moreover, issue entrepreneurs were successful in securing federal concessions through quieter avenues than congressional legislation. Thus, even in the absence of federal legislative solutions that could preempt their subfederal policies and increase public scrutiny, issue entrepreneurs were able to secure favorable federal action in an enforcement-only direction.

Under these background conditions, restrictionist issue entrepreneurs (a) engendered federal legislative gridlock, (b) squeezed substantial political mileage out of complaining about that federal inaction, and then (c) filled that legislative vacuum by proliferating subfederal immigration laws that feature uncompromised versions of their restrictionist agenda.

With respect to ethnic nationalism, issue entrepreneurs such as Lou Dobbs tried different ways to cast Latin-American immigrants as a security threat. With concerns over terrorist threats becoming less salient with each year since 9/11, and economic anxiety not yet on the horizon during the early years of restrictionist fervor, aspects of immigrant criminality suddenly seemed very salient. Thus, for instance, elected representatives such as Lou Barletta from Hazleton and Russell Pearce from Arizona justified their restrictionist efforts by claiming a rise in violent crime among Mexican immigrant residents, and the possibility of clandestine cross-border arms networks. Law enforcement officials such as Arizona Sheriff Joe Arpaio affirmed such claims. Finally, media personalities such as Lou Dobbs amplified the anxiety by running stories on immigrants and crime, suggesting that gangs of illegal immigrants from Latin America were prompting a rash of new crimes in the country.[127]

These claims mostly did not stand up to empirical scrutiny: While the isolated stories about particular crimes involved were not false, the idea of widespread immigrant criminality was belied by evidence. In fact, scholarly study indicated the contrary; immigrants committed fewer crimes than did native-borns,[128] and immigrant-heavy cities like Houston and states like Arizona were actually facing significant declines in violent crime.[129]

Nevertheless, such misinformation or uncertainty regarding the underlying empirical facts did not deter policy proliferation. Legislative epidemics are most likely when an entrepreneur's message is especially sticky, not necessarily when it is supported by evidence. Undoubtedly, the trope of immigrant criminality is not new to issue entrepreneurs or to this last decade of immigration discourse. Indeed, the message of immigrant and foreign threat to domestic prosperity, security, and cultural values is a long-held and well-ingrained trope in American political and legal history.[130] It is so entrenched in the American political imagination that it resists empirical refutation.[131] Despite data from economists and sociologists showcasing national welfare gains from more liberal migration laws[132] and the lack of correlation between immigration and crime,[133] public perception about the negative impact of increased migration remains largely unchanged.[134]

While the use of the trope of immigrant criminality is cliché, what was innovative about issue entrepreneurs in this specific time period, however, was the connections they drew between the purported immigrant criminality, homeland security, and subnational immigration policy. They successfully blamed so-called sanctuary cities for facilitating and sheltering dangerous immigrant criminals and illegal immigrant gangs.[135] Conversely, if certain cities' lenient policies were in part responsible for the flourishing of immigrant criminal activity, then the corollary must be true: states and cities could and should be part of the solution, thereby justifying local police participation in immigration enforcement. Protecting domestic security in a post 9/11 world, then, was not just about national border control, but also required the elimination of sanctuary cities, and the increased participation of states and cities in criminalizing illegal immigration and enforcing immigration law.

Enter Kris Kobach. While entrepreneurs, media personalities, and elected officials were making the rhetorical case for the necessity of state and local solutions, Kobach designed legislation for localities, using his background in constitutional law to ensure a colorable legal basis for his proposals. On July 13, 2006, Hazleton, Pennsylvania, enacted a Kobach-authored law, in a well-publicized, real-life instantiation of this theory of state and local control.

A scant four days later, on July 17, 2006, the city of Valley Park, Missouri, enacted a similar ordinance, also authored by Kobach, targeting landlords and local employers. In a few months, Escondido, California, followed suit. From that point, with significant media coverage focused on those and similar enactments, subnational immigration lawmaking gained significant momentum. In our analysis of data from the National Council of State Legislatures, the most significant spike in restrictive state legislation also occurred during this time, more than tripling from 2005 to 2006 (from fifteen to forty-nine), and then doubling in 2007 (to ninety-eight laws enacted). Again, it is worth recalling that this surge began during a national economic boom, with low unemployment; retrospective analysis of the restrcitionist trend based on the deteriorating economic conditions after 2008 fail to capture the start of the restrictionist trend.

Obama First Term (2009–2012) During the Bush Presidency, issue entrepreneurs built their organizations and began organizing their multi-level strategy. In the early part of the decade, they took advantage of a post-9/11 context, which allowed them to conflate terrorism and immigration concerns, and increase party polarization, which allowed them to solidify a restrictionist stance as a lame-duck president's influence within his party waned. By the time Obama began his first term, restrictive issue entrepreneurs were riding the strong momentum of their victory in derailing 2007 bipartisan federal reform, and the enactment of several high-profile subfederal laws, like the Legal Arizona Workers Act of 2008 and Hazleton-type laws in places as far flung as Farmers Branch, Texas, and Riverside, New Jersey. During Obama's first term in office, issue entrepreneurs grew prominent and entrenched, and their work became systematized and evident.

While party polarization has generally stalled many initiatives at the federal level, Obama was successful in mobilizing federal legislative majorities to end "Don't Ask Don't Tell" and to pass a federal health care overhaul. Despite being able to herd enough votes to pass health care legislation – an area of traditional state dominance with strong individual liberty valences – the Obama administration was unable to make any progress on immigration – an area traditionally relegated to federal control. Indeed, in late 2010, Congress was unable to pass the DREAM Act, one of the most popular individual pieces of the 2007 comprehensive reform package (and even now a measure with broad public support).[136] In a coordinated effort, FAIR and NumbersUSA, along with the Center for Immigration Studies, ensured that the DREAM Act proposal would not survive a Senate filibuster. Completing the project begun in 2001, issue entrepreneurs' exacerbation of party polarization on immigration meant that by the 2010 DREAM Act vote, no moderate Republicans remained to help break the filibuster, and effectuate national majoritarian preferences.[137]

Indeed, entrepreneurs had pushed so hard for state-centric enforcement policy that they not only helped derail federal efforts at reform and integration, but also opposed changes at the federal level that reflected the restrictionists' own agenda. This was perhaps most starkly evident in May 2011, when Kris Kobach expressed his opposition to a congressional bill mandating the use of the federal E-Verify database to check the immigration status of all employees in the United States. His stance appeared odd, as Kobach and other restrictionists supported the Legal Arizona Workers Act, which mandated the use of that same database for employers within the state (and was upheld by the Supreme Court in *U.S. Chamber of Commerce v. Whiting* (2011)). Kobach explained than an analogous federal mandate would "defang[] the only government bodies that are serious about enforcing immigration law – the states." Noting the political interconnectedness between federal and state legislation, on the one hand, and federal judicial activity, on the other, Kobach continued: "The timing couldn't be worse. The bill stabs Arizona in the back, just after it won a victory in [*Whiting*]."[138]

While that federal legislative effort stalled, administrative agency attempts at increased border security and enhanced enforcement by the Department of Homeland Security continued through 2012. In efforts to bring enough Republicans (sufficient to break the filibuster) to the negotiating table on the DREAM Act or other immigration reforms, the president used his executive power to make enforcement concessions that angered his own party's base, but appeared designed to bring polarized restrictionists to the negotiating table and begin bipartisan reform. For example, President Obama used his executive power to order National Guard troops to the border, and deported immigrants at record rates.[139] These executive concessions, however, did not succeed in breaking the hold of issue entrepreneurs over the number of lawmakers necessary to overcome a filibuster and enact immigration reform or popular parts of such reform.

Stepped up national enforcement, moreover, did not mollify restrictionist critics, either at organizations such as NumbersUSA or among conservative media personalities. With the departure of Dobbs from CNN in 2009, groups such as FAIR now rely more heavily on conservative talk radio hosts and special events such as the annual "Hold Their Feet to the Fire" conference in Washington, DC, where the organization brings together dozens of conservative radio hosts to focus on illegal immigration and immigration enforcement, combined with rallies, visits to wavering legislators, and guest appearances by sympathetic members of Congress.[140] As the New York Times noted, such events allow FAIR to maintain its own race-neutrality, while its associates are free to invoke ethnic nationalist frames: "This year's event mixed discussion of job losses among minorities with calls to use Tomahawk missiles on Tijuana drug lords, while a doubter of President Obama's birth certificate referred to 'the undocumented worker' in the White House."[141] And concerns about national security and sovereignty remained salient, as prominent radio personalities such as Roger Hedgecock continue to press the notion that Mexican drug cartels controlled vast portions of the Southwest.[142]

Meanwhile, during Obama's first term, subnational legislative activity continued apace, most notably at the state level. Even as the Department of Justice sued to enjoin one enactment, issue entrepreneurs created others, each one subject to federal challenge, and each consuming federal prosecutorial and judicial resources. Moreover, each subsequent enactment expanded the boundaries of state and local enforcement activities, adding increasingly punitive policies with each step. Discussing a provision of the Alabama law he authored, Kobach noted that a new provision made that state "the first ... to invalidate all contracts entered into with illegal immigrants. A strict reading of the law could mean that any contract, including mortgages, apartment leases and basic work agreements, can be ruled null and void."[143]

While expanding the scope of subnational laws with each enactment, entrepreneurial strategy also matured and systematized with regard to venue selection. Prospectively, the Polarized Change model utilizes the mechanics of the decentralized and federated party system to unlock the predictive power of party polarization. Partisan dynamics at the state and local level allowed observers to predict where the entrepreneurs are likely to strike next. Like the putative copycats for California's Proposition 187 in the 1990s, rather than looking to areas of significant demographic or economic change, issue entrepreneurs in the late 2000s and early 2010s looked to areas of Republican party domination with enterprising candidates and officials, regardless of the underlying demographic factors.[144]

Thus, for instance, the November 2011 switch of the Mississippi House of Representatives from Democrat to Republican for the first time since Reconstruction meant that the Mississippi House would no longer be able to bottle up legislation in committees controlled by Democrats.[145] Notably, Mississippi ranks as the third lowest state in terms of immigrant share of the resident population (2 percent of the total population in 2010), and this grew from about 1.5 percent of the population in 2000. Finally, even in states with more sizable new immigrant populations, such as North Carolina, partisan dynamics seemed to be of paramount importance, as NumbersUSA reported on the conditions in North Carolina for its State and Local Alert: "with Republicans now in control of the state legislature in North Carolina, efforts have begun to pass similar, statewide legislation to crack down on illegal immigration."[46]

Thus, during the first Obama presidential term, we witnessed the fruition of the restrictionist entrepreneurial vision: engendered gridlock at the national level at key moments of potential bipartisan compromise, providing the rhetorical hook and policy vacuum necessary to proliferate state and local legislation. This legislative landscape became so normalized that presidential hopeful Mitt Romney promised that his putative administration would "stand with the states" in immigration enforcement. Far from the 2000–2001 Bush platform of bipartisan federal reform, focused on meeting labor needs and increasing legal immigration, this alternate vision imagined states and localities as equal partners in a hard-line restrictionist stance, not co-opted by the federal government alone.

As we have shown, the networked activity of issue entrepreneurs at both the federal and subfederal levels is critical to explaining and understanding the general policy climate on immigration after 2001, and genesis and proliferation of state and local restrictionist laws for several years, beginning in 2004. The work of Kris Kobach and the Immigration Reform Law Institute were particularly important. In sharp contrast to the uncoordinated and sporadic nature of the Proposition 187 effort we detailed in Chapter 2, the revival of state-level restriction was far more sophisticated in terms of legal expertise. The effort also had considerable institutional backing and resources from national organizations such as FAIR and NumbersUSA, and it was not waiting around for congressional action. Indeed, congressional inaction was a key prerequisite for the proliferation of state-level restriction, and we saw issue entrepreneurs like Kobach resist attempts to pass a national E-verify law so as to keep state E-verify laws viable, both in present form and in future iterations. In fact, the state-level restrictionist strategy was so powerful that it started to make an impact on national public opinion. The Gallup poll in April 2010 found that three-quarters of Americans had heard of Arizona's immigration enforcement law, and among those who had heard of it, a majority supported the legislation.[47] Support for SB 1070 was particularly high among Republican voters, with 75 percent in favor and 17 percent opposed among those who were aware of the law. It was little surprise, then, that Republican candidates for the presidency all lined up in favor of more Arizona-type laws, with Mitt Romney even going so far as to seeking Kris Kobach's endorsement and declaring Arizona's law a model for the nation.[48]

As it turned out, however, Romney's endorsement of the Kobach strategy proved to be the high-water mark of state-level immigration restriction. As we detail in the next chapter, 2012 brought about significant legal and political changes that tipped the scales against immigration restriction at the subfederal level, and hastened the frequency and scope of pro-immigrant legislation. Immigration federalism, as it later became clear, was not solely a strategy that would be touted by restrictionists or Republicans advocating for states rights in general. Instead, the fight over immigration federalism was a multi-jurisdictional turf battle to instantiate competing visions of desired national immigration policy. We provide a detailed look at this integrationist bent in Chapter 5, as we seek to explain its seemingly sudden rise and its spread across a select set of states and localities. We save a more integrated analysis of both restrictionist and integrationist activity for Chapter 6, where we note that both appear to have had some lasting consequences for our doctrinal and theoretical understandings of immigration federalism.

# 5

## A Shifting Tide in 2012: Pro-Integration Activists Gain the Upper Hand

Just as restrictionist fervor had begun to wane in 2012, a countertrend was beginning to emerge, and a growing number of states began passing pro-integration legislation. This development did not emerge out of nowhere. Indeed, it owed its origins in some important ways to the prior restrictive movement, as various state-based groups battled restrictive efforts, both at the legislative stage through lobbying and coalition-building efforts and at the implementation stage through lawsuits. Many of these same state and local groups had also been gaining political skills and legal experience in confronting federal enforcement, from persuading the Obama administration to slow down its record pace of deportations and, when those strategies failed, exploring ways to legally resist them.

And yet, 2012 represented a dramatic shift in the balance of power between pro-immigrant and restrictive forces at the subfederal level. While previously, many pro-immigrant groups had been playing defense, battling what they considered to be very harmful legislation and administrative action, these same groups now began to play offense, working across jurisdictions and in partnership with national actors to turn the tide toward pro-immigrant legislation. This development was significant in and of itself: as late as 2008 and 2009, the major national immigrant advocacy organizations had thought of federal legislation and litigation as the best way to deal with the spate of restrictive laws at the state and local level.[1] This strategy seemed to be the most efficient since it relied on the hope of federal preemption, either by passing congressional legislation or by getting federal courts to beat back the growing reach of restrictive state and local laws. It was a high-risk strategy and one that counseled patience: the political opportunities had to be aligned in order for preemptive legislation to pass, and advocates would have to wait months or years for cases to wend their way through federal courts, with considerable uncertainty over the ultimate outcome (the Supreme Court's decision in *Whiting*, for example, was far from reassuring).

After the failure of the DREAM Act in 2010, however, even those national advocacy groups primarily focused on comprehensive immigration reform began to recognize the near-term futility of federal legislative efforts. They also began to see state legislation as an opportunity to push for pro-immigrant policies, and to coordinate efforts across jurisdictions. As we detail below, this strategy echoed in important ways the federated and networked strategy of restrictionist issue entrepreneurs such as Kris Kobach and the Federation for American Immigration Reform (FAIR).[2] While previously pro-integration organizations at the state level were struggling to be heard, after 2010 they began receiving more attention and funding to implement pro-immigrant laws at the state level and to try proliferating model legislation across jurisdictions. These efforts included ways to mitigate or resist federal enforcement efforts, and to legislate in other ways to improve the lives of undocumented residents, including issuing municipal identification cards and providing expanded access to driver's licenses, public higher education, public welfare, and professional licensing.

What accounts for this dramatic shift in fortunes on state-level immigration legislation, what are the new kinds of policy changes being envisioned, and what explains their adoption in some states but not in others? These are the central questions animating this chapter. In seeking answers to these questions, we also revisit the Polarized Change model from Chapter 4, to see if key aspects of the model (such as the centrality of political factors, the involvement of issue entrepreneurs, and the linkage between national and state legislative dynamics) are also applicable to the post-2012 period of pro-integration legislation. This chapter proceeds as follows: first, we provide important context to three major changes in the legal and political opportunities available to restrictionist and pro-integration forces alike in the realm of immigration federalism. Next, we provide a detailed examination of the kinds of pro-integration laws that were being proposed and passed in various states. Finally, just as in our analysis of restrictive laws in Chapters 3 and 4, we conduct statistical analyses and qualitative empirical work, to ascertain the factors and processes responsible for the development and spread of pro-integration legislation.

## WHY WAS 2012 A TURNING POINT?

Why did the tide turn so decidedly away from restrictive legislation and toward pro-integration efforts at the state level? And, to repeat a question we asked earlier with respect to the surge in restrictive legislation: are the dominant explanations to be found with respect to demographic change or changes in economic conditions, or are they to be found in the realm of

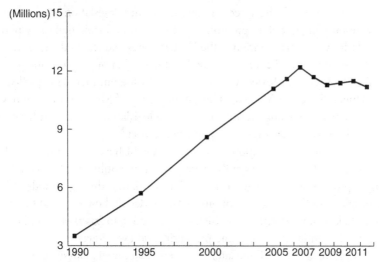

FIGURE 5.1. Estimates of the unauthorized population in the United States. *Source*: Pew Hispanic Center, 2014.[3]

politics, with political opportunities and issue entrepreneurs playing critically important roles? As we detail below, the answers we find with respect to the surge in integrationist legislation are very similar to the explanations we found for the sudden rise in restrictionist activity. The critical factors that explain this momentum shift in 2012 are not attributable to any sudden change in the demographics of migration. Instead, they are related to political and legal developments that simultaneously weakened the power of restrictive issue entrepreneurs and strengthened the hand of pro-immigrant advocates.

Just as macroeconomic and demographic explanations were unhelpful in explaining the rise of restrictive legislation at the state and local level after 2004, they are also limited in explaining the strong uptick in pro-immigrant legislation after 2012. First, there was no sudden drop in the unauthorized population in 2012 that made pro-integration legislation more favorable. As research by the Pew Hispanic Center has shown, the number of unauthorized immigrants had declined a few years earlier, from 12.2 million in 2007 to 11.3 million in 2009, and remained relatively stable thereafter (Figure 5.1). As the Pew data indicate, changes in state-level unauthorized populations mirrored those at the national level.[4] If changes in the unauthorized population were the major driving force behind state legislation on immigration, then we should have seen relatively high levels of state-level restrictive legislation after

1996, and we should have seen a tapering of such legislation after 2007 and a corresponding uptick in pro-immigrant legislation during that same period. Similarly, Mexican migration to the United States had reached "net zero" status between 2005 and 2010, meaning that the number of people coming to the United States from Mexico was canceled out by the number of people leaving the United States for Mexico.[5] Thus, if the easing of Mexican migration were the impetus for passing pro-integration state legislation, we should have seen these efforts gather steam many years prior to 2012.

Finally, improving economic conditions might have helped the proliferation of pro-integration laws at the state level, as it would have been challenging to promote pro-immigrant integration legislation during periods of high unemployment or sluggish economic growth. Recall, however, that the sharpest uptick in state restrictive legislation (from 2005 to 2007) occurred during a time of even greater economic prosperity and even lower unemployment.[6] Furthermore, as we shall see later in our cross-sectional analysis of state legislation, the state unemployment rate and poverty rates from 2011 through 2013 bore no significant relationship to the passage of integrationist legislation. Indeed, the state that passed the most progressive legislation on immigrant integration, both in numbers and scope, was California – a state whose unemployment rate remained well above the national average and was among the highest in the country in 2012 and 2013.[7]

Finally, even if favorable or improving economic conditions are necessary but insufficient factors for pro-integration legislation (which might help account for why restrictive legislation was dominant in 2007 despite very favorable economic conditions), this still does not account for why there was a sudden shift in state legislative momentum in 2012. The economic trend data after 2010 were moving in a gradual and linear fashion, making it an unlikely explanation for more sudden policy change. Thus, we need to look elsewhere to understand why there was a sudden shift in the immigration policy landscape in 2012.

As we discuss below, three prominent developments in 2012 – the *Arizona v. United States* decision, President Obama's announcement on Deferred Action for Childhood Arrivals (DACA), and the 2012 election results – fundamentally restructured the legal and political opportunities available to restrictionist and pro-integration advocates alike. First, the United States Supreme Court struck down several provisions of Arizona's SB 1070 in June 2012, dealing a significant legal blow to Kobach and the state/local strategy of attrition through enforcement. This meant that many pro-immigrant organizations at the state level could shift their resources away from litigation and toward pro-integration legislation. Around the same time as the *Arizona v. United*

*States* decision, President Obama announced the Deferred Action for Child Arrivals (or DACA) program in a Rose Garden announcement. Although DACA was a program of the federal government, it necessitated state cooperation in some policy areas, and more generally marked a turning point toward more integrationist policies toward immigrants. Finally, with Barack Obama's reelection in November 2012 and Mitt Romney's massive loss among Latino voters, the state-centered strategy of immigration enforcement suffered a significant political rebuke. For about a year, this presidential defeat and related post-mortem recommendations from Republican Party leaders bolstered the morale of pro-immigration interest groups. However, after the drawn out partisan fight over the implementation of the Affordable Care Act and the government shutdown of 2013, the prospects for national legislation on immigration dimmed once again, leaving states as the only plausible arena for pro-integration legislation.[8]

### Arizona v. United States

The first major development that helped shift policy momentum at the state level was the Supreme Court's decision in *Arizona v. United States* that struck down most of the challenged provisions of Arizona's SB 1070. As we noted in Chapter 4, SB 1070 was chiefly authored by Kris Kobach, and introduced to the state legislature by state Senator Russell Pearce in 2010. After SB 1070 was enacted, the legislature also passed HB 2162 that amended SB 1070 with provisions intended to address the racial profiling concerns in the law. Almost immediately after SB 1070 went into effect, the U.S. Department of Justice filed suit to enjoin its enforcement, claiming that federal law preempted the state enforcement efforts. The federal government's conspicuous involvement in the litigation was itself unusual. Even though immigration federalism suits have generally involved preemption claims, the federal government is rarely involved in litigation, and even more rarely the actual litigant in the case.[9] Indeed, several other advocacy groups and individuals, including the American Civil Liberties Union, had also filed suit against SB 1070. Thus, the Obama administration's decision to sue the state, and bring to bear the litigatory power of the federal government, represented an especially robust attempt to control the terms of state involvement in immigration and the contours of the national immigration debate.[10]

The law contained several provisions, ranging from one intended to prevent localities from enacting sanctuary ordinances, to others that required state officers to determine immigration status, required the carrying of alien registration documents, criminalized work solicitation by day laborers, penalized unauthorized employment, and permitted warrantless arrests if the immigrant was suspected of having committed a removable offense. Another section of the law made the concealing, transporting, or harboring undocumented persons a state crime. Despite these myriad provisions, by the time the case reached the federal appeals court and the Supreme Court, only four provisions were at issue[11] – the section requiring police officers to check the immigration status of those they encountered under certain conditions, the section penalizing immigrants for not carrying alien registration papers, the section criminalizing unauthorized employment, and the section permitting police officers to arrest those they suspected of having committed a removable offense.

In 2012, the Supreme Court struck down three of the provisions on various preemption theories (discussed in Chapter 6), leaving in force Section 2(B), the "show me your papers" provision, requiring police officers to check the immigration status of suspected undocumented persons they encounter. In the wake of the Arizona ruling, federal appeals courts that were awaiting the high court's decision, similarly enjoined most provisions of the respective state and local laws at issue – from Alabama, South Carolina, Georgia, and cities like Farmers Branch, Texas, and Hazelton, Pennsylvania[12] – significantly limiting these enforcement efforts, and leaving the future legal status of much restrictive enforcement legislation in doubt.

In addition, federal courts in Arizona took up remaining issues left unanswered by the Supreme Court's ruling on SB 1070. Immediately after the Arizona ruling, a suit was filed against Section 2(B), arguing that although the section passed constitutional muster as written, it violated Fourth Amendment and equal protection guarantees as applied. While that litigation is still pending, in other litigation, lower federal courts have struck down the SB 1070 provisions that penalized solicitation of work by day laborers,[13] and the smuggling and transporting provisions.[14] In short, the federal courts' rulings (including the Supreme Court's) of 2012 and following clarified that, as a matter of legal theory, courts have been much more likely to side with the long-standing notion of federal supremacy on immigration enforcement than to side with the theories of Kobach and others who claim inherent authority for states to engage in the policing of immigrants.

### Deferred Action for Childhood Arrivals (DACA)

Another important development in 2012 that changed the balance of power between restrictionist and pro-integration efforts was the announcement and rollout of Deferred Action for Childhood Arrivals (DACA), a program implemented by the Department of Homeland Security. As per the program, unauthorized immigrant youth, who fit several criteria, may apply for two years of deferred prosecution from federal authorities (later, this deferral was extended to three years).[15] Those who receive DACA status are also eligible to receive an Employment Authorization Document (EAD), allowing them to seek employment without violating federal law. As a purely administrative program, DACA recipients are lawfully present for the period of deferred action (although they are not granted lawful status, which only Congress can provide through legislation).

As we show later in this chapter, the rollout of DACA played a significant role in getting states to reconsider their driver's license policies, a process that ultimately led several states to expand access to driver's licenses to all unauthorized residents. Even before its implementation, however, DACA had significant political effects on immigration federalism, helping push the thrust of public opinion in favor of integrationist solutions rather than restrictive ones such as Arizona's SB 1070. While the president's political calculations on DACA were primarily interpreted as a move to energize Latino voters and mollify critics of mass deportations,[16] the White House also framed its announcement in a politically savvy manner for a broader presidential electorate. First, it crafted the policy of deferred action as one explicitly involving children, a frame that public opinion research has shown to increase support for immigrant legalization.[17] In addition, the White House chose to announce the policy on June 15, 2012,[18] timing it to coincide with the thirtieth anniversary of the *Plyler v. Doe* decision that guaranteed unauthorized immigrant children the right to a public education (for more on *Plyler*, see Chapters 2 and 6). In the event that the broader electorate may have missed the "children connection" between *Plyler* and DACA, the White House also made sure that this symbolism was part of the promotional materials made available to reporters.[19]

Finally, by announcing DACA, the White House implemented, as an administrative matter, what Senator Marco Rubio (R-FL) had been attempting to do through congressional legislation. This strategy, too, likely played a significant role in shoring up public support for DACA, which drew 64 percent support among registered voters in September 2012, including 58 percent among Independents and 50 percent among Republicans.[20] Thus, the announcement and rollout of DACA in 2012, combined with the Supreme Court decision in *Arizona*, tipped the political scales away from restrictionist solutions to immigration policy and toward immigrant integration. Not only did these developments help shift news coverage and the policy conversation toward immigrant integration (there were about five times as many news stories on DACA as stories on SB 1070 in the latter half of 2012),[21] they also helped bolster public support for more welcoming policies and, more generally,

boosted the morale of pro-integration organizations. After 2012, these organizations could afford to worry less about state enforcement legislation like
Arizona's SB 1070 and its copycats, and they could count on more support
from a White House that had previously focused its executive authority on
border enforcement and record levels of deportation.

### 2012 Presidential Election

Just as the Supreme Court decision in 2012 served as a *legal* repudiation to the
restrictionist theory and strategy of attrition through state enforcement, Mitt
Romney's spectacular loss in the 2012 election served as a *political* repudiation,
at least when it came to presidential politics. As we noted in Chapter 4, the
work of restrictive issue entrepreneurs such as Kris Kobach and the Federation
for American Immigration Reform (FAIR) reached their apex in the 2012 presidential primary, as the leading Republican presidential candidates voiced their
support for restrictive legislation like Arizona's SB 1070. Indeed, Mitt Romney
touted the endorsement of Kris Kobach in January 2012 as he tried to shore up
conservative voter support in advance of the South Carolina primary,[22] and the
candidate declared on his blog that his future administration would "support
states like South Carolina and Arizona that are stepping forward to address this
problem [of illegal immigration.]"[23] Romney did not moderate his stance on
immigration enforcement during the general election, and he signaled that he
would discontinue DACA if he won the presidency.[24] It was little surprise, then,
that he lost to Obama by record margins among fast-growing electoral constituencies like Latino voters (27 percent to 71 percent)[25] and Asian Americans
(31 percent to 68 percent).[26] These voting patterns were a far cry from the modest losses Republicans faced in 2004 when President George W. Bush lost the
Latino vote by 9 percent and the Asian American vote by 12 percent.[27]

Soon, many Republican officials began calling for the party to move swiftly
in favor of immigration reform as a way to win back some of these voters
and remain viable in the 2016 presidential election and beyond.[28] Even conservative opinion leaders on immigration such as Sean Hannity and Bill
O'Reilly dropped their prior opposition to immigrant legalization and started
calling for comprehensive immigration reform at the national level.[29] A few
Republican jurisdictions that had previously been hotbeds for immigration
restriction also began passing resolutions in support of immigration reform,
including states such as North Carolina and Missouri[30] and localities such as
Riverside County, California.[31]

Absent this trifecta of developments in 2012 – Arizona v. United States,
DACA, and Romney's defeat - it would have been very difficult to envision

such a drastic shift in policy momentum. Perhaps most obviously, a Court ruling in favor of Arizona's SB 1070 would have instantly made viable similar laws that were passed in other states. It would also have breathed new life into efforts to proliferate enforcement legislation in even more states,[32] thus perpetuating a dynamic where pro-immigrant groups would be forced to play defense, focusing on combating restrictive legislation rather than promoting pro-integration laws. Similarly, a Romney victory in 2012 would have further emboldened state restrictionists, particularly as the presidential candidate had indicated support for Arizona-type enforcement laws and would most likely have used presidential discretion in ways to support similar legislation rather than fighting them in federal court. Finally, it is plausible that a shift toward pro-integration legislation would have occurred even without the announcement of DACA in 2012. However, as we indicate later in this chapter, the implementation of DACA proved critical in shifting state momentum on driver's licenses and other policies in a decidedly pro-integration direction. Thus, a counterfactual analysis largely supports our contention that the Arizona decision, DACA, and the 2012 presidential election were critical factors that helped engender an abrupt momentum shift toward more pro-integration laws at the state level.

At the same time, these three factors were unlikely to have been the only ones that mattered. As we discuss below, these factors certainly structured the political opportunities for pro-immigrant legislation, much in the same way that the September 11 attacks structured political opportunities for restrictive legislation in the prior decade. Just as with our Polarized Change model on restrictive legislation, however, we also need to take into account the role of resource mobilization and legislative innovation by issue entrepreneurs. Before we discuss the post-2012 relevance of the Polarized Change model, however, it is important to first take stock of what types of state legislation were being considered and passed. In the following section, we provide a detailed examination of what these pro-integration policies looked like, and what they sought to achieve.

## THE VARIETIES OF PRO-INTEGRATION POLICIES
### AT THE SUBFEDERAL LEVEL

As we did with restrictionist legislation, here we individually examine several different types of integrationist policies that either arose, or picked up significant momentum, as part of the new immigration federalism. Below, we provide details on efforts to mitigate federal enforcement and the provision of municipal identification cards, state driver's licenses, tuition benefits and education financing, public welfare, and professional licensing. The goal of this review is to help better understand the policies advanced by pro-immigrant activists, before attempting to explain why they have emerged, and what implications they hold in our developing immigration federalism jurisprudence.

## Mitigation of Federal Enforcement

For a few decades now, several localities have conspicuously positioned themselves as "sanctuary" cities.[33] It is a broad term intended to describe jurisdictions that have placed limits on the efforts of local law enforcement officials to discover and investigate immigration status and the amount of assistance they will provide to federal enforcement authorities in enforcing immigration laws.[34] State and local policies that mitigate federal enforcement began to appear soon after the start of this third era of immigration federalism. Various political crises in Caribbean countries, Cuba, and Central American countries led to an increased presence of unlawfully present immigrants from those countries in the United States.[35] At the same time, the concept of unlawful presence had gained much more traction in federal immigration law than ever before, and these individuals became potential targets for federal enforcement efforts in line with post-1965 immigration enactments.[36] The state and local sanctuary ordinances of the late 1970s, 1980s, and 1990s placed limits on the efforts of state and local law enforcement officials to discover and investigate immigration status, and the amount of assistance they provide to federal enforcement authorities. Some jurisdictions, such as New York City, went further and attempted to stop any communication between local officers and federal authorities for the purpose of alerting federal authorities to the presence of unlawfully present migrants (a policy expressly preempted by later enacted federal law).[37] One of the primary goals of sanctuary, or noncooperation, policies is to enhance community-policing efforts and improve relationships between local law enforcement and immigrant communities who would otherwise be reluctant to contact the police for fear of their immigration status.[38]

While sanctuary jurisdictions have been present for some time, more recent federal enforcement efforts have spurred newer forms of noncooperation and enforcement-resistance policies in the past few years. These attempts to remove immigration enforcement functions from local law enforcement have gained support from various quarters, including a range of associations of law enforcement officers,[39] but they have also encountered resistance in some states and from the federal government. States such as Colorado, Arizona, and Alabama, in their major restrictionist enactments in, respectively, 2006, 2010, and 2011, passed laws forbidding localities from implementing sanctuary ordinances. From 2008 to 2014, the federal government operated the Secure Communities (S-Comm) program, effectively co-opting local law enforcement authorities into providing federal immigration authorities with information regarding undocumented persons regardless whether that jurisdiction was a sanctuary jurisdiction.[40] S-Comm's replacement, the Priority Enforcement Program (PEP), also requires state participation regardless of sanctuary status.

Initiated by the U.S. Department of Homeland Security in 2008 and then tested and implemented nationwide over the past six years, S-Comm was an information-leveraging program that forwarded information about every arrestee in a local jurisdiction to a federal database that checks for lawful status.[41] When local law enforcement authorities entered information about an arrestee into the FBI's national crime database to check for outstanding warrants or past criminal history, that criminal background check also resulted in an immigration status check. Thus, even if local officers, pursuant to a sanctuary policy, endeavored not to investigate or discover the immigration status of an individual they takes into custody, the federal immigration authorities still received information about that individual's immigration status. At that point, federal officials may decide to further investigate or prosecute the individual in question, often beginning their process by issuing a "hold request" or "immigration detainer," requesting the local agency to hold the individual in custody until federal enforcement officials can interview or otherwise take custody of the individual.[42]

Although the federal government declared the program mandatory,[43] some states and localities resisted aspects of S-Comm. Specifically, a detainer resistance movement or anti-cooperation trend developed across several jurisdictions from 2011 to 2014, with the National Day Laborer Organizing Network playing a central role in crafting model legislation and working with local immigrant rights partners to get them passed in various cities and states. Santa Clara County in California, for example, passed resolutions that effectively declined to honor immigration detainer requests from Immigrations and Customs Enforcement, or ICE.[44] These jurisdictions offered varied policy reasons for resisting ICE hold requests, including the high costs of detention, the desire to focus on more pressing public safety priorities, and the risk to law enforcement's relationship with immigrant communities, who might be less willing to come forward and contact the police if they fear they could be put into removal proceedings for doing so.[45]

The legal argument for detainer resistance is premised on well-established Supreme Court jurisprudence forbidding the federal government from commanding or directing local law enforcement to enforce federal law. This principle – based on the Tenth Amendment, known as the "anti-commandeering" doctrine – means that a federal immigration detainer amounts at most to a request from federal authorities. While the federal government can incentivize and encourage state and local compliance with ICE holds, they cannot force local officials to use their own resources and personnel to hold noncitizens. The federal court of appeals for the Third Circuit adopted this reasoning in holding that Lehigh County, Pennsylvania, was not obligated to comply with an ICE detainer that resulted in the unlawful detention of a U.S. citizen.[46] In addition, because the holds are issued without warrant or probable cause, they may violate the Fourth Amendment's prohibition against unreasonable searches and seizures, and the risk of racially inequitable application threatens to violate equal protection guarantees.[47]

Along with Santa Clara County, Cook County, Illinois; Miami-Dade County, Florida; the Newark Police Department, and Washington, DC, also maintain policies that function as refusals to respond to federal detainer requests.[48] In addition to this type of resistance, other jurisdictions have passed civil detainer statutes that limit their response to some, but not all, federal detainer requests. California and Connecticut maintain such policies at the state level through their TRUST Acts, and at least seventeen other local jurisdictions or county penal institutions maintain some form of a detainer-resistance or anti-cooperation policy.[49] This makes a practical difference because local enforcement agencies and officials are likely to have informational advantages over federal officials in terms of identifying, locating, and interacting with potentially removable persons. Notably, in California, the number of immigrants made available to ICE for deportation sank considerably in the first year of TRUST Act implementation.[50]

In 2014, as part of the president's announcements on expanding deferred action through the DACA and DAPA programs, he also announced the end of S-Comm. Critical to the administration's discontinuance of S-Comm was the state and local resistance in the form of detainer-resistance policies and TRUST Acts. As Secretary Jeh Johnson admitted in his memorandum on the end of S-Comm:

> The goal of Secure Communities was to more effectively identify and facilitate the removal of criminal aliens.... But the reality is the program has attracted a great deal of criticism, is widely misunderstood, and is embroiled in litigation; its very name has become a symbol for general hostility toward the enforcement of our immigration laws. Governors, mayors, and state and local law enforcement officials around the country have increasingly refused to cooperate with the program, and many have issued executive orders or signed laws prohibiting such cooperation.[51]

Thus, this form of subfederal resistance appears to have influenced federal enforcement policies. The PEP program, which replaced S-Comm, still utilizes local law enforcement agencies to provide notice and information to federal authorities (and thus may still raise serious concerns),[52] but it was clearly formulated to attempt to assuage the growing resistance movement across various states and localities.

Finally, states have also voiced noncooperation stances on employer verification and employer sanctions. For example, California passed a law expressly stating that neither the state nor jurisdictions within it could mandate use of the federal E-Verify database.[53] Illinois and Rhode Island maintain similar policies intended to limit E-Verify use and bar localities from requiring it.[54] These states' policies cannot prevent employers' voluntary use of the database, and other federal laws that prohibit employment of unauthorized workers still apply.[55] These states' anti-E-Verify bills stand in sharp contrast to Arizona's approach with the Legal Arizona Workers Act (see Chapter 3 for more on LAWA). Notably, Utah passed a unique set of laws creating a state-sanctioned guest worker program for undocumented workers in 2011.[56] State lawmakers, however, recently put the program on hold, and in any case, would require a federal waiver to proceed; if eventually implemented, the program would raise serious constitutional concerns.[57]

### State Driver's Licenses

The REAL ID Act of 2005 maintains minimum standards for state-issued licenses and identification cards if those cards are to be used for federal purposes, such as access to federal buildings, identification for airline travel, and proof of identity for accessing benefits. Importantly, REAL ID provides states with the discretion to issue federally approved licenses to unlawfully present persons who are recipients of deferred action.[58] Using this statutory discretion, many states maintained a policy even prior to 2012 of allowing temporary immigrants and undocumented persons who had received deferred action and obtained employment authorization documents, or EADs, from the federal government to apply for driver's licenses. States, however, may maintain more stringent standards than the minimum allowed by REAL ID[59] or may choose to provide licenses that fail to meet the minimum federal status-verification standard with the understanding that such licenses may not be acceptable for federal purposes once the REAL ID Act becomes fully implemented.[60]

While a few states had provided licenses to undocumented persons prior to REAL ID, the trend during the recent restrictionist heyday was clear. Seven states that previously granted driving privileges to undocumented immigrants stopped doing so from 2003 to 2010, by either rescinding or overturning their policies.[61] By early 2012, only three states remained that allowed undocumented persons to apply for driver's licenses. The Obama administration's implementation of the Deferred Action for Child Arrivals program in mid-2012, however, appears to have galvanized a significant reversal in that trend.[62] In the wake of DACA, 46 states now offer driver's licenses to DACA recipients who are eligible to receive EADs during the time of deferral.

More broadly, the momentum created by DACA moved state policy on driver's licenses for undocumented persons generally. Ten states, along with Washington, DC, and Puerto Rico, currently provide or are preparing to provide licenses regardless of immigration status.[63] Of those twelve jurisdictions, nine changed their policies within eighteen months of DACA's announcement, most likely as a response to the policy climate created by DACA.[64] Further, other states, such as New York, New Jersey, Pennsylvania, and Massachusetts, are considering a similar change.[65]

Because of REAL ID Act requirements, however, states issuing licenses to unauthorized persons must either designate or mark those licenses differently, so that it is clear they cannot be used for federal purposes, or accept that none of their residents will be able to use their state-issued identification cards and licenses for those purposes. Several states that have recently changed their policies on driver's licenses have opted to designate or mark the licenses provided to unauthorized persons in a manner that renders them unusable for federal concerns.[66] Notably, at this early stage in license availability, general concerns regarding turning over information to government officials has kept some undocumented immigrants from taking advantage of their newfound eligibility in enacting jurisdictions.[67]

The decision of most states to provide driver's licenses to DACA recipients seems to have been born out of practical necessity and the need for consistency. First, DACA created hundreds of thousands of beneficiaries who had work authorization,[68] and states had to consider the transportation needs of these residents with work authorization. Indeed, many states were already offering licenses to those who had previously received deferred action with employment authorization, an individual-level determination before the Obama administration created a class of beneficiaries under a broad set of rules. For these states, in particular, granting driver's licenses to DACA beneficiaries was not much of a stretch, although it did entail clarification of rules – either via legislation, executive action, or bureaucratic determination.

Pragmatic concerns have also animated the arguments of advocates who pushed states further, to make driver's licenses more broadly available to unauthorized migrants, couching their arguments in public safety concerns rather than framing the issue as one involving immigrant rights or immigrant benefits. Thus, they have argued that broader provision of licenses allows states to ensure that more drivers are insured, which in turn improves traffic safety and reduces the cost of auto insurance. They have also pointed out the fact that driver's licenses also operate as identity documents, facilitating inter-action between immigrants and state agencies, including law enforcement.

Although a significant number of states are now welcoming undocumented driver's license applicants and the overwhelming majority allow DACA recipients to apply, at least two states have conspicuously bucked this trend. Both Arizona and Nebraska have announced their intention to deny driver's licenses to DACA recipients and subsequently engaged in litigation over their policies. The Ninth Circuit Court of Appeals struck down Arizona's policy as a violation of equal protection, as it prohibited DACA recipients, but not other recipients of deferred action, from license eligibility.[69] In May 2015, Nebraska passed a law granting driver's licenses to DACA recipients.[70]

## Municipal Identification Card Programs

Beginning with the city of New Haven, Connecticut, in 2007, several cities began issuing municipal identity cards to local residents regardless of immi-gration status.[71] In San Francisco – the second city to offer a resident card – applicants must show some form of identification – such as a foreign passport or consular card, which many undocumented persons possess – and proof of residency within the city, such as a utility bill.[72] Although any city resident can theoretically obtain and use the cards, they present the greatest utility to groups such as the undocumented or the indigent, who generally do not have or are prevented from obtaining driver's licenses and other forms of federal or state identification. In other jurisdictions, such as Mercer County, New Jersey, the card is technically offered by a nongovernmental nonprofit advo-cacy group but is endorsed and accepted by several county agencies.[73]

As with driver's licenses that fail to meet federal standards, the REAL ID Act prevents these resident cards from being used for any federal purpose, and they do not provide proof of lawful status. Moreover, private businesses and other localities are not required to accept the cards. Despite these limitations, the cards remain useful for undocumented immigrants within the enacting jurisdictions. Within those cities, the cards have enabled holders to access local medical clinics, interact with and receive services from city agencies, borrow books from local libraries, and some resident cards also have debit card functionality. In addition, many private businesses within those cities have been receptive, allowing holders to use the cards as sufficient identification to pick up packages, cash checks, or open bank accounts.[74] The cards may also facilitate interaction with local law enforcement, especially in jurisdictions that also maintain sanctuary policies. Moreover, the cards provide a form of local documentation for many undocumented persons that creates a sense of belonging and membership to the local community.[75]

The San Francisco municipal identification program survived a preemption challenge in state court, with the court dismissing the claim that the card violated the federal prohibition on harboring an unlawfully present person.[76] Such programs have not otherwise been tested in litigation. In addition to New Haven and San Francisco, Los Angeles, Richmond, and Oakland, California, as well as Trenton and Mercer County, New Jersey, and Washington, DC, maintain some form of local identity card that can be obtained by undocumented residents.[77] In 2015, New York City began offering such a card, and Iowa City and Philadelphia are currently considering similar policies.[78]

## Education and Tuition-Equity Laws

The 1996 federal immigration law, IIR-IRA, restricted the states' ability to provide residency and in-state tuition benefits for undocumented students. Specifically, the law prohibits states from making undocumented students eligible for any postsecondary education benefit on the basis of state residency, unless a U.S. citizen from another state would also be eligible for that benefit.[79] Since the enactment of that federal law, several states have, as Florida House Speaker Will Weatherford characterized it, "realiz[ed] that there are a lot of kids who are not being given an opportunity [for higher education]" and decided to offer in-state tuition benefits to undocumented students, with Texas starting the trend in 2001.[80] Such enactments continued from 2001 through 2013, with seventeen states currently offering admission and in-state tuition rates to undocumented students attending public institutions of higher learning.[81] Three additional state university systems allow the same benefit.[82] In addition, six states – California, Illinois, Minnesota, New Mexico, Texas, and Washington – also offer certain forms of access to financial aid to undocumented students.[83] Although these tuition-equity laws began in 2001 with California and Texas, and continued through 2006 with several other states enacting laws providing in-state tuition rates for undocumented students, there was a notable gap in that momentum from 2007 to 2011.[84] In that time of restrictionist fervor, Wisconsin enacted a tuition equity law in

2009, but repealed it in 2011. However, momentum started again in 2011 with Connecticut's enactment, and accelerated in 2013 and 2014 when five states – Colorado, New Jersey, Minnesota, Oregon, and Florida – all passed in-state tuition policies.[85]

These policies have not been litigated in the U.S. Supreme Court, but the California Supreme Court has upheld the state's in-state tuition policy against a challenge – from Kris Kobach, among others – that it violated the 1996 federal law. The California Supreme Court rejected the challenge and found the programs constitutional.[86] California overcame the federal prohibition by allowing anyone, including undocumented students or U.S. citizens from other states, who attends three years of high school in the state to pay in-state tuition at state colleges and universities, and many other states have followed this lead. In contrast to this trend of facilitating postsecondary education for undocumented students, five states have denied tuition equity, with two states taking the further step of prohibiting unlawfully present immigrants from attending state institutions of higher learning.[87]

As for other education-related laws, the recent round of federal appeals court and U.S. Supreme Court decisions has not altered the existing status quo on state-level education policy regarding unauthorized immigrants. Importantly, the federal appeals court reaffirmed in *United States v. Alabama* the now 30-year-old constitutional principle, established by the Supreme Court's 1982 decision in *Plyler v. Doe*, that states and localities may not exclude or otherwise deter undocumented students from attending public primary schools. Alabama's attempt to discover the immigration status of such students or their family members was dismissed by both the trial court and the appeals court, and thus far, the Supreme Court has shown no inclination to overturn *Plyler*.

## Public Welfare Laws

The major legislative changes to state welfare schemes vis-à-vis noncitizens took place in the wake of the federal government's 1996 Personal Work Opportunity and Reform Act. PWORA rendered many groups of noncitizens ineligible for important federal benefits such as Temporary Assistance for Needy Families (TANF), Food Stamps, Supplemental Security Income (SSI), Medicaid, and the Children's Health Insurance Program (CHIP).[88] The act purported to devolve some decision making over noncitizen eligibility for jointly funded federal-state programs and state-only public assistance programs to state governments.[89] Importantly, states that desired to provide public assistance to unauthorized immigrants would have to do so through enactment of affirmative legislation after 1996.[90] Indeed, some high immigrant population states have used their discretion under federal law to provide more generous welfare assistance to immigrants. In the years following the passage of PWORA, most states restored some aspect of welfare eligibility to those legal permanent residents who had arrived prior to 1996,[91] with California being the most generous.[92] Many states have also provided some health care access to unauthorized immigrants through provisions for prenatal care and child health insurance. In 2002, the U.S. Department of Health and Human Services gave states the option to provide prenatal care to undocumented immigrant women by extending CHIP coverage to unborn children.

Today, states have expanded immigrant access to prenatal health care in three ways: laws granting access to CHIP for unborn children (sixteen states as of September 2014), laws granting access to presumptive eligibility (PE) for pregnant women to obtain immediate temporary Medicaid coverage (seventeen states), and states setting up more comprehensive low-income insurance for pregnant women through state funded programs (Massachusetts, New York, and New Jersey).[93] Many states have also expanded health care access to immigrant children, with twenty-three states providing lawfully resident children access to CHIP regardless of their year of entry, and five states – California, Illinois, Massachusetts, New York, and Washington – provide immigrant children access to health insurance regardless of legal status.[94] Finally, a bill recently proposed in the California Senate would extend state medical coverage to undocumented immigrants, directing the state health agency to seek a federal waiver to allow undocumented Californians to get insurance coverage through the state health care exchange, operated as part of the federal Affordable Care Act.[95]

### Professional Licensing

A few states, such as California, New York, and Florida, have also contended with the question of undocumented law students applying for admission to the state bar. Although this is not a wide-ranging concern that affects a significant portion of the undocumented population, the underlying issues are both legally and symbolically important. State bar admission explores the possibility of states providing certain benefits, such as professional licenses, to undocumented immigrants in a manner consistent with federal law. In addition, it is likely that issues of professional licensing will become of increasing concern as more students begin taking advantage of DACA.

Licenses to practice law are primarily a matter of state law, generally left to state bars and state supreme courts. The State Bar of California, for example, preliminarily reviews applications and then sends recommendations to the California Supreme Court. The California Supreme Court was presented with an undocumented applicant in 2012 who had completed law school and passed the state's bar exam and whose admission was recommended by the state bar association.[96] The legal hurdle for the applicant was a provision of the 1996 IIRA-IRA that generally prohibits states from conferring a "public benefit," including a professional license, to an unauthorized immigrant unless the state affirmatively enacted a state law providing the benefit after 1996.[97] Just weeks after oral argument in the case, the California legislature enacted such a law, expressly providing for the possibility that undocumented applicants could become members of the state bar.[98] Relying on that statute, the state supreme court ruled to admit the undocumented applicant.[99] A similar dynamic occurred in Florida, where the State Supreme Court initially rejected the application of an undocumented bar applicant,[100] but that decision was made moot when the Florida legislature passed a bill, in accordance with federal law, that granted undocumented immigrants the ability to become members of the bar.[101] A similar suit regarding bar admission is pending in New York.[102]

Of course, even if they gain admission to the state bar, undocumented licensees still face federal prohibitions that would prevent employers from hiring them without obtaining employment authorization or benefitting from a change in federal law.[103] Nevertheless, even without federal reform, such professional licensees might work as self-employed, work on a pro bono basis, or practice in a foreign country. Currently, Sergio Garcia works for his own law practice, as a civil litigation attorney in northern California.[104]

Finally, California expanded access to professional licensing one step further: In October 2014, Governor Jerry Brown signed a law, SB 1159 that "requires all 40 licensing boards under the California Department of Consumer Affairs to consider applicants regardless of immigration status by 2016."[105] Just as in the case of lawyers, these individuals could, if they met their licensing requirements, practice their profession without needing a social security number: a federal individual tax identification number (ITIN) would suffice. So far, no other state has followed California's lead. Others may do so in the future, although the demand for such legislation may become less strong, as more and more professionals get work authorization through federal expansions of deferred action programs.

### Local Integration Agencies and "Welcoming" Initiatives

Several states and localities with high foreign-born populations have created governmental offices that are intended to provide residents with access to services to which they are already entitled, by providing resources such as information on state and local services, job training, language assistance, and information about federal services and programs including naturalization and deferred action. At the state level, Illinois, Massachusetts, New York, and Michigan maintain agencies and offices that are dedicated to these goals,[106] and California has recently introduced similar legislation to coordinate policy implementation, interagency coordination, and public outreach on the many state benefits passed in the last decade.[107] In addition to these state efforts, some cities also maintain their own local organizations. New York City, for example, runs the Mayor's Office of Immigrant Affairs (MOIA), which offers a variety of services to immigrants, including those who have recently arrived and may be undocumented.[108] The MOIA alerts noncitizens about the city's policies on protecting information regarding their immigration status, provides DACA resources, social services information, and lists nonprofit organizations that may help noncitizens, including those who are undocumented. Similar to New York City, Boston, Chicago, and Los Angeles also maintain such offices, tasked with coordinating services and information for immigrants regardless of status. Through its newly created Task Force on New Americans, the White House aims "to support existing efforts and encourage additional local governments to develop and implement integration strategies tailored to their communities' needs."[109]

In addition to activities directed exclusively by state and local government agencies, the past few years have also seen a growth of public-private partnerships aimed at creating more welcoming communities. Indeed, the White House Task Force on New Americans drew attention to two such national-level efforts in its inaugural report in April 2015: [110] the National Partnership on New Americans, which coordinates the efforts of statewide and regional immigrant advocacy organizations primarily from traditional immigrant destinations,[111] and the Welcoming America network, which brings together local governments, nonprofits, and local industries primarily from newer immigrant destinations. [112]

The Welcoming America network, in particular, is important for federalism concerns because it engages with local governments as they embark on plans to attract immigrant residents and revitalize their economies. As a first step, local governments in the Welcoming network pass legislative resolutions that recognize and celebrate the presence of immigrants, and the potential economic windfalls of foreign trade and commerce.[113] The resolutions themselves are nonbinding and generally do not create legal obligations or prohibitions. At the same time, these resolutions are only the first step: As the "commitment form" for the Welcoming Cities and Counties Project indicates, local jurisdictions also pledge to adopt policies and practices that promote inclusion, appoint at least one key municipal staff contact for the project, and participate in conference calls and annual meetings with other members of the network.[114]

As of April 2015, fifty-two cities and counties were participating in the program and most were new immigrant destinations, varying from large cities such as Atlanta, Georgia, and Nashville, Tennessee, to medium-sized cities such as Boise, Idaho, and High Point, North Carolina, to smaller cities such as Dodge City, Kansas and Clarkston, Georgia.[115] This was a significant jump from twenty-nine jurisdictions from the prior year.[116] So far, the early evidence from some welcoming programs indicates that they might indeed be helping to revitalize local communities. For example, Dayton, Ohio, a city facing big problems with abandoned housing and population decline, adopted a welcoming program that drew support from various government agencies, community organizations, and local nonprofits. As the *New York Times* noted, "The city found interpreters for public offices, added foreign-language books in libraries and arranged for English classes.... Local groups gave courses for immigrants opening small businesses and helped families of refugees and foreign students."[117] Dayton also partnered with local universities to help high-skilled immigrants better translate their skills and credentials to the local labor market, and the police department decided to no longer check on the legal status of immigrants for minor offenses. The overall effort "cost them one salary for a program coordinator and some snacks for meetings," and the benefits of reversing depopulation and reviving the local economy seem to be taking root.[118]

Since many welcoming efforts in other cities are still in their early stages, there have not yet been extensive studies of their effectiveness in promoting economic growth, bolstering local housing markets, and improving attitudes among native-born and foreign-born populations. What is clear, however, is that these efforts open up new possibilities for the study of immigration federalism moving forward, not only with respect to state and local laws but also other policies related to workforce development and economic growth that are explicitly tied to attracting more immigrant residents.

Finally, local governments are also moving beyond integration efforts oriented towards immigrant residents, to organizing politically across jurisdictions. Perhaps the most notable example in this regard was the creation of Cities United for Immigration Action, which launched immediately after the president's announcement of his DACA expansion and institution of other deferred action policies in November 2014.[119] The forty-seven members on the CUIA steering committee expressly state that their purpose is to "shape[]"

the national debate," and "work[] together on implementation."[120] Although a significant part of their stated purpose is to lobby Congress for immigration reform, the twenty members from the collective who met in New York City in December 2014 focused their discussion on the implementation of inclusive, immigrant-friendly policies at the local level consistent with the president's actions.

These integrationist trends in the past few years have showcased the power of building coalitions across localities that share ideas and purpose, with an eye toward creating de facto national policies and affecting national legislative output in the future. As Professor Judith Resnick notes, these types of translocal governmental organizations can cross territorial lines to help shape and spread policies.[121] In this way, and often with the help of policy entrepreneurs, integration efforts in the new immigration federalism have taken on a horizontal dimension,[122] in addition to its more traditional vertical component.

### State Citizenship Proposals

Finally, perhaps the most ambitious and far-reaching integrationist proposals in the new immigration federalism have been state citizenship bills. Thus far, only one in New York has even made it to the state legislature for consideration, and none have been passed. The *New York Is Home Act* would allow undocumented immigrants to vote in state elections, hold state office, qualify as recipients for Medicaid coverage, seek the protection of all state laws, and be eligible to receive professional licensing, tuition assistance, and driver's licenses.[123] Undoubtedly, many of the provisions included as part of the bill, including provisions on licenses, professional licensing, and tuition assistance, are not novel and have been part of state policies in New York and elsewhere for some years. Indeed, even political rights like voting were once available to noncitizens in several states.[124]

What is striking about the proposal, however, is its bold claim to creating a highly meaningful form of geography-based citizenship separate from the idea of national citizenship. Although the proposal has not yet been put to a vote and the chances of passage appear slim,[125] it nevertheless represents a resurgence of a robust version of state sovereignty in a pro-integration direction. Indeed, defenders of the bill justify it on the federalism theory of dual-sovereignty, with states possessing the constitutional authority to determine the rights of those within their political community.[126] "Alien suffrage," itself is not new, as several states permitted noncitizen voting throughout the 1800s and early 1900s.[127] But the time of robust political participation by noncitizens occurred at a time when immigration laws were racially biased, "illegal immigration" did not have the legal or social meaning it has today, and the noncitizens permitted to vote were white noncitizens. More recent forays into immigrant voting have been in smaller venues, like municipal and school board elections, although successful passage of local noncitizen voting has been rare, with Takoma Park, Maryland, as the only local jurisdiction that allows noncitizen voting.[128]

At the same time, the main legal architect of the *New York Is Home Act*, Professor Peter Markowitz, sees the proposal of state citizenship as a "lodestar" in the immigrant rights movement, guiding states and localities along a continuum with full political and civic inclusion as the ultimate prize.[129] Thus, the New York state bill is qualitatively different than past enactments in the state, and the more comprehensive set of benefits that has accumulated over time in a state like California, as it codifies the notion of state citizenship (and its attendand rights, obligations, protections, and identity) alongside our present-day, dominant understanding of national citizenship as our primary source of formal affiliation.

### ACCOUNTING FOR THE SPREAD OF INTEGRATIVE LAWS

What factors account for the spread of integrationist legislation toward immigrants, particularly unauthorized immigrants? Mirroring the analysis we did in Chapters 3 and 4, we conduct a statistical analysis across jurisdictions to see which factors are statistically predictive of pro-integration legislation, and then we conduct an institutional analysis that takes into account changes over time, and the role of various institutional actors in a federalism framework.

### Statistical Analyses

**Political Context** Local political contexts are important across most of these types of integrative policies. First, the only states that have provided access to health insurance for undocumented children – California, Illinois, Massachusetts, New York, and Washington – are those controlled by Democratic legislators. Next, Democrat-leaning areas are also much more likely to resist federal enforcement efforts than are Republican-leaning areas.[130] The relationship is even stronger in the case of municipal identification laws, which have been passed only in cities with Democratic majorities. Finally, most states that have expanded access to driver's licenses to unauthorized immigrants have Democratic-controlled legislatures. Utah is a notable exception in this regard. As we show in Appendix C, party control of the legislature is the strongest predictor in a regression model that controls for the share of agricultural jobs in the state and the proportion of Latinos and naturalized citizens in the state. The strength of the partisanship factor is on par with the strength of the proportion of Latinos in the state.

Partisanship also plays a significant role in predicting whether or not a state allows in-state tuition for undocumented residents, although it is important to note that there are four Republican-led states – Florida, Kansas, Texas, and Utah – that have provided this benefit, along with fourteen states with Democratically controlled legislatures and one nonpartisan legislature (Nebraska). Finally, when it comes to the provision of financial aid, Texas is the only Republican-controlled state that provides financial assistance of any kind, whether public or private. At the same time, we should also acknowledge that partisanship did not play a significant role in state provision of driver's licenses for DACA recipients, with most Republican-controlled states (save Arizona and Nebraska) granting this privilege.[131]

Finally, although state agricultural interests played a significant role in making restrictive legislation less likely, this factor is not important for the pro-integration laws that we consider. However, this relationship might become significant in the future as more states contemplate expanding access to driver's licenses or in-state tuition.

**Size of the Latino Electorate**: In addition to partisanship at the state level, the size of the Latino electorate, and the immigrant electorate more generally, makes a difference. States with a greater proportion of Latinos and naturalized immigrants are significantly more likely to pass legislation providing driver's licenses and financial aid for unauthorized immigrant residents. States with a high proportion of naturalized immigrants in the electorate are also more likely to grant health insurance to undocumented children. At the same time, it is also important to remember that these statistical findings may not explain some notable outlier cases such as Arizona, which has a sizable Latino population that accounts for 30 percent of the state's population,[132] but also a Republican-dominated state legislature since 1992.[133] As we noted in Chapter 4, the combination of issue entrepreneurship and partisan opportunities have played a significant role in Arizona, as Republican primary voters have pushed their elected officials further to the right on immigration and other issues, largely by mounting primary challenges from the right.[134] By contrast, New Mexico has not had a similar partisan dynamic, even though it is also a border state with a sizable Latino population. Indeed, when we specify the model a little differently, by interacting Latino population share and the party control of state legislatures, we find that larger Latino populations are associated with more expansive driver's license policies in states controlled by the Democratic Party but not in those controlled by Republicans.

### THE POLARIZED CHANGE MODEL REVISITED

While it is helpful to know that partisanship is statistically predictive of pro-integration legislation at the state level, with very few Republican-controlled states passing such legislation, it still does not provide an adequate explanation of *how* political factors and political processes have made a difference in successfully pushing pro-integration legislation. To do so, we turn once again to the Polarized Change Model that we laid out in Chapter 4, to see if the same model (or some variant thereof) can help us account for why, and how, pro-integration forces were able to make a significant set of legislative breakthroughs after 2012.

### The Role of Party Polarization and DACA

Recall that, in the case of restrictive legislation, key background factors included the rise of party polarization in Congress and the growth of ethnic nationalism after the September 11 attacks. Party polarization is still an abiding feature of Congress; indeed, historical data indicate that party polarization has gotten even stronger in Congress in the past decade,[135] and it has also gotten stronger in many state legislatures.[136] By contrast, the effects of 9/11 seem to be more diminished today than before, although attacks on U.S. nationals in far-away places such as Libya and Syria have, at times, found their way into political discourse about homeland security and the U.S.-Mexico border.[137]

While these background factors still remain relevant, they present a different set of constraints and opportunities for pro-integration advocates based on whether they are operating at the national level or at the state level. For advocates working on congressional legislation, party polarization and anxieties over border security present challenges to winning passage of comprehensive immigration reform. This was particularly true after 2012, as champions of immigration reform needed to secure support among a significant number of Republicans in the Senate and a majority of those in the U.S. House.[138] At the state level, however, pro-integration advocates can take advantage of party polarization in places where Democrats are dominant. This certainly was the case in California, as the state legislature achieved a two-thirds Democratic majority in 2012 and a governor from the same party. Thus, pro-immigrant advocates in California did not need to appeal to Republican legislators or a Republican governor to pass any pro-integration legislation. In other, more closely divided states, however, pro-integration advocates needed to appeal to moderate legislators (Republican and/or Democrat), which might explain, in part, why California has passed the most far-reaching set of immigrant integration measures when compared to other states.

At the same time, unified Democratic Party control has not been a guarantor of pro-integration legislation. Indeed, prior to 2013, California Governor Jerry Brown, a Democrat, had signaled his opposition to providing driver's licenses for unauthorized immigrants,[139] and he vetoed the TRUST Act (a detainer resistance law) when it reached his desk in September 2012.[140] Thus, while Democratic Party control at the state level may be strongly associated with the likelihood of pro-integration legislation, recent history from the "most likely" case for a party control explanation suggests that other factors may also be important.

As we have already indicated, there are a few national-level developments in 2012 – most notably the passage and implementation of DACA and the political repudiation of the restrictionist strategy in the November elections – that made pro-integration legislation more likely to succeed in 2013 and 2014 than just two years prior. Indeed, there is good reason to believe that DACA, in particular, had a significant and independent impact on the expansion of driver's licenses at the state level. But how did these mechanisms work? How did DACA end up getting California and several other states to expand access to driver's licenses to all unauthorized residents?

To be clear, we are not claiming the presidential administration *intended* these state-level policy changes when it implemented DACA. Indeed, there is no mention of state driver's licenses in any of the federal government's documents outlining the contours of DACA or its effects on potential beneficiaries. Our interviews with pro-integration advocates who were party to discussions with the White House about DACA also indicate that state laws on driver's licenses, or any other policy matter, was not part of the conversation.[141] At the same time, the administrative creation of a large class of persons who now are temporarily lawfully present despite their unlawful status virtually necessitated some state-level response. With a group of a few hundred thousand DACA recipients openly attending schools and seeking employment, and necessitating transportation to take advantage of both, DACA helped ease the policy climate for states desirous of accounting for all residents, regardless of immigration status.

This process – of an exogenous shock (this one prompted by the president's decision on DACA) prompting a rash of changes in state policies on driver's licenses – comports very closely to what Frank Baumgartner and Bryan Jones have called a "punctuated equilibrium," in which a status quo of policy inertia is upended by an exogenous development, which subsequently catalyzes processes that propel toward rapid change.[142] The reason why the president's action on DACA is exogenous is that the administration was not seeking to change state policy on driver's licenses when it announced its policy in June 2012.[143] And the policy reverberations from the 2012 executive action continue to be felt. As DACA recipients renew their status and continue to establish deep ties to their communities through education, work, and family ties, they appear more and more as a permanently non-deportable group. By regularizing, without legalizing, hundreds of thousands of previously unauthorized immigrants, the president's action catalyzed states and localities into dealing with the everyday needs of these residents and their families.

### Change in Strategy among Funders and Organizations

While DACA may account for the sudden changes in state driver's license policies after 2012, our analysis of news coverage and in-depth interviews indicate that the broader increase in integrationist legislation was also due to changes in foundation strategy and organization mobilization. Of course, this makes sense from a theoretical perspective; as theories of social movements and policy change would suggest,[144] and as we saw in the case of restrictionist efforts in Chapter 4, the opening of political opportunities only lay bare the possibilities that are available to interest groups. For these groups to capitalize on those opportunities, they needed to have sufficient organizational resources and politically viable ideas in order to successfully change policy.

After the failure of the DREAM Act in 2010, there was a growing recognition among the immigrant-rights funding community[145] that comprehensive immigration reform might not happen for the foreseeable future.[146] Prior attempts at reform had failed, even when Democrats controlled both chambers of Congress, and the prospects for reform looked fairly dim with a Republican majority in the U.S. House starting in January 2011. These prospects grew even weaker after the drawn-out partisan fight over implementation of the Affordable Care Act and the government shutdown of 2013. Thus, a realization that dawned after the 2010 congressional election had crystallized by 2013: Presidential action and state/local legislation seemed like the only plausible scenarios for pro-integration policies.[147] Consequent to this realization, national funders of immigrant rights organizations began to devote more resources to those states where pro-integration legislation seemed most favorable.

Another important factor was state-level organizational capacity: an increase in resources would have provided little benefit in states that lacked a prior infrastructure or experience in building support for immigrant rights. Certainly, in many states that had seen the passage of restrictive legislation, assistance from national funders largely flowed to organizations providing technical assistance and convening a broad coalition of stakeholders, to beat back future efforts at restriction and slowly build support for pro-integration policies.[148] In many of these places, immigrant-rights and civil-rights organizations often teamed up with clergy, police chiefs, labor unions, state chambers of commerce, and other business organizations to pass legislation that is pro-integration.[149] Indeed, much of the work in building conservative stakeholder coalitions for immigrant integration was being done by the National Immigration Forum, with financial support from various national foundations and corporate donations.[150] Still, most nationally funded efforts in 2011 and 2012 were aimed at preventing restrictive state legislation in the wake of enforcement laws in Arizona and Alabama, and building support for comprehensive immigration reform in traditionally conservative areas.[151]

The organizational infrastructure for pro-integration organizations was quite different, however, in states with Democratic-controlled legislatures and an immigrant rights infrastructure that had been built up over a decade or more. This was perhaps most evident in California, which passed various restrictionist measures in the 1990s, including Proposition 187 in 1994. As we noted in Chapter 2, the politics surrounding immigration restriction in 1994 actually hastened the demise of future restrictive legislation in California, as Latino voter registration soared and contributed to the dominance of Democrats in the state legislature beginning in 1996. The reaction to Proposition 187 also affected the political sensibility of a new generation of Latino legislators in Sacramento who had "cut their teeth" by organizing immigrants.[152]

Immigrant rights organizations grew stronger in the aftermath of Proposition 187 as well. In the late 1990s, they scored some early policy victories by getting the state to restore most welfare benefits to legal permanent residents that were stripped away by federal legislation in 1996.[153] And they managed to get Democratic Governor Gray Davis to restore driver's licenses to undocumented immigrants as he faced a voter recall, although this victory was short-lived as Republican Arnold Schwarzenegger won the election, pressured lawmakers to repeal the measure, and vetoed further attempts to restore driver licenses.[154] During the Schwarzenegger administration, however, the immigrant rights movement built its organizational capacity and grew more politically sophisticated. A network of statewide funders poured significant resources over several years to build up a regional infrastructure of immigrant advocacy organizations.[155] These organizations, in turn, started coordinating on legislative and advocacy strategies that have included acts of civil disobedience by immigrant youth, outreach to business organizations and clergy, and research on messaging strategies designed to sway public opinion toward more welcoming strategies.[156] This cross-regional strategy in building organizational capacity proved useful over the years, as immigrant rights organizations helped elect more pro-integration legislators to state office and kept those representatives accountable by holding large-scale protests and rallies in their home districts. Thus, they could push for legislation such as driver's license bills or the TRUST Act in successive legislative sessions, each time building greater legislative and public support to eventually secure enactment.

In addition to California, statewide organizations and networks grew stronger in states like New York (*New York Immigration Coalition*), Illinois (*Illinois Coalition for Immigrant and Refugee Rights*), Massachusetts (*Massachusetts Immigrant and Refugee Advocacy Coalition*), and Oregon (*CAUSA*). Indeed, in 2010, these organizations and eight others joined forces to form the National Partnership for New Americans (NPNA), which promotes cross-regional efforts at immigrant integration.[157] At the same time, the building of state organizational capacity was no guarantee of success, as was evident in Oregon. While the statewide immigrant rights organization (CAUSA) was able to work effectively with a range of stakeholders in 2013, such as agricultural groups, labor unions, police chiefs, and clergy, to support a series of pro-integration measures, this coalition was unable to overcome a ballot referendum challenge to the driver's license measure in 2014. Andrea Silva's case study of the Oregon measures indicates that the closing of political opportunities made a critical difference in the case of driver's licenses in Oregon.[158]

Nevertheless, even if we include the example of the driver's license defeat in Oregon, the story more generally – of a shifting political landscape after DACA and the failure of comprehensive immigration reform, increased funding for state and local efforts, and growing organizational capacity among immigrant rights coalitions – still goes a long way in explaining the surge in pro-integration legislation after 2012. To sum up this development in a pithy formulation we often heard from our interviews with pro-integration organizations: these groups moved "from defense to offense" and, in doing so, could rely on some significant organizational capacity that they had built up along the way.

### The Role of Networked Issue Entrepreneurs: Similarities and Differences

Now that we have outlined the role of important background factors such as the stalemate on comprehensive immigration reform, and of important organizational actors in particular states in pushing pro-integration legislation, it is important to ask the broader question of whether the Polarized Change model still "works" in the same manner when applied to the surge in integrationist legislation after 2012, when compared to the surge in restrictionist activity in the prior period.

Certainly, there are similarities to these two processes: the proliferation of both restrictionist and integrationist legislation depended in some critical ways on the failure of comprehensive immigration reform at the national level. They also both included coordinated activity across states and regions, with model legislation often being deployed by people with critical legal expertise (Kris Kobach and the Immigration Reform Law Institute on the restrictive side, and the National Day Laborer Organizing Network, the National Immigration Law Center, and various university-based law clinics on the pro-integration side). Indeed, our interviews with several pro-integration activists indicate that they learned some important lessons from the prior wave of restrictionist activity, including pushing the boundaries of current legal doctrine and sharing model legislation, framing techniques, and organizing tactics.

At the same time, there are some important differences between these two manifestations of the Polarized Change model. First, unlike in the case of restrictionist organizations that were few in number and highly coordinated between federal and state action, there were many more pro-immigrant advocacy organizations working on different aspects of immigration reform at the national and state levels. Our analysis of news coverage of pro-integration legislation as well as interviews with several national and state-level organizations indicates that the pro-integration side contains a far greater number of actors than does the restrictive side. Key DC-based groups receiving frequent mention include: National Immigration Forum, Center for American Progress, America's Voice, NCLR, Asian Americans Advancing Justice, SEIU, AFL-CIO and the National Immigration Law Center (NILC). Most of these groups had been focused on national-level efforts until 2012, with the notable exception of NILC, which for many years has been working on national as well as state-level issues as they affect low-income immigrant residents. In more recent years, United We Dream and Center for Community Change have also joined NILC in working simultaneously at the federal and subfederal levels.

At the same time, there have been various efforts outside of Washington, DC, that have played an important role in shaping a different vision of immigrant integration that has built up over time and, in some fundamental ways, reshaped immigration policy at the federal and state levels. While many of these efforts have been focused on particular states and cities, nationally networked groups like the National Day Laborer Organizing Network

(NDLON), Immigration Advocates Network, Center for New Community, and Progressive States Network also played important roles in helping to coordinate campaigns across multiple jurisdictions. Finally, as we have already discussed, groups like National Partnership for New Americans and Welcoming America were coordinating activities across the country, including finding ways for local governments to share information about best practices and providing logistical support for federal government efforts.

So, while we saw in Chapter 4 that proliferation of state legislation on immigration restriction emerged from a change in strategy among only a handful of actors, the pro-integration landscape was far more dispersed, making a coordinated strategy between the federal and subfederal levels far less likely. Indeed, the process of changing strategy in the pro-integration landscape was far more contested and messy. Certainly, a growing recognition after 2010, of the importance of state activity among national-level organizations and their funders, helped provide more resources to state-level organizations. At the same time, this changing balance of power (and financing) between organizations focused on national policy change and state/local reforms remains hotly contested. Indeed, there are significant differences of opinion and strategy among some of the major immigration advocacy organizations on important matters of immigration federalism such as resistance to executive enforcement, starting with 287(g), and continuing through Secure Communities and the Priority Enforcement Program – in general, many DC-based organizations with access to the White House have have stayed focused on comprehensive immigration reform and have kept relatively silent on the administration's immigration enforcement, while immigrant rights organizations outside the Beltway have been far more public and vocal in opposing these enforcement programs.[159]

Another important difference emerges in the interplay between national policy gridlock and state/local proliferation. Unlike the restrictionists who generated legislative gridlock at the national level in order to justify state action (see Chapter 4), state-level integrationists merely benefited from the growing realization among funders that national legislation might not be achieved in the near or medium term. More pointedly, state-level integrationists were not committed to derailing comprehensive immigration reform, even when such legislation contained enforcement and timeline provisions that they found unpalatable. Thus, a national legislative strategy for comprehensive immigration reform could proceed in parallel with state-level actions on immigrant integration.[160] By contrast, restrictionists were vehemently opposed to any federal legislation that contained a pathway to citizenship, even if such bills included important enforcement provisions such as beefed-up border security, national employee verification, and stricter penalties for immigration violations.

Thus, while in some ways, we can say that the pro-integration activists on state legislation borrowed some of the strategies from the restrictive-issue entrepreneurs who preceded them, there were nevertheless some important differences in the structure and operation of their advocacy networks, especially between the federal and subfederal levels. And yet, in "moving from defense to offense," pro-integration activists at the local level helped reinforce the importance of states and localities as important venues for immigration legislation. The strategy of relying on Congress to pass preemptive legislation, or for courts to invalidate all restrictive schemes, was no longer operative. If pro-integration activists wanted to protect the rights and promote the interests of unauthorized immigrants, they would have to do so at the state and local level.

# 6

## Implications for Legal Theory on Federalism and Immigration Law

In this chapter, we pivot from answering the "what" and "why" questions of this new immigration federalism, to more fully considering its implications for law and legal discourse. The state and local enactments we described in the preceding chapters are part of a developing new surge of immigration federalism. To recap, the third era of immigration federalism occurred against the backdrop of some major changes in the immigration policy regime: the dismantling of legal temporary worker programs; increased political and legal salience of the line between lawful and unlawful presence; and limiting lawful migration from Mexico and other countries of high immigration. In the immediate aftermath of these changes to the immigration regime, states and localities in the 1970s responded with restrictionist policies, such as excluding undocumented immigrants from employment, erecting barriers for undocumented children attending public schools, and restricting jobs and welfare for noncitizens generally. These policies, in turn, elicited the judicial and academic responses of the late 1970s and 1980s, as courts and commentators attempted to make sense of the rapidly evolving meaning, policy regime, and statutory background of lawful and unlawful migration.

Federal legislative responses to these state and local enactments also took on a different flavor during the third era of immigration federalism. Unlike the prior immigration laws of the twentieth Century, congressional efforts in 1986 and 1996 specifically accounted for the increased presence of states and localities in the regulation of unauthorized migrants. These federal laws responded to subfederal lawmaking and trends, and provided exceptions and opportunities for state and local participation in policies that affected the lives of immigrants. For example, 1986's IRCA expressly addressed several state laws prohibiting the employment of unauthorized workers, preempting those state sanctions (but including a "business licensing" exception that would become significant thirty years later in the *Whiting v. U.S. Chamber of Commerce* case dealing with Arizona's renewed employer sanctions law enacted in 2007).[1] The federal welfare overhaul in 1996 provided states with the leeway to restrict welfare provision to immigrants – even some lawfully present immigrants – in ways they could not before.[2] Concurrently, the 1996 immigration overhaul provided opportunities for state and local enactments to benefit unauthorized migrants, including provisions for in-state tuition benefits and professional licensing.[3]

At the state level, in the lead up to the restrictionist laws of the early twenty-first century, California's Proposition 187 in 1994 represented another significant milestone. Like the state enactments of the 1970s and 1980s, Prop. 187 also spurred a judicial response and scholarly ruminations about the proper role of states and localities in immigration matters. Although that state effort did not expand beyond California, it garnered significant national notoriety and brought to the fore questions of the importance of immigration policy at the state level, thus revealing the potential of state action to influence national immigration politics. Although it ultimately failed because of its several legal defects and the lack of an orchestrated and networked political movement behind it, careful study of those flaws seemed to provide the blueprint for the proliferation of state and local laws that would follow a decade later.

Even with this backdrop, however, significant state and local involvement in immigration regulation was still rare in the 1990's, especially on matters of enforcement.[4] California's Prop. 187 indicated the potential political and legal salience of the issue, but as we discussed in Chapter 2, such policies failed to proliferate, and the law itself suffered from fatal legal flaws. Subsequent federal laws seemed to reestablish federal dominance to the exclusion of such state enactments.

However, Post-9/11 and, more specifically, since 2004, state and localities have become resurgent in immigration federalism. The federal statutory overhauls of 1986 and 1996 provided opportunities and possibilities for state involvement in a wide variety of areas affecting immigrants' lives.[5] At the same time, these federal laws only provided potential openings; it would take nearly a decade for conservative issue activists to exploit the opportunities more fully. As Chapter 4 details, restrictionist issue entrepreneurs took lessons from past failures, such as Prop. 187, and exploited party polarization and post-9/11 security concerns to proliferate highly publicized state and local regulations across multiple jurisdictions. More recently, there has been a surge of pro-integration laws at the state level, both in numbers and types of bills, and a corresponding decline in restrictive legislation. Importantly, the weight of pro-integration legislative activity has shifted from efforts at comprehensive reform at the national level to proliferation efforts at the subfederal level.

In response to this decade of dizzying changes, courts and commentators have struggled to understand how this most recent activity fits into the legal theories and narratives used to capture the phenomenon of subfederal immigration. Here, we offer perspective on this concern, showing how our model of polarized change with its focus on partisanship and political context necessarily changes the way in which we should view, assess, and account for state and local lawmaking.

We explore the implications of our empirical assessment in two parts. Part I of this chapter addresses the conceptual and theoretical changes wrought by our politicized model of immigration federalism. Here, start with a bird's-eye view of policy proliferation and federalism theory, fitting our empirically investigated model into frameworks that better capture the method and utility of the type of policy proliferation we have seen over the past decade. In Part II, we turn our focus to individual cases, and how courts have developed the legal doctrine of the new immigration federalism. Here, we critique the structural power framework used by courts, arguing that the doctrine must incorporate analytic methods better suited to capturing the realities of polarized policy proliferation.

In both our theoretical and doctrinal critiques, we argue that traditional federalist narratives and ideas are used as a guise. Federalism provides the structure and the scaffold for this new round of subfederal decision making, but invocations of subfederal variegation, experimentation, and sovereignty are conjured primarily to achieve immigration policy goals unrelated to addressing pressing problems of public policy, state autonomy, or governmental competency. Rather, federalism has become the convenient rhetorical and constitutional hook for a multi-level, multi-jurisdictional partisan contest over immigration policy. Doctrinally, the federal court response to these recent state and local enactments reveals the instability of a structural powers framework. Continued reliance on preemption analysis, we argue, suppresses judicial attention to the discrimination and equality concerns that should be motivating courts' consideration of subfederal immigration regulations.

## TOWARD A REIMAGINED DYNAMIC OF IMMIGRATION FEDERALISM

The new immigration federalism is changing the way in which scholars, courts, and policy analysts might conceive of state and local dynamics in immigration policy making. Mainly, these conventional assessments have centered on the propriety of state and local involvement in the immigration arena, engaging federalism debates about the virtues of decentralized policy experimentation versus the notion that immigration regulation and enforcement are best left to the federal government alone. Our Polarized Change Model, however, suggests not only that courts rely on improbable assumptions in their analysis, but also that some existing scholarly theories may rest on premises at odds with our quantitative and qualitative empirical investigation of state and local immigration lawmaking. At minimum then, both current doctrine and discourse, and the assumption on which they are founded, must be carefully reexamined.

If stylized and traditional federalism narratives fail to capture the empirical reality of immigration federalism, what theoretical frames should we apply? First, our evidence of partisanship-based federalist expansion calls into question traditionally accepted notions of the potential value of state and local variegation and experimentation. Second, the Polarized Change model of state and local policy proliferation may require reimagining other models to explain the relationship between demographic factors and immigration policy dynamics at the federal and subfederal levels. Here, we argue that a cascade model of policy proliferation fits our empirical data better than functionalist or "steam valve" models that attempt to explain state and local immigration regulation. Finally, our thick description of the process of state and local policy making in immigration supports the viability and importance of emerging theoretical models of federalism that are now paying closer attention to the role of partisanship and politics. This use of our federalist system also suggests that the current immigration federalism is less about the virtues of decentralized and region-specific lawmaking than it is about providing alternate forums for large-scale immigration policy debates. With Congress stalemated on immigration reform for the foreseeable future, state and local jurisdictions have become the primary legislative turf for articulating differing and competing visions of what should be our national immigration policy.

### Challenges to Traditional Assumptions of Federalism

Our Polarized Change model suggests that policy proliferation in the immigration sphere is the product of a coordinated, networked system that is highly dependent on political factors. Recognizing this modus operandi conveys an image that is at odds with the hallowed view of federalism, which posits that state and local variations are organic responses to regional needs that are self-evident and driven by objective conditions. Our rich description of the process of subfederal immigration proliferation contributes to the evolution of scholarly voices rejecting or questioning conceptions of federalism that focus solely on governmental units, and treat each entity's domain as distinct spheres, with pockets of concurrent authority.[6] As noted scholar Judith Resnik maintains, "at a both descriptive and normative level, this [essentializing of rights, roles, and jurisdictional allocations] is misguided."[7] As she and others, including ourselves, have argued the multiple outlets for policy production afforded by a federalist system ensure dynamic relationships between federated units, and further, provide multiple opportunities for entrepreneurs to advance their policy objectives.[8] The critical presence and work of these entrepreneurs in the immigration field demonstrates that the "'who' of federalism" is not limited to the actors imagined in most judicial and scholarly accounts of immigration federalism that usually only account for legislative bodies at the federal and state level. This narrow focus limits the value of traditional federalism discourse in determining the value, legality, and normative desirability of state and local variegation in immigration policy.

As the voluminous federalism literature suggests,[9] proliferating subfederal legislation helps unlock the theoretical benefits of federalism, to wit: (1) providing more responsive government by matching local problems with local solutions; (2) allowing for policy innovation through variegated experimentation; (3) promoting intergovernmental competition, resulting in desirable outcomes for the citizenry; (4) helping states fulfill their roles as a bulwark against federal tyranny; and (5) increasing democratic participation. Because of these benefits, courts, at least in matters outside of the immigration context, have articulated, and sometimes applied, a "presumption against preemption," when adjudicating such questions.[10] The mechanism of politicized legislative growth we uncover, however, casts doubt on several of these justifications proffered by courts and commentators invoking federalism-based policy. We consider these in turn.

First, the new immigration federalism does not appear to be especially responsive to unique local conditions or regional variations. As we showed in Chapter 3, demographic changes and related economic stresses are, for the most part, not unique to the localities proposing and enacting local immigration regulations. Indeed, the vast majority of jurisdictions facing the same demographic changes, language isolation, and economic stresses do not even consider (let alone pass) immigration regulation.

For example, New Mexico experienced a rate of increase in its unauthorized immigrant population that is similar to that in Arizona,[11] but the state has not passed any significant restrictionist measures. The partisan conditions have not been favorable in New Mexico, which has had an electorate that has averaged 47 percent registered Democratic voters and just 33 percent Republican.[12] Furthermore, demographic change is often unrelated to subfederal policy responses, as many enacting jursidictions are states and localities with comparatively and objectively low levels of immigration and immigrants (and the attendant social and economic challenges that would follow). This has certainly been the case in restrictive states such as Alabama, Indiana, and Oklahoma, where the proportion of unauthorized immigrants (2.5 percent, 1.8 percent, and 2.0 percent in 2010, respectively)[13] has been significantly below the national average (3.7 percent).[14] If, in fact, objective and regionally specific policy concerns could explain this current trend in subfederal lawmaking, we would expect demographic factors to emerge as highly salient predictors of such laws. Instead, we found that partisanship and political dynamics explain the trend.[15]

More broadly, these findings belie functionalist explanations for state and local immigration lawmaking. Many scholars have evaluated the potential utility of state and local immigration regulations, and the value of abandoning exclusive federal control over all matters immigration.[16] In defending constitutional leeway for such enactments, scholars have sometimes assumed that these nonfederal policy expressions arise as inevitable responses to demographic shifts and variations.[17] The explanation and evidence we offer, however, suggest that for recent immigration federalism, this functionalist, demography-based explanation is an incomplete one.

Subfederal immigration policy largely reflects naked political preference and the opportunistic use of party polarization by issue entrepreneurs.[18] Professor Cristina Rodríguez has argued that what is "missing" from debates over the constitutionality of subfederal enactments is "a functional account that explains why state and local measures have arisen ... over the past five to ten years, and how this reality on the ground should reshape our conceptual and doctrinal understandings of immigration regulation."[19] Indeed, we agree with Professor Rodríguez that purely legal constitutional debates over subfederal involvement in immigration focusing on federalism questions miss crucial on-the-ground factors that should influence judicial and policy evaluations of these laws. However, we argue that the missing reality is *not* primarily the new demography and geography of immigration; rather, it is the new politics of immigration and rise of issue entrepreneurs willing to capitalize on this partisan context.

Undoubtedly, functionalist accounts of subfederal legislation serve the important purpose of carving out a normative space for local involvement, especially in the integrationist efforts. It may very well be preferable to locate and institute such measures at the local level, rather than at the national level. Additionally, we agree with Professor Rodriguez's underlying point that uniformity in immigration policy across the nation may not be necessary or normatively desirable.[20] However, our data show that local immigration restrictionism from the past decade did not necessarily occur, and is not necessarily occurring, in places that are particularly affected by immigration. Furthermore, perpetuating the assumption that demographic changes explain policy responses lends credence to the claims of legal necessity proffered by states like Arizona and cities like Hazleton. In contrast, we have shown that states and localities that pass immigration laws often experience little "need" for such regulation – at least not in the functional or instrumental sense.

Second, this process of politicized change does not produce the type of policy experimentation and innovation envisioned in Justice Brandeis's famous laboratories metaphor – that any given state may independently serve as a "laboratory" for "social and economic experiments."[21] As commentators have argued, in order for subfederal policies to be effective as policy experiments and innovations, states must (1) internalize costs and (2) provide replicable approaches.[22] When measured against these standards, the context of immigration federalism limits the ability of states to innovate in meaningful ways and to serve as "laboratories" of reform.[23]

Often jurisdictions enacting restrictionist legislation fail to internalize costs.[24] Even assuming that unauthorized immigrants exacerbate the economic and social problems in states like Arizona and Alabama, the ability of such ordinances to meet those challenges by incentivizing immigrant movement out of the jurisdiction means that these laws will almost certainly recreate and export those burdens to neighboring jurisdictions.[25] Moreover, individual states cannot deport or expel persons from the country; only the federal government can. Thus, enacting jurisdictions may be reducing the incentive to remain within their borders, but they are unlikely to achieve attrition of the unauthorized population from the United States. This is especially true as long as the federal executive maintains enforcement priorities at odds with state and local enforcement efforts.

It is possible, of course, that these types of spillovers might actually have salutary effects on national policy making. Heather Gerken and Ari Holtzblatt argue that state-to-state spillovers from state policy decisions might induce political engagement with the policy issue in states affected by the spillover, and such engagement might in turn force national compromise and legislative response.[26] Importantly, to the extent these benefits are realizable, they are not the ones imagined in a "states as laboratories" conception, in which states learn from policy innovations in another.

In addition, our politicized model undermines the viability of the replicability precondition for successful experimentation.[27] Undoubtedly, the restrictive policies of high-enforcement states mimic each other,[28] but this mimicry is not the type celebrated in federalism theory. Because the state and local laws generally do not respond to critical on-the-ground challenges, other states and localities cannot glean much about the utility of such laws in addressing any policy challenges posed by unlawful migration.[29] When issue entrepreneurs shop premade immigration solutions to jurisdictions based on partisanship and ripe political factors, the resultant policies are bound to be similar.[30] While this is "replication" in a strict sense, it is manifestly not replication as part of a meaningful process of effective reform.

Our model proposes that restrictive subfederal immigration laws proliferate in jurisdictions when political conditions are ripe, not because the legislation presents a unique method of addressing an emerging policy challenge. Accordingly, it is far from clear that "local experimentation will be of tremendous value in this context."[31] The "experimentation" currently occurring in the immigration field has little demonstrative value to other jurisdictions if the object is to address a pressing public policy need.[32] Such proliferation could have other important effects for entrenching policy positions or stimulating national debate on desirable immigration policy, but it does not necessarily respond to region-specific, on-the-ground problems.

Third, politicized policy proliferation, with the political and structural entropies described in Chapter 4, undermines competition between governmental bodies, at least along the vertical dimension between federal and state entities.[33] Certainly, the rhetoric surrounding the enactments focus on the relative significance of a particular policy to a particular state, and the ability of that state or locality to deal with the problems caused by unauthorized migration in a superior manner to the federal government. But, the underlying dynamic is a contest of political and partisan ideologies that use varying levels of government as sites for enactment, not necessarily because states and localities are functionally superior to the federal government in addressing migration concerns.

The type of competition between governments for votes and resource-based attempts to enact superior public policy seems to envision distinct sovereign entities operating in wholly different spheres. But, the connective tissue between national and subnational governments is increasingly thick.[34] Given the influence of state primary contests and policies on national politics, mediated through national political parties, competition across the federalism dimension is increasingly one between parties and ideologies, not between the various levels of government. On the restrictionist side, productive competition is less likely when a key competitor – here, the federal government – is hamstrung by groups and individuals outwardly decrying federal failure while at times fomenting the very failure they lament.[35] The only comparisons for the prefabricated policies instantiated in receptive restrictionist jurisdictions during the period from 2004 to 2012 were identical or similar policies, framed by the same issue entrepreneurs, enacted in other receptive jurisdictions.

Finally, in our evidence-based description of immigration legislation, state and local lawmaking ceases to be a vital bulwark against federal tyranny. Instead, issue entrepreneurs appear to be using states and localities in the immigration legislative landscape as "battering rams" to effectuate a minority position.[36] In this strategy, interested individuals and organizations might provide states and localities with legislation and attempt to enact laws in as many jurisdictions as possible, seeking eventually to influence public opinion and federal policy.[37] The success of the strategy depends on marrying a substantive policy position – here, restrictive immigration policy – with states' rights discourse.[38] In doing so, subfederal entities are able to tie their purported demographic challenges and restrictionist goals with the "classic trope[]" of challenging the national government's violation of the nation's deepest commitments.[39] In effect, the restrictive immigration federalism of the past decade showcases how national immigration priorities can be co-opted by the tyranny of the minority rather than by that of the majority, at times fomenting the national gridlock that suppresses diffuse national majorities from achieving policy success.[40]

Integrationist policy proliferation suffers from less friction with these stylized views of federalism, at least in regard to the relationship between subfederal policies and federal inaction.[41] Although integrationist entrepreneurs eventually turned to state and local arenas during this period of extended congressional intransigence, they are not averse to the possibility of federal reform. This is true even if that federal reform would include provisions for enhanced border and interior enforcement. Fundamentally, while federal gridlock provided motivation for subfederal integrationist efforts, it has never been a necessary precondition for it.

To be clear, we are not arguing that opposing federal immigration reform renders the restrictionist movement illegitimate; neither are we suggesting that legislative expression of political preference, regardless of region-specific challenges or demographic pressure, is an illegitimate or unconstitutional use of state and local authority. Rather, our more modest interest is to match the reality of state and local proliferation to scholarly and judicial theories of federalism. What is clear, especially for restrictionist state laws, is that justifications based on traditional notions of state and local policy variance and the benefits of such federalist variations are incongruous with the underlying reality of restrictionist subfederal laws.

If the Polarized Change model of immigration policy proliferation undermines the saliency of traditional conceptions of the value of federalist variegation, then what models of federalism more appropriately capture the politicized policy making we see today in the immigration field? What value, if any, does state and local policy making serve in the immigration arena?

## Legislative Cascades versus Conventional Immigration Federalism Narratives

As with traditional federalism narratives articulated by courts and federalism proponents, the primary problem with most scholarly appraisals of immigration federalism is their choice of conceptual frame to describe the trend. Commonly used theoretical models assume the responsiveness of public policy to regional or unique demographic concerns. But, we have shown that in the context of the recent immigration federalism, demography is not destiny. The presence of more immigrants generally, or great numbers of unauthorized migrants specifically, entering a region does not automatically explain why certain jurisdictions pass restrictive immigration regulations and others do not. Instead, we show that a more complex and dispositive set of political and entrepreneurial factors are at play in producing the state and local interventions of the past ten years.

This nuanced context of networked, partisan-based enactments suggests this recent policy proliferation resembles a "cascade" phenomenon similar to that described by scholars in other policy areas.[42] The saliency of partisanship – and not demography – in subfederal immigration regulation indicates that this recent spate of state and local immigration regulation is a real-time illustration of Professors Cass Sunstein and Timur Kuran's model, which highlights the influence of information deficits and reputational concerns on public policy.[43] As they note, in a policy debate, sometimes a minority position or one based on empirically dubious claims can triumph in the legislative and political sphere by exploiting the cognitive biases of the public and elected officials.[44]

In such cascades, interested persons take advantage of limited, sometimes incorrect, information about an issue or apparent problem to drive public policy.[45] Taking advantage of information scarcity and cognitive biases, they explain, "availability entrepreneurs" are able to create public concern on a topic and proliferate policy solutions, regardless of the necessity, efficacy, or proportionality of those solutions.[46] Sunstein and Kuran explain how these costly cognitive errors have manifested in cascades in water and environmental pollution policy, pesticide contamination of food, and high-profile human tragedies (such as plane accidents).[47] Situating this information-deficit manipulation within the larger legislative context of policy proliferation, others have argued that rapid legislative momentum develops across several jurisdictions when (a) few, intensely interested actors, (b) armed with a sticky message, (c) operate in a receptive context.[48] Examples from drunk driving, three-strikes, and sex-offender laws to show how legislative cascades initiate and spread at particular moments in our social consciousness, given ripe political and historical factors.[49]

Our qualitative empirical work has already identified the intensely interested actors in the restrictionist immigration policy context – those groups including FAIR, IRLI, NumbersUSA, and individuals such as Tom Tancredo and Kris Kobach – whom we have referred to as restrictionist issue entrepreneurs.[50] Armed with prefabricated model legislation[51] and predesigned legal defenses, these issue entrepreneurs found willing allies in elected officials such as Arizona Governor Jan Brewer, Arizona state Senator Russell Pearce, and former Hazleton Mayor Lou Bartletta. Foremost among the informational deficits exploited by restrictionist issue entrepreneurs are generally assumed beliefs that often do not stand up to rigourous empirical scrutiny – that immigrants are causing uniquely insurmountable public policy problems that require enforcement-heavy responses, the same propositions undermined by our empirical inquiry. These informational claims are particularly sticky in the immigration context, persisting despite the experience of jurisdictions that passed restrictionist legislation –for example, Riverside, New Jersey; Oklahoma; and Alabama – and then suffered greater economic distress *after* the legislation passed and have, subsequent to the passage of restrictionist legislation, seen a substantial labor source and an important consumer base driven away.[52]

Our theoretical orientation based in a cascading legislative momentum, draws distinctions with, and identifies the weaknesses of, current scholarly models. As we already noted, any model or theory of subfederal immigration action that relies primarily on functionalism or responsiveness to demographic factors to explain state and local restrictionism must be reassessed. As another example, a "steam-valve" type of model and its variants must also be critically examined and potentially abandoned.

According to that theory, as its chief proponent Professor Peter Spiro maintains, leeway for isolated, subfederal anti-immigrant regulation relieves pressure to promote those restrictive policies by way of federal legislation.[53] Accordingly, even if subfederal restrictionist measures primarily reflect raw political preference (and not necessarily responses to pressing policy problems), those measures in isolated localities could serve a normatively desirable purpose by providing a relatively contained outlet for anti-immigrant feelings.[54] As per the theory, allowing nativist legislative sentiments to find legislative expression at the local level dissipates the pressure to seek federal instantiation of the same policies; in effect, the local expression relieves the pent-up pressure (as a steam valve on a pressure cooker would) caused by restrictionist policy momentum.[55]

To be sure, the historical antecedents of the Page and Chinese Exclusion Acts in the late 1800s, and the federal immigration enactments of 1996 may lend credence to this notion. Indeed, as we describe in Chapter 2, both the federal Page Act, denying admission to Chinese women on morality grounds, and the federal Chinese Exclusion Acts mirrored prior legislative efforts from California that had been passed and subsequently struck down by courts, leading Californians to lobby the federal government for redress. And, the defeat of California's anti-immigrant Proposition 187 presaged the federal efforts that led to the enforcement-heavy 1996 federal immigration reforms contained in IIRIRA and PRWORA.[56] Those federal enactments contained some of the provisions that the state had attempted to enact.

However, the policy dynamics between the federal and subfederal governments, as well as the politicized method of restrictionist state and local legislation seems to have evolved since these antecedents. The use of political party structures, party polarization, and the stoking of ethnic nationalism have interacted to make this a new strain of immigration federalism, one that does not necessarily look to federal legislative success as its ultimate goal. Indeed, our analysis of the past decade of restrictionist state and local immigration lawmaking suggests that the causal paths are reversed: Suppression of subfederal lawmaking does not necessarily promote restrictionist measures at the federal level;[57] rather, purposeful suppression of federal lawmaking provides the receptive legislative backdrop for promotion of extreme measures at the subfederal level.

The critical difference between a cascade understanding of state and local immigration lawmaking and a steam-valve theory is that in the cascade model, the issue entrepreneurs' goal is to continue proliferation of immigration laws and policies in every jurisdiction that is politically ripe for legislation. Each successive enactment builds, rather than dissipates, horizontal momentum across multiple subfederal jurisdictions; it is a strategy that appears targeted toward building a de facto national immigration policy through several subfederal enactments that emphasize heavy enforcement and denial of benefits to noncitizens. Specifically in the restrictionist context, it appears that interested policy activists sometimes coordinate activity between the local and federal levels so that legislative activity at the federal level does not stand as an obstacle to further subfederal proliferation.[58] A stark example of this dynamic is Kris Kobach's antipathy toward the 2011 federal E-Verify bill proposed in

or violated due process and equal protection standards. As Gerken and Holtzblatt note, when states move on an issue like immigration, "outside money often pours into the legislative fights. It's not because people elsewhere think that those regulations will have an immediate effect on their own lives. It's because they fear that these efforts will eventually lead to the imposition of a *national* policy."[82]

In public discourse then, the state law raised fundamental disagreements over the nature of unauthorized migration, and the propriety and necessity of increased enforcement against the group.[83] Indeed, the U.S. Department of Justice's decision to sue Arizona indicated just how nationally important the issue of state-level enforcement had become, and how desperately the federal executive desired to frame the national debate around immigration enforcement. Further, that law, and similar ones, re-ignited debates over the use of social services, the cost to taxpayers of unauthorized migration, and the necessity of border vigilance and domestic enforcement priorities.[84] In essence, the real stakes in the battle over state immigration law were about gaining the upper hand in broader debates about national immigration policy.

The several enactments, both restrictionist and integrationist, that have followed have kept alive this same national ideological contest, with both money and political support for various proposals flowing across state and local lines. In short, the new immigration federalism is a national debate being waged on state and local turf.[85] The various enactments, both integrationist and restrictionist, may be an end in and of itself, or may provide a blueprint for, and flesh out the spectrum of, policies that federal lawmakers will have to consider when and if comprehensive federal legislation becomes a viable option.

To sum up: the recent surge in state and local immigration policy making, and its empirical foundation that we have uncovered, has evolved and altered existing conceptions of immigration federalism. Long-held assumptions about the inevitability of certain state and local enactments must be reconsidered. Demography, we argue, is not destiny. Therefore our legal theories and responses to the phenomenon cannot rest on conventional assumptions regarding the functionality of these subfederal responses. Second, the deep connections we uncover between federal and subfederal lawmaking caution against viewing policy making at these different levels of government as untethered and separate processes. They are intertwined in ways that challenge traditional conceptions of federalist activity. As in other areas, state and local participation in immigration is mediated by the federal government in important ways, and those jurisdictions are increasingly becoming sites of national political and partisan contestation. The new immigration federalism is forcing reconsideration of the nature of federalism itself, as the ways in which states and localities are becoming involved in immigration policy, and the consequences of that involvement, are transforming.

## DOCTRINAL IMPLICATIONS OF THE NEW
## IMMIGRATION FEDERALISM

While it is clear that the politicized proliferation of subfederal immigration policy is moving us to a federalism discourse that can account for empirical realities, entrepreneurial activity, and partisan influence, how has it affected doctrinal development in immigration federalism? While scholars have been busy attempting to empirically investigate and contextualize the new immigration federalism, several federal courts, including the Supreme Court on two occasions in the past few years, have been busy attempting to determine the legality of these various enactments. In doing so, they have attempted to utilize the federalism doctrines described in Chapter 2. But, as we argue later, that effort has lead to inconsistent and undertheorized rationales and results, showcasing the limitations of a purely structural powers judicial approach.

Before delving into the particular cases and legal reasoning, an initial observation about the ideological and political commitments of federal judges on both immigration and federalism is worth mentioning. It is not original or terribly revealing to suggest that judges are political creatures heavily influenced by their own political and policy preferences, and not just by principled legal arguments. The various and predictable camps into which justices on the Supreme Court fall, for example, have been discussed ad naseum in both the media and academia. Generally, in other areas such as tort liability and commercial regulation, conservative justices have supported federal preemption as a way, perhaps, of vindicating their anti-regulatory preferences; in those same cases, less conservative justices have often supported concurrent state authority, in line with their comfortability with governmental regulation. In immigration federalism cases, the traditional conservative versus liberal judicial views on state power and regulation tend to flip-flop in ways that betray the instability of the underlying doctrine and the policy preferences of the justices. As Professor Ernest Young put it, "In [*U.S. Chamber of Commerce v. Whiting*] ... it was hardly edifying to see the conservative Justices who so frequently vote for preemption switching places with the nationalists who most often oppose it, to all appearances simply because both sides have more specific preferences about immigration policy."[86] Interestingly, while immigration federalism cases expose this contradiction, in other ways they are quite predictable. The anti-preemption position of conservative justices in both *Whiting* and *Arizona v. United States* comports with the high-enforcement, restrictionist position favored by many Republicans; meanwhile, the pre-emption position favored by the court's more liberal wing comports with the calibrated-enforcement, integrationist position favored by many Democratics.

Leaving aside these general observations about the political leanings of justices and how those commitments play out in immigration federalism cases, judicial responses to the new immigration federalism reveal more specific concerns with preemption methodology used to evaluate the legality of these state and local immigration regulations. In the sections that follow, we first identify the ways in which the doctrine has evolved in the past few years, including its attempt to address the robust versions of sovereign exclusivities that dominated early judicial thinking, its erstwhile invocation of plenary federal immigration authority, and its uncertain ruminations on the role of executive discretion in defining immigration policy.

After examining these changes and identifying weaknesses in courts' analysis, we turn to the assymetrical nature of immigration federalism cases; that is, the fact that extant doctrines generally treat the restrictionist regulations of Chapter 3 differently than the integrationist laws of Chapter 5. We argue against the false equivalency of viewing anti-immigrant and pro-integration state and local laws in the same light: most integrationist laws are either expressly contemplated by federal law, or fit within the limited, but established, boundaries of state sovereignty. More importantly, we argue that both as a historic and empirical matter, restrictionist laws often play on misperception and group stereotypes and explicitly call out particular groups for differential treatment. By contrast, many of the integrationist measures passed by state legislatures have couched their policies in universalistic terms, and often do not make reference to particular classes of persons. In that sense, these integrative efforts are *equality-promoting*, bringing them into line with the constitutional evolution of the latter half of the twentieth century.

As such, we conclude by offering a prescriptive account of immigration federalism doctrine grounded in anti-discrimination norms. Both theoretical shortcomings identified earlier – the limitations of preemption and the incongruity between restrictionist and integrationist laws – can be resolved by more prominently featuring an equality-based analysis. These rationales must move from the implicit periphery to the explicit core of judicial and scholarly understanding.

## The Problems With Immigration Preemption

We first concern ourselves with the ways in which the recent spate of subfederal restrictionist legislation, and attendant scholarly and judicial responses, has posed challenges for preemption analysis in immigration federalism. The cases assessing recent restrictionist laws – *Whiting v. U.S. Chamber of Commerce* (2011), *Arizona v. United States* (2012), and various post-*Arizona* federal appeals court decisions – reveal three ways in which the doctrine has been forced to evolve, and in doing so, exposed its limitations. First, some judges appear to still invoke dual federalism notions of separate sovereigns with segregated spheres of regulatory authority, a view belied by the expansion of both federal and state regulations on immigration and the factual underpinnings of state and local immigration laws. Second, immigration preemption analysis inevitably rests on the specialized nature of the immigration context. Courts implicitly and inconsistently factor the federal plenary power doctrine into their assessment of subfederal enactments, and scholars explicitly invoke the singular nature of the INA in justifying outcomes in immigration federalism cases. Third, and relatedly, recent judicial opinions unveil an inchoate accounting of the role of executive action and its preemptive effect. Most recently, *Arizona v. United States* conspicuously raised and, at least in part, relied on the federal executive's enforcement discretion in its preemption analysis, but failed to articulate a coherent account of this doctrinal move.

## Reevaluating the Distinction between Immigration Law vs. Alienage Law

Before assessing contemporary cases, we begin by briefly revisiting the comparison between *Chy Lung v. Freeman* and *Yick Wo v. Hopkins* that we laid out in Chapter 2.[87] These opinions from the late 1800s offer insight into the initial, oftentimes implicit, categorical decision in all immigration federalism cases: Has the state implemented "immigration law" or, has it enacted law that affects noncitizens but does not directly cover admissions and removals (i.e., has the state implemented "alienage law"?).

In theory, the answer could matter a great deal.[88] If the court decides that a state has enacted the former, it is essentially determining that the state had no power to regulate at all. In comparison, if the court decides that the state has instead enacted alienage law, it is essentially conceding that the state has some authority to regulate the subject matter, and then the question is whether the state has properly exercised that authority within constitutional and statutory limits. As we noted, these characterizations are often difficult to cleanly distinguish in practice, and are better understood as differences of degree rather than kind. Accordingly, consequences of this initial categorical division become problematic as the variety of state and local enactments stray from, for example, a city's regulation of laundry structures at issue in *Yick Wo*, and veer closer to the "immigration law" end of the regulatory spectrum.

Prior to this recent spate of state and local laws, the category of alienage law in this modern era was mostly populated from cases in the 1970s and 1980s that curbed noncitizens' access to public benefits or specific types of public employment.[89] In comparison, in the past decade states and localities have taken bolder steps, unilaterally deciding who they wish to remain within their borders with a clear eye toward discouraging the movement of foreigners across the national border.[90] The porousness of the line between the two analytic categories is evident in court cases responding to the recent round of restrictionist state and local ordinances, in which federal appeals judges and Supreme Court justices struggled with the ordinances that bore many similarities to regulations of entry and exit, and were intended as such.

Both the omnibus state immigration enforcement schemes, Arizona's SB 1070 and Alabama's HB 56, illustrate this unequivocal intent of migration control. The Arizona legislature expressed SB 1070's purpose as causing "attrition [of the unlawfully present population] through enforcement," clarifying that the provisions of the law were created to "work together to discourage and deter the unlawful entry and presence of aliens and economic activity by persons unlawfully present in the United States."[91] Similarly, the Alabama legislature chronicled the supposed economic hardships and lawlessness caused by unauthorized migration and then stated that "the State of Alabama declare[s] that it is a compelling public interest to discourage illegal immigration."[92] Any doubt about the way in which these ordinances were conceived as regulating exit from the country, was erased by Kris Kobach, the former law professor who drafted the laws and served as legal counsel for many of the enacting states and localities, when he clarified "If we had a true nationwide policy of self-deportation, I believe we would see our illegal alien population cut in half at a minimum very quickly."[93] In other words if enough states were to enact restrictionist measures, unauthorized immigrants would leave in large numbers.

Understandably, judges and justices noted the very direct impact on entry and exit that these types of state laws could have, even as they regulated areas that courts have traditionally found to fall within the purview of state police power. Specifically addressing the portion of Alabama's law that invalidated contracts entered into by unauthorized immigrants, the Eleventh Circuit Court of Appeals opinion characterized the state as "craft[ing] a calculated policy of expulsion."[94] The contracting provision, according the circuit court, was a "thinly veiled attempt to regulate immigration."[95] As a result, the Eleventh Circuit recognized the possibility of structural preemption, reasoning that because the power to expel aliens from the states "is retained only by the federal government, [the contracting provision] is preempted by the *inherent power* of the federal government to regulate immigration."[96]

Other enactments regulating rental properties, for example, were also viewed by several federal judges as "immigration law" even if those laws were not stopping people at the border or a port of entry. The various concurring opinions in the Fifth Circuit's en banc enjoinment of a Texas city's rental ordinance illustrate the point. Judge Dennis's concurrence noted that by effectively excluding certain noncitizens from parts of the United States, the rental ordinance "violates the principle that the removal process is entrusted to the discretion of the Federal government."[97] Similarly, Judge Reavley's concurrence pointedly articulated: "I repeat what the [Fifth Circuit] panel said about the Farmer's Branch ordinance: Because the sole purpose and effect of this ordinance is to target the presence of illegal aliens ... and to cause their removal, it contravenes the federal government's exclusive authority on the regulation of immigration."[98]

But, the same type of provisions were read differently by the Eighth Circuit in its contemporaneous ruling on a rental ordinance in Fremont, Nebraska. There, the appeals court rejected any characterization of rental ordinances as functionally equivalent to expulsion or entry/exit regulation: "Laws designed to deter, or even prohibit, unlawfully present aliens from residing within a particular locality are not tantamount to immigration laws establishing who may enter or remain in the country."[99] And, it could be argued that such regulations have the effect of incentivizing movement to other states and localities, but not necessarily out of the country. As such, that court upheld Fremont's rental ordinance under statutory preemption principles. A few years prior, the Eighth Circuit had also upheld an immigrant employment ordinance similar to the one struck down by the Third Circuit.[100] As the Supreme Court declined certiorari in these cases, this circuit split remains, with the possibility of rental ordinances and employment ordinances still viable in the seven states covered by the Eighth Circuit (Arkansas, Iowa, Minnesota, Missouri, Nebraska, North Dakota, and South Dakota).

In the end, despite certain judges' characterizations of state policies and attendant exclusivity rhetoric, majorities in both the Fifth and Eleventh circuits decided the cases using structural preemption analysis, in essence implicitly treating these muscular state restrictionist laws as alienage regulation. But the variation in judicial conceptions of the same state policies illustrates indeterminacy of the categorical distinction prompted by *Chy Lung* and *Yick Wo*.[101] It is a taxonomy built on a conception of separate sovereigns operating in distinct spheres. Today, however, it is increasingly clear that federal power over immigration is more than just control over entry and exit, and that

state power over alienage can seriously influence and incentivize the movement and residency of noncitizens. But, in neither case has the Court clarified
the extent of these concomitant enlargements, making this formal categorical
inquiry meaningless for the most part.

Acknowledging this doctrinal shift is important because it helps emphasize the erosion of robust versions of sovereignty and exclusivity that dominated early judicial discussions of immigration federalism. While such a shift
is unexceptional in areas outside of immigration law, the erstwhile invoked
notion of immigration as a species of foreign affairs prerogatives has permitted
immigration to retain the vestiges of the dual federalist approach still extant in
foreign affairs federalism.[102] As we discuss further later, the federal government
itself has contributed to this erosion by creating opportunities for state involvement in immigration enforcement and integration. Whatever its cause, judicial responses would benefit from expressly confronting the untenability of
robust sovereign exclusivities. This is increasingly important as the presence
of states and localities in immigration matters becomes more normalized.

This evolution away from structural or categorical preemption correspondingly places great weight on more conventional analyses, like statutory preemption, in immigration federalism analysis. For decades, scholars have
debated the concept of immigration exceptionalism in constitutional and
statutory adjudication, arguing that immigration law and doctrine should be
(or is) constrained by general applicable constitutional norms, rather than
more obscure and specialized doctrines.[103] The move away from structural
preemption analysis in immigration federalism forces the application of generally applicable constitutional principles, and accordingly, contributes to
the domestication of immigration law. Despite this doctrinal move, however,
even statutory preemption remains far from unexceptional in immigration
federalism. As the following sections on plenary power and executive power
demonstrate, even within the framework of statutory preemption, the new
immigration federalism raises unique concerns.

### Plenary Immigration Power and Preemption

Assuming that the Court genuinely attempts to measure state immigration
regulations against the federal INA, judicial responses to recent enactments
expose the limitations to the doctrine in the immigration arena. The Supreme
Court's last word on immigration federalism, *Arizona v. United States* in
2012, illustrates these immigration-specific quirks in two ways. First, the case
showcases the centrifugal pull of the plenary power doctrine on preemption
decisions. Second, it highlights the role executive discretion in immigration
enforcement plays in the preemption context.

To those outside the immigration field, Justice Kennedy's majority opinion in *Arizona* must appear odd. He begins the substantive portion of the opinion with several platitudes about the expansiveness of federal immigration power:

> The Government of the United States has broad, undoubted power over the subject of immigration and the status of aliens. This authority rests, in part, on the National Government's constitutional power to "establish an uniform Rule of Naturalization," and its inherent power as sovereign to control and conduct relations with foreign nations.[104]

It is an incantation seemingly more appropriate in a suit challenging the limits of Congressional immigration authority, rather than one challenging the legality of a state law. The introduction begins to address federalism when, in emphasizing the plenary power of the federal government, it cites *Chy Lung* and *Hines v. Davidowitz* for the proposition that the nexus between immigration law and foreign relations requires that the federal government speak for the nation with one voice.[105]

After setting this rhetorical stage, however, the operative portions of the opinion do not require proof of, or references to, the impact of these regulations on foreign affairs or entry regulations. Indeed, despite his invocation of federal preeminence and exclusivity, the actual analytic framework applied to each challenged section was grounded in conventional preemption inquiries typical in cases dealing with areas of concurrent regulatory authority.[106] It is this set of standard preemption questions to which Justice Kennedy turned after his initial exposition of the unique and plenary nature of federal immigration power. His majority opinion found SB 1070's section 3 (alien registration) field preempted, and sections 5(c) (seeking unauthorized employment) and 6 (authorizing warrantless arrests of aliens suspected of deportable offenses) conflict preempted. Section 2(B), obligating local law enforcement officers to verify immigration status, however, was deemed not to be impliedly preempted – that is, it neither conflicted with or presented an obstacle to federal law, nor did it intrude on a field the federal government had occupied. It was left un-enjoined with the caution that detention or custody of noncitizens for any unreasonable or prolonged time to investigate their immigration status could raise serious constitutional infirmities.[107]

So why did Justice Kennedy frame his ultimate use of standard preemption doctrines by first describing the extent of federal plenary power? One possibility is that courts will oftentimes intermingle these theoretically distinct concepts to bolster their preemption rationale in the alienage context. Professor Kerry Abrams appropriately terms this doctrinal move "plenary power preemption"[108] to highlight the idea that even though it appears that the Court is applying the same preemption analysis across multiple policy areas (e.g., environmental law, criminal law, labor law, immigration, and alienage law), preemption in the immigration/alienage arena is uniquely affected by the plenary power doctrine, with its attendant concerns about states' burdening of national concerns like foreign affairs.[109] By averring to plenary power in this way, courts in the alienage preemption field can, without expressly stating it, help overcome the traditional "presumption against preemption" canon often articulated in preemption cases in other doctrinal areas.[110]

This use of plenary power platitudes thus enables the Court to engage in a preemption analysis with hazy parameters, varying the preemptive force of federal immigration laws and policies depending on whether, and to what extent, the Court invokes the plenary power doctrine.[111] In contrast to *Arizona*, the Court in *Whiting* eschewed the plenary power doctrine in adjudicating state sanctions against employers who employed unauthorized workers Instead, the Court invoked the notion of traditional state authority over business licensing to prime an anti-preemption position. This internal inconsistency within immigration federalism cases reveals the Court as unpredictable and ad hoc in its determinations whether state statutes implicate national concerns or local ones. Moreover, it relies on outdated conceptions of "truly national" versus "traditionally local" concerns, under conditions in a case such as *Whiting*, in which Arizonans enacted LAWA at least in part for the purpose of deterring unlawful migration.

In addition, the erstwhile appearance of the plenary power rationale in immigration federalism cases distinguishes these cases from preemption analysis in other regulatory areas.[112] Of course, as Professor Ernest Young reminds us, the Court's differing approaches to preemption based on subject matter may not necessarily indicate an incoherent doctrine; it may be based on the diversity of the background statutory regime, with the INA, in the case of immigration federalism, necessitating an eclectic jurisprudential mode. Without entering that debate, it is worth noting that one of the byproducts of this distinct plenary power preemption in immigration is the Court's willingness to consider factors beyond statutory text and congressional intent. The most prominent example is the majority opinion in *Arizona v. United States* invoking executive enforcement memoranda – which are guidance documents and not enacted by Congress, or through notice and comment administrative procedures – in its ruling mostly striking down the challenged provisions of the law. The invocation of plenary federal power facilitates this move, and we turn to the role the executive plays in immigration federalism adjudication below.

## Presidential Power and Immigration Preemption

The apparently dispositive assumption of the Arizona majority is that executive enforcement discretion is part and parcel of federal immigration policy for preemption purposes. Prominently featured in the briefing and opinion in *Arizona* was the role of executive enforcement priorities, embodied in agency guidance memoranda issued by various administrative officials, which noted the executive branch's priorities for use of its limited enforcement resources.[113] State and local enforcement, however, need not, and likely would not, focus on these same enforcement priorities. This logic, at least in part, informed the Arizona majority's holding that sections of SB 1070 were preempted.

This accounting for executive enforcement policy is significant for two reasons. First, numerous cases have articulated that "the purpose of Congress is the ultimate touchstone in every preemption case."[114] Although accounting for executive action does not necessarily contradict this established doctrine, it certainly requires rigorous theorization. Second, as a matter of practical consequence, excluding executive policies lends much more credence to the "mirror image" argument advanced by Kris Kobach and the state of Arizona in defense of SB 1070.[115]

As per the mirror-theory argument, Congress defined unlawful presence, and a state's adoption of those congressional standards to help vindicate congressional intent as embodied in the statutory text would ostensibly operate as the mirror to the federal statute. Under the mirror theory, executive enforcement decisions, which may tolerate a certain level and/or type of unlawful migration and presence, cannot supplant state and local efforts to vindicate federal statutory goals and reduce that level. Indeed, such an argument appears to have helped carry the day for Arizona in its defense of LAWA in 2011. There, discussing the implied preemption claim, the Court in *Whiting* reasoned that because LAWA "closely tracks [INA provisions] in all material respects" and requires federal verification of unauthorized status, "there can by definition be no conflict between state and federal law as to worker authorization."[116]

That same argument applied to the context of omnibus state enforcement laws like SB 1070 would appear to require the same result of upholding most parts of the state law.[117] Approximately 11 million people are currently unlawfully present in the United States as per the INA's presumptive classification. However, only a fraction of those people have been, will be, or are likely to be discovered, prosecuted, and deported by the federal government. The gap between the number of potentially removable persons and the number actually prosecuted and removed facilitates the claim that states and localities must help the federal government fulfill legislative mandates. As Professor Adam Cox notes, this type of "enforcement redundancy" between subfederal and federal authorities is commonplace and legally unproblematic in several regulatory areas.[118] And, the restrictionist laws of the new immigration federalism relied on federal definitions of unlawful presence and unauthorized work, avoiding the legal pitfalls that sunk California's Prop. 187's legal prospects nearly two decades earlier.

Undoubtedly, even without factoring in executive policy decisions, the mirror-theory argument can be undermined on its own terms. First, ideas similar to the mirror-theory were advanced – and defeated – in prior cases such as *Takahashi* and *Hines*, as detailed in Chapter 2.[119] Second, one can contest the argument's interpretation of congressional intent vis-à-vis the deportation of all persons suspected of being unlawfully present and the limits of state and local participation.[120] Finally, federal law specifically limits the circumstances under which states and localities may participate in enforcement efforts, either through agreements with the federal government or for particular immigration crimes.[121]

Even so, factoring executive enforcement practices into the equation certainly makes the preemption calculus easier. Again, compare *Whiting* to *Arizona*. The federal executive's enforcement practices on employer sanctions law was essentially irrelevant to the Court in *Whiting*; in comparison, an extensive discussion of executive enforcement priorities was critical to the majority's rationale in *Arizona*. Indeed, within the *Arizona* case, a key distinction between the majority and dissents in *Arizona* was their respective characterizations of the executive's role in defining federal immigration policy. The majority noted that a "principal feature of the removal system is the broad discretion exercised by immigration officials," and that "[t]he dynamic nature of relations with other countries requires the Executive Branch to ensure that enforcement policies are consistent with this Nation's foreign policy."[122] In sharp contrast, Justice Scalia's opinion, dissenting in part and concurring in part, dismissed the role of the executive in defining the boundaries of federal immigration policy. He responded to the majority's concern about the prerogatives of the federal enforcement apparatus by arguing that the although state actors might not adopt federal enforcement priorities, "[t]he State has the sovereign power to protect its borders more rigorously if it wishes, absent any valid federal prohibition. The Executive's policy choice of lax enforcement does not constitute such a prohibition."[123] In his conception of federalism, the immigration field provided no special reason to transcend the presumption against preemption or traditional conceptions of concurrent and robust state sovereign authority.

Thus, the new immigration federalism, proliferating during a time of extended congressional deadlock, has brought into sharp focus the role of the executive branch, and its constituent role in defining immigration policy as a matter of practical reality and doctrinal import.[124] Prominent scholars have defended the elevation of executive enforcement priorities to the level of supreme federal law for preemption purposes based on the unique context of immigration laws. They point to the mass delegation of authority by Congress to the executive branch in the INA, and the chasm between the immigration "law on the books" and immigration policy in practice as justifications for this view of preemption. But, it is worth noting that such an elevation is a doctrinal move that could have far-reaching consequences if applied outside of immigration federalism.[125] As such, it relies on understanding the INA, including its delegations of authority to the executive branch, as a special creature in relation to other similarly broad federal statutes.

Furthermore, the propriety of imbuing executive priority setting with preemptive power is not a consensus view. Since *Arizona* was decided (and DACA was contemporaneously implemented), a contentious debate has developed in scholarly, political, and popular discourse over the proper constitutional role of the president in immigration enforcement., and what effect that role should have in judicial determinations.[126] This debate has become even more intense in recent months, as the president in late 2014 unveiled a new deferred action plan that builds on and broadens the relief offered with his 2012 DACA program, applicable for up to 4 million unauthorized immigrants.[127]

The scholarly and political debate on this issue highlights the extent to which the Supreme Court undertheorized these concerns. First, the Court provides no rationale as to why its apparent reliance on a mirror-theory type reasoning in *Whiting* gives way to a more robust preemption analysis in *Arizona*, akin to the one motivating the *Hines* decision decades earlier. Indeed, the Court's non-enjoinment of 2(B) begs the question of why the same executive enforcement priorities that were prominent in the Court's assessment of the other sections did not similarly wield preemptive power over 2(B). The Court's decision to leave that section in force cuts against the thrust of other parts of the opinion, and opens significant ground for discriminatory state practices.[128] Finally, the opinion fails to account for the background context in which it was federal executive branch policies in the aftermath of September 11 that initially encouraged and incentivized state and local participation in immigration enforcement in the first place.[129]

These questions will become more pressing as Congress remains unlikely to pass new, comprehensive immigration legislation in the near future. The emerging cases and conflicts call for a more theoretically cohesive account of what constitutes federal immigration policy, and what types of executive action warrant preemptive effect. In doing so, courts and commentators will also have to wrestle with the question whether preemption works differently in immigration than it does in other fields, accounting for both the centrifugal pull of the plenary power doctrine and the challenge of accounting for executive enforcement policy, as those executive actions become more prominent features of the overall immigration policy landscape.

### Integrationist Policies and Asymmetrical Federalism

These deficits in immigration preemption doctrine were mostly revealed in cases occasioned by the restrictionist subfederal policies of the past ten years that captured the national spotlight. But, what about the integrationist and pro-immigrant policies of states and localities that were the focus of Chapter 5? For many years, states and cities have also maintained immigrant-friendly policies that seek to incorporate noncitizens – even unlawfully present ones – into local communities, provide social services to them, or help shield them from federal enforcement. This trend has accelerated since 2012, the year the Supreme Court struck down parts of Arizona's SB 1070, President Obama won reelection, and his administration implemented its DACA program.

Because courts have struck down many restrictionist laws under a federalism framework that disfavors state and local policy making related to immigrants, it would stand to reason that integrationist laws would suffer a fate similar to restrictionist laws. After all, one might argue that New York City's immigrant-friendly policies act as a magnet to putative migrants, encouraging them to enter or remain in the country unlawfully, knowing that the city's policies will offer assistance and shield them from federal prosecution. Thus far, however, integrationist policies have almost uniformly been upheld, or, in the majority of instances, not challenged at all. Aware of this apparent inconsistency, the U.S. Department of Justice stated when it filed suit against Arizona's SB 1070, "There is a difference between a state or locality saying they are not going to use their resources to enforce a federal law, as so-called sanctuary cities have done, and a state passing its own immigration policy that actively interferes with federal law."[130]

One reason for integrationist policies not being contested in federal court are the extant jurisdictional doctrines limiting the types of claims a federal court will adjudicate. In general, using principles like standing or the political question doctrine, courts have routinely turned away cases against the federal government claiming lax immigration enforcement.[131] With many integrationist state laws, opponents may have trouble convincing a court that they have suffered a legally sufficient personal injury by a policy that, for example, makes undocumented persons eligible for driver's licenses. We do not dwell on this threshold jurisdiction question, and simply note that this current doctrinal limitation may motivate some to push for changes in standing doctrine that would allow for both restrictionist and integrationist laws to be similarly tested in court.[132] Leaving that question aside, we ask whether, even assuming standing, there is good reason for most integrationist laws to survive while many restrictionist laws are struck down.

Our initial response is that integrationist laws require different judicial outcomes than do restrictionist ones even under a structural powers framework. To see why, we begin by dividing integrationist policies into two broad categories: (1) those that resist, undermine, or otherwise incentivize noncooperation with federal enforcement; and (2) those that provide affirmative benefits, protections, and recognition to noncitizens, and especially to unauthorized migrants. Integrationist laws in the former category require constitutional defense based on the autonomous sovereign power of states, whereas most – but not all – in the latter category are contemplated and thus, preapproved, by existing federal law. In other words, many integrationist enactments exist because of politicking and compromises hashed out in Congress and federal administrative agencies.

While these sanctuary jurisdictions have been present for some time, more recent federal enforcement efforts, such as Secure Communities (S-Comm), have spurred new forms of state and local enforcement–resistance and noncooperation policies.[133] Federal responses to these sanctuary and noncooperation policies have been markedly different than federal responses to state and local efforts to enhance or aid federal enforcement. The solicitor general's office sued to enjoin Arizona's SB 1070, but has generally declined to litigate against jurisdictions resisting federal enforcement. The decision not to pursue litigation against noncooperating jurisdictions is likely because such assertions of state power are based on one of the last remaining contexts in which state sovereignty and independence are constitutionally protected.[134]

Justification for state noncooperation with federal authorities is founded in the Supreme Court's anti-commandeering doctrine derived from the Tenth Amendment to the U.S. Constitution.[135] As we noted in Chapter 5, for the most part, critics of a robust role for the Tenth Amendment have prevailed in the Supreme Court.[136] The one area, however, that the Court carved out where Tenth Amendment claims still have salience is when states' argue that federal policies directly commandeer or control state legislative or executive officials and resources. In other words, despite a general trend toward dismissing claims based in state sovereignty, the Court draws the line when it appears that federal authority is commanding state authorities to act in a particular way.[137]

Under this conception of the Tenth Amendment, sanctuary and noncooperation ordinances are protected from legal assault.[138] Although states cannot stop federal officials from enforcing federal law, federal law cannot mandate state and local participation in immigration enforcement.[139] Certainly, federal authorities could entice or incentivize state and local enforcement participation, or condition the receipt of federal resources on the state's participation.[140] Indeed, this is how the federal S-Comm program ensured state and local compliance during its period of operation. The program implicitly conditioned state and local access to the federal crime database on providing immigration status information to the federal government. Nevertheless, the anti-commandeering rationale maintains significant practical import even as federal enforcement authority remains unchecked and the nature of federal co-optation of state and local resources becomes more encompassing. In dismantling major aspects of the S-Comm program as part of President Obama's suite of executive actions in November 2014, the Department of Homeland Security noted these various acts of state and local resistance to S-Comm as reasons for the program's discontinuance.[141] Indeed, the Priority Enforcement Program created by DHS to replace S-Comm shares some similarities to the various state TRUST Acts that permitted local authorities to comply with ICE holds only for certain enumerated crimes.

The second category of integrationist laws – those that affirmatively grant privileges, rights, or social benefits to noncitizens, especially unauthorized migrants – mostly need not rely on assertions of independent state sovereignty under the anti-commandeering doctrine. Rather, these types of integrationist laws generally fit within federal statutory schemes that expressly permit state provision of certain benefits to noncitizens. In other words, state authority to enact many of these integrationist measures derives from permissions, exceptions, and gaps in federal statutes.

This form of federalism, in which federal statutory provisions expressly contemplate that some states and localities may be more magnanimous toward unauthorized migrants than is the federal government, describes subfederal integrationist efforts regarding public benefits, in-state tuition, professional licensing, and driver's license provision. In all of these instances, federal laws – many passed in 1996 – establish conditions for state and local intervention in these areas.[142]

The federalism concerns occasioned by these types of enactments raise fewer theoretical, constitutional, and practical concerns than enforcement-enhancing measures. Here, the extent and power of state sovereign prerogative are less relevant (and perhaps not at all relevant) than the political debates and compromises in federal legislative debate that resulted in the statutory leeway for these state and local actions. As such, it is difficult to see how a preemption suit against these integrationist enactments could prevail. In the in-state tuition context, the most notable challenge ended with the California Supreme Court ruling in *Martinez v. Board of Regents*, that federal law did not preempt the state's provision of in-state tuition to unauthorized migrants attending state universities and colleges.[143] Further, it noted that California had complied with the exceptions to federal law, and had therefore structured its program in a lawful manner. Congress, the court essentially ruled, foresaw and intended this type of integrationist state law. This same type of analysis prevailed in the California Supreme Court's decision to uphold the admission of an undocumented applicant to the state bar.[144]

Buttressing these federal statutory permissions are arguments based on the role of prosecutorial discretion and executive enforcement in preemption decisions. The de facto and de jure acquiescence by federal authorities to a large undocumented population, and targeted enforcement against certain high priority deportation categories, leaves several millions of individuals in the care and jurisdiction of state and local authorities. For example, the formalized 2012 and 2014 deferred action programs, and their attendant conferral of employment authorization to unauthorized migrants, requires, in many instances, considering admissions and financial aid policies at state institutions of higher education, as well as driver's licenses for transportation to work or school for beneficiaries of the programs. These policies under state and local control are vital to actualizing the intended goals of the federal executive's conferral of deferred action and decision to de-prioritize removal of the beneficiary classes.[145] Thus, the expenditure of state and local resources and community systems to recognize and aid those individuals is consonant with federal executive discretion, so long as those state and local interventions do not promise immunity from federal enforcement.

More difficult federalism concerns, however, arise with two other forms of integrationist state and local policies – provision of municipal ID cards and recent proposals for state citizenship.[146] One potential legal concern with these types of integrationist laws is the claim that they operate to create a form of local or state membership or citizenship arguably at odds with the concept of national citizenship.[147] This is most obvious in emerging proposals for state citizenship, which provide for a formal state affiliation and membership despite the inability of an undocumented individual to achieve any lawful federal status or presence. Although neither this state citizenship bill nor the municipal ID card programs purport to, or for that matter can, confer national citizenship or neutralize federal immigration consequences, they nevertheless grant what appears to be meaningful forms of belonging.[148]

According to legal scholar Peter Markowitz, these forms of robust sub-federal citizenship were commonplace in early American history, existing as primary forms of allegiance even into the first several decades under the Constitution.[149] However, the first clause of the Fourteenth Amendment – that entrenching national citizenship as a matter of birth or naturalization in the United States – forged national citizenship as the primary basis for allegiance and political identity. As such, these proposals more squarely present a conflict between state's sovereign power to define their own political membership and federal constitutional structure than do other types of integrationist measures. Markowitz nevertheless defends state citizenship proposals on the theory that the federal Constitution sets a "floor, not a ceiling" for state citizenship, allowing states the discretion to extend membership rights to a broader class than those granted federal citizenship by the Constitution.[150]

This is certainly a plausible defense, but our broader point is that these proposals, unlike many other integrationist measures, may require a justification built on a robust version of state sovereign authority to create alternate forms of membership. Such a tack cuts against the more general historical, theoretical, statutory, and doctrinal trend of deemphasizing notions of segregated and strong state sovereign powers. Moreover, such an emphasis might have unintended consequences for immigration advocates. Indeed, Justice Scalia's partial dissent in *Arizona* also conjured a vibrant conception of state sovereignty as the rationale for upholding SB 1070.

In the end, however, these membership policies are only one form of integrationist enactments. The remainder, as we noted, rely primarily on federal statutory permission and well-established constitutional boundaries on federal lawmaking authority.

## Equality and Non-Discrimination Norms

We conclude this chapter by suggesting a way out of the doctrinal inconsistencies, limitations, and quandaries of preemption law and structural power analysis. The entire realm of integrationist state and local laws – both enforcement mitigation policies and those conferring affirmative benefits – are also defensible on a more encompassing theory based in other important constitutional and statutory provisions. Structural questions and individual rights considerations should work together, in Professor Gerken's metaphor regarding the Court's assessment of marriage equality claims, like two "interlocking gears."[151]

Immigration federalism, however, has long eschewed explicit equality and rights talk for a debate formally waged solely on structural power turf. Although discrimination concerns and fears of racial and ethnic bigotry have been a part of the language of judicial opinions and, perhaps, silently may be influencing courts in certain cases, these interests have rarely found expression in judicial analysis and discourse. Here, we conclude this chapter by providing doctrinal, historical, and empirical support for the explicit recognition of equality and rights claims in the evaluation of state and local immigration laws, both integrationist and restrictionist. In doing so, we adopt Dean Harold Koh's observation that there is something intuitively disquieting about consistently applying a structural power context to understand lawmaking that is, at its core, also about the disparate treatment of individuals based on accidents of birth and veiled racial categories.[152]

Importantly, we do not suggest that federalism, structural power analysis, and preemption should play no role in immigration federalism determinations. As we noted, sometimes state laws fall into accepted and trans-substantive areas of state prerogatives. And, in many instances, federal law includes provisions that expressly contemplate integrationist – or at least, non-discriminatory – state and local policy making. Such enactments may sometimes require interpretation as to their scope and effect on state lawmaking. But what has mostly been missing from judicial discourse has been a doctrinally consistent role for anti-discrimination and equal protection norms. Incorporation of an integrated analysis in the immigration federalism arena would help explain why courts should be both skeptical of restrictionist laws and predisposed to integrationist ones. In both instances, courts and commentators could sidestep many thorny questions of sovereignty, the scope of the plenary power doctrine, the degree of tension between federal and subfederal policies and the preemptive effect of executive action.

To be sure, the constitution and courts permit the federal government to classify and discriminate based on national origin and immigration status in a variety of important ways.[153] Historically, federal immigration law used explicit racial and national origin disqualifiers for both admission and naturalization.[154] Even now, immigrant visas are determined on a per-country basis.[155] This disproportionately delays applicants from Mexico, China, India, and the Philippines, which are countries accounting for a significant percentage of unlawfully present persons.[156] And, citizenship status is not always regarded as a prohibited basis for state discrimination either.[157] This is especially true when the legislation classifies on the basis of unauthorized status.[158]

Despite this background, however, the development of immigration federalism doctrine since the late nineteenth century has concomitantly always betrayed a special concern for those state and local enactments that might produce the possibility of discrimination based on race, religion, or national origin even as the legislation ostensibly targets citizenship status. This concern can be traced back to the very first significant federal immigration policy, the Burlingame Treaty of 1868. Concerned with the nativist and anti-Chinese sentiment in states and localities, the federal government included a provision that operated as an equal protection guarantee for the Chinese immigrants who would be coming to the United States under the treaty.[159] That provision was added to allay concerns over the discriminatory state and local anti-Chinese laws. Since that time, in rare instances – *Yick Wo, Graham*, and *Plyler* – the Supreme Court also explicitly relied on constitutional equality standards for striking down state or local policies.

Of course, only one – *Plyler* – specifically dealt with state regulation of unauthorized migrants, as opposed to lawfully present noncitizens. And, to be sure, that case has proven to be a limited legal precedent, and did not inspire a wholesale change in immigration federalism doctrine. Although the Court struck down a Texas law discriminating against unauthorized children, it declined to label unauthorized immigrants (or even the unauthorized immigrant children at issue) a "suspect class" for constitutional equal protection analysis.[160] Moreover, since *Plyler*, the Court has shied away from its equal protection jurisprudence. [161]

Nevertheless, beyond these explicit invocations of equality principles, the other key foundational immigration federalism cases have consistently evinced an implicit meshing of both federalism and equal protection doctrine. Thus, despite their formal fidelity to principles of structural power allocation, many cases starting from the late nineteenth century were acutely concerned with the discriminatory origins and effects of state and local restrictionism. *Yick Wo* provides one of the earliest examples of this intermingling. The Court, in support of its striking down the city's laundry ordinance on equal protection grounds, curiously cited *Chy Lung v. Freeman*, the quintessential structural preemption case. Moreover, it did so for the proposition that a facially neutral law that was discriminatorily applied against a particular group was unconstitutional. This use of *Chy Lung* suggests that the Supreme Court, just a decade after that case was decided, understood that a critical problem with California's admissions law was its targeting of Chinese women, and not just the state's incursion into an exclusively federal domain.

As we elaborated in Chapter 2, this same pattern of intermingled reasoning is evident in several other cases, including *Truax v. Raich, Takahashi v. Fish & Game Commission, Hines v. Davidowitz*, and *Graham v. Richardson*.[162] In all of these cases, the Court's ostensible reliance on structural power dynamics between the federal government and subfederal ones obscures its irrepressible worries that such laws promote discrimination on the basis of race or national origin. As if by involuntary reflex, the Court cannot seem to avoid mentioning discrimination concerns even when it seems to be formally relying on federalism grounds.

This link – or a conspicuous attempt to disentangle the link between restrictionist state laws and racial discrimination or national origin discrimination – was clearly evidenced during oral argument in *Arizona v. United States*. Before U.S. Solicitor General Donald Verrilli, Jr. could begin his argument as to why SB 1070 was unconstitutional, Chief Justice Roberts awkwardly interjected to stave off an entire line of federal government's potential argument:

> Chief Justice John G. Roberts: Before you get into what the case is about, I'd like to clear up at the oustet what it's not about. No part of your argument has to do with racial or ethnic profiling does it?
> Mr. Verilli Jr.: That's correct
> Chief Justice Roberts: Okay. So this is not a case about ethnic profiling.[163]

Despite General Verrilli's reassurance, however, he could not help but raise SB 1070's potential for ethnic and racial discrimination:

> Mr. Verrilli Jr.: Now, we are not making an allegation of racial profiling; nevertheless, there are already tens of thousands of stops ... even in the absence of SB 1070. It stands to reason that ... the [Arizona] legislature thought that that wasn't sufficient and there needed to be more. And ... given that you have a population in Arizona of 2 million Latinos, of whom only 400,000, at most, are there unlawfully, there—
> Justice Antonin Scalia: Sounds like racial profiling to me.[164]

This breaching of the hermetic lines the Chief Justice and Justice Scalia attempt to draw – and General Verilli improvidently ceded at the argument's inception – is unavoidable. A hard line between structure and rights in immigration law may be easy to draw in Supreme Court briefing and argument but, in practice, it is far more difficult to do. Indeed, similar to the anti-Chinese laundry ordinance in *Yick Wo*,[165] SB 1070 was also altered during state legislative deliberations to attempt to cleanse it of potential concerns about racial and ethnic profiling. After hearing these concerns, the Arizona legislature hastily passed HB 2162 to amend the originally proposed version of SB 1070. That amendment expressly stated that law enforcement officers could not consider, race, color, or national origin when enforcing SB 1070. And, ultimately, even though the Court refused to enjoin SB 1070's § 2(B), it noted that the section might eventually be struck down if litigants could prove that its implementation caused problems related to the Fourth or Fourteenth Amendment. As further example of the connection between structural power and rights concerns, the U.S. Department of Justice filed suit and prevailed against one of SB 1070's most vociferous proponents, Maricopa County Sheriff Joe Arpaio, accusing him of unconstitutionally discriminating on the basis of race, color, and national origin.[166] More generally, Jennifer Chacon has argued that provisions of state enforcement laws, like SB 1070's section 2(B), are only saved from preemption when the Court ignores or "de-emphasizes the antidiscrimination goals and rationales of federal immigration policy."[167]

This intermingling of equality concerns with preemption questions is necessary to understand an important reason why integrationist laws cannot be evaluated along the same federalism metric as can restrictionist ones. Because racial, ethnic, or national origin discrimination possibilities are unavoidable in immigration federalism cases – either implicitly in many instances or explicitly in a few – the question whether a state law is equality-undermining or equality-promoting should be a dispositive one. And, because integrationist laws, at minimum, avoid concerns with ethnic and racial profiling (and indeed, attempt to legislate solely on the basis of residency or presence in a jurisdiction), the asymmetry in judicial treatment between restrictionist and integrationist policies is inevitable in addition to justifiable. This equality-driven explanation thus extends not just as a political buttress to integrationist laws embedded within a federal statutory scheme, but as a powerful legal defense for other integrationist policies that are based on assertions of independent state authority.

We are not the only academics to suggest this. As scholars such as Hiroshi Motomura and Lucas Guttentag have argued, integrationist laws can be understood as equality-promoting enactments, thus justifying the asymmetry in judicial and scholarly treatment between integrationist and restrictionist laws.[168] Professor Motomura further suggests that *Plyler* might reveal a connection between preemption doctrine and equal protection. Courts may seek to limit subfederal activity because doing so constricts the number and variety of actors involved in immigration enforcement, and as a consequence, the possibility of discrimination by a more varied and larger group of potential enforcement agents.[169]

In addition, as Motomura and other notable commentators have argued, *implicit* consideration of a state and local law's discriminatory potential or the influence of background federal statutory civil rights standards, may be motivating judicial consideration of restrictionist subfederal immigration laws. Motomura notes that at the trial testing the city of Hazelton, Pennsylvania's anti-illegal immigrant rental ordinance, for example, the challenger introduced significant evidence of the potential for racial and ethnic discrimination against Latinos if the ordinance were to go into effect. Although the trial court (and later the appeals court) based its decision to strike down the ordinance on statutory preemption grounds, Motomura conjectures that the evidence of discrimination played a significant role in motivating the court's ruling.[170] In essence, under this theory, courts are folding equality concerns into preemption decisions, with concerns regarding decentralized immigration lawmaking providing the formal legal language that allows unauthorized migrants and other noncitizens to obliquely address the latent discriminatory potential of subfederal enforcement.[171]

Motomura and other scholars may be correct on both accounts. Clearly, current equal protection doctrine provides a fairly high constitutional bar for discrimination claims, requiring a showing of intentional and purposeful discrimination or animus to strike down offending policies.[172] Thus, it makes practical sense why litigants and challengers of recent state and local laws have stuck with the conventional structural powers claims. And, one may reasonably maintain that from the perspective of unauthorized migrants and advocates, it does not matter what motivates judicial reasoning, so long as that judicial reasoning reaches the normatively desirable result. We believe, however, that such a concession exacts long-term costs on doctrine and immigrants themselves. Reifying preemption and federalism concerns as the dispositive rationale in well-publicized decisions such as *Arizona* further embeds the notion that laws targeting noncitizens, and especially undocumented immigrants, are legitimate state and local pursuits but for their excessive aggrandization of subfederal power. Further, the formal judicial avoidance of the possibility of ethnic and racial antipathy ignores empirical realities. As such, it allows the legislative use of immigration status to immunize the deep-seated racial underpinnings of many restrictionist laws.

As such, the argument we present here is intended to move the terms of this battle, by showing that the historical doctrinal concerns and current empirical realities should force courts into bringing these equality concerns from the periphery to the fore. Combined with emerging data regarding the ethnic antipathy fueling the popularity of these laws within enacting jurisdictions, our evidence-based inquiry calls for courts to explore the import of the rights-based claims advanced in immigration federalism cases.[173] The first step is for courts to be skeptical of the typical justifications proffered for restrictionist immigration regulation, which rely on conventional narratives about demographic necessity and public policy crisis. As we have shown in Chapters 3 and 4, the empirical reality undermines, if not outright contradicts, many of these purported motivations. If courts are willing to investigate those state claims without simply accepting them as true, the second step is to ask hard questions about the motivations and genesis of such laws. We maintain that the discriminatory potential for restrictionist subfederal laws inheres, not only in their potential execution, but also in their inception and in the public and political discourse around state and local restrictionism that gives rise to these laws in the first place.

To begin, the salience of ethnic nationalism in the genesis of the new immigration federalism that undergirds the Polarized Change model described in Chapter 4, begs a greater role for equality-based jurisprudential norms.[174] First, political actors have been, and are, aware of the underlying connection between immigration law, state and local law, and race. While enacting SB 1070, Arizona's legislature and governor amended original language in the bill in an attempt to address concerns raised by advocacy groups about the potentially racially disparate effects of state and local immigration enforcement.[175] Thus, while denying that immigration regulation and enforcement are inextricably tied to characteristics like race, national origin, and color, subfederal jurisdictions have nevertheless conspicuously attempted to quash concerns that the laws arose out of illegitimate prejudices or inevitably will be enforced in illegitimate ways.

Second, elected officials and restrictionist issue entrepreneurs have successfully packaged the new immigration federalism within the post–September 11 historical narrative, imbuing immigration discourse with the language necessary to covertly indulge the racial and cultural prejudices of particular voters.[176] With post–September 11 national security considerations adding a level of legitimacy and plausible deniability to the role of racial antipathy in nativist sentiment,[177] issue entrepreneurs conjured this dimension frequently in their advocacy of state and local laws.[178] A glaring example of this elision is the first attempt by the city of Farmers Branch, with the assistance of Kris Kobach, to enact an anti-illegal immigrant rental ordinance. The ordinance directly conjured the spectre of 9/11 in its first paragraph:

> Whereas, in response to the widespread concern of future terrorist attacks following the events of September 11, 2001, landlords and property managers throughout the country have been developing new security procedures to protect their building and residents.[179]

In several other instances, undocumented immigrants frequently were lumped together with terrorists in discussions ranging from the U.S.-Mexico border crossing[180] to the attempt by states to grant driver's licenses to unauthorized immigrants,[181] to the unaccompanied child migrant surge and Ebola panic of 2014.[182]

Indeed, as Professor Jennifer Chacón notes, the term "border security" emerged only after September 11. Prior discussions of "border control" took on military metaphors and subsumed concerns about homeland security and terrorism.[183] She also notes that immigration enforcement and detention, after 9/11, became the primary focus of domestic anti-terrorism policy.[184] Further, as Professor Leti Volpp explains, terrorism and terrorists have been discretely racialized in contemporary social and legal discourse.[185] Not surprisingly, each new terror or public health threat has instigated a flurry of predictable responses claiming that unwanted persons crossing the porous southern border will be the conduit for the threat du jour. This was again demonstrated most recently with the surge in unaccompanied child migrants from central America, with those favoring more stringent enforcement policies conjuring the fear of disease and other foreign-coded threats across the southern border. Thus, the conflation of terrorism and unlawful immigration creates a distinct racial context for subnational immigration laws.[186]

Third, emerging social science research undermines the notion that sub-federal immigration laws are free from the taint of racial and ethnic prejudice *in their creation*, and not only in their execution. The key findings in this data are: (1) The use or perceived use of a foreign language pushes voters, especially Republican voters, to adopt more restrictive stances on immigration proposals;[187] (2) media references to Latino immigrants produce greater anxiety and provoke greater support for restrictive action than do similar references to European immigrants;[188] (3) voters are more likely to hold negative views of illegal Mexican immigrants than of illegal immigrants from Asia or Europe;[189] and (4) voters are more likely to monitor the legal status of Latino immigrants than European immigrants for the purposes of granting public benefits.[190]

Also, the link between restrictionist state and local laws and their role in *producing* or *enhancing* prejudicial attitudes about race and ethnicity has become the subject of increased empirical scrutiny. Scholar Emily Ryo, for example, has begun to study the effects on public attitudes toward Latinos after having simply been exposed to a law like Arizona's SB 1070.[191] This field of study, steeped in the academic literature on the expressive and sybmolic features of law,[192] suggests that the very proposal, presence, and persistence of a restrictionist law enhances explicit discriminatory feelings about Latinos. The development of this type of research shows that restrictionist enactments have subtle equality-deteriorating effects on public perceptions. While such effects alone do not trigger unconstitutionality, they help explain why the distinction between immigration status and race is more apparent than real.

Thus, we argue that ethnic antipathy is an essential ingredient of these laws *at their inception*. These conclusions bolster the argument for a strong judicial role in monitoring and deterring the use of unlawful and illegitimate characteristics in the genesis of subfederal immigration law. These findings do not rely on disparate or coincidental effects;[193] they show that racial concerns animate laws premised on ostensibly neutral immigration status.[194] While these findings may not yet reflect the level of intentionality required to initiate a claim of racial discrimination,[195] they support the idea that structural power frameworks fail to capture the nuanced racial dynamics actually at play in the creation of subfederal immigration law. Moreover, our empirical refutation of the public policy–based justifications for restrictionist subfederal legislation leaves open the possibility of a competing explanation of what motivates such laws. This contextual and sociological evidence on xenophobic and racialized impulses provides the most likely alternative account.

Again, as scholars like Motomura have maintained, some courts may already be aware of this latent racial dynamic, implicitly folding equality considerations into their preemption analysis when striking down state and local laws.[196] Professor Kerry Abrams has made a similar point, suggesting that courts may invoke the principle of plenary power in preemption cases to find a way to incorporate anti-discrimination norms. Indeed, recently, a federal appeals court enjoined Arizona's attempt to deny driver's licenses to undocumented persons granted deferred action under DACA, concluding that the state's policy appeared to be based in animus against DACA beneficiaries.[197] Our evidence and explanation of ethnic nationalism lends further weight to these intuitions, suggesting that they can and should be prominently featured in judicial and political discourse rather than implicitly accounted for.

These findings are consistent with what we might expect to arise out of the discourse of states' rights rhetoric applied to regulation of wide swaths of the population. Indeed, racial segregation throughout the late nineteenth and early twentieth century was also defended on federalism grounds. The ultimate repair for racial discrimination in that context was Supreme Court recognition that the claim merited equal protection analysis, followed by substantial federal law concerned with the equality problems caused by segregation and its effects.[198] Undoubtedly, immigration regulation is different from racial segregation, but fundamentally both remind us to be wary of allowing structural power battles to obscure the racial antipathy animating parts of subfederal public policy.

Fundamentally, our legal and political discourse would be more productive and match the underlying empirical reality of immigration federalism if inchoate equality norms were moved to the fore. Of course, under current jurisprudence, moving to explicit equality-driven determinations in immigration federalism would be a difficult task. But, the consistent presence of discrimination concerns in cases from throughout immigration federalism history, and our evidence regarding the proliferation of restrictionist laws combined with this emerging empirical work regarding the connections between restrictionism and racial discrimination should at least move courts to reconsider their silence on equality concerns in immigration federalism cases.[199] At a minimum, more empirical research in this area is warranted, with an eye toward reimagining judicial and scholarly discourse on the viability of restrictionist state and local immigration regulations.

The empirical foundation of the new immigration federalism has required that we re-evaluate long-held explanations for the proliferation and utility of state and local policies, and the assumptions undergirding judicial consideration of these laws. This re-evaluation has helped us discover alternative models of legislative action to explain this type of policy proliferation, one that accounts for the outsized role of issue entrepreneurs and political parties, players not typically covered in traditional accounts of immigration federalism. Fitting our model within the frameworks of legislative cascades and partisan-based federalism also uncovers new ideas about the relationship between subfederal lawmaking on immigration and national policy dynamics.

Meanwhile, this shift in conceptual understandings of state and local immigration lawmaking also effects doctrinal considerations as they pertain to individual cases in front of federal courts. The deterioration of sovereignty-based approaches to immigration federalism, and continued pressure on the structural powers framework, clears doctrinal room for heretofore less recognized judicial methodologies based on anti-discrimination norms to become more central in the adjudication of immigration federalism.

In Chapter 7 that follows, we build from these ideas and look to the future of immigration federalism, and its place in our national political, legislative, and judicial landscape.

by some state-level immigrant rights advocates to push for stronger legislation at the state level than what could be achieved at the national level.

## THE STATE(S) OF IMMIGRATION FEDERALISM TODAY

As the preceding chapters detail, immigration federalism is a variegated landscape with room for states to maneuver on both restrictionist and integrationist policies. Congress, since 1996, has essentially been unable to move on any comprehensive immigration efforts, including any that deal with the state or local role.[1] This extended congressional silence virtually ensures that states and localities will seek to fill the legislative void, as motivated policy activists and opportunistic party officials push the envelope on entrepreneurial activity. Without federal legislative rebuke, such policies stand and gather momentum unless and until federal courts strike them down. But, in the meantime, such laws galvanize constituencies, and become expected and normalized fixtures in the national legislative landscape.

This certainly was the case with restrictionist states and local laws, which from 2004 through 2011 witnessed an unprecedented rise in the proposal and passage. While sophisticated issue entrepreneurs like Kris Kobach played a state-level game of rapid proliferation, immigrant advocates were still focused on the federal picture, placing their faith in Congress to proactively stifle the state efforts and in federal courts to stem the restrictionist tide. The integrationists, for the most part, prevailed in federal courts, but the restrictionist campaign left an indelible mark. Some state enforcement possibilities were left blessed by the Supreme Court and remain viable, along with other restrictionist policies created during that period. More fundamentally, the notion of inevitable state and local participation in fashioning immigration policy, for 140 years relegated to the margins, had moved to the center of the American political and legal consciousness. And, the integrationists' expected victory in Congress during that time never occurred. Even they would eventually adopt the state and local strategy that we see developing today.

Certainly, after 2012, the universe of constitutionally permissible restrictionist legislation has become more limited, as *Arizona v. United States* struck down several key provisions of SB 1070. States may not create state penalties for violations of the alien registration requirements, or penalize unauthorized workers for seeking employment. And, they may not authorize local law enforcement officers to arrest those they suspect of being deportable. Prior to reaching the Supreme Court, a federal court had already struck down the provision of Arizona's law that penalized day laborers from soliciting work. More recently, a federal court struck down another provision of Arizona's SB 1070 that criminalized the smuggling, transport, or harboring of undocumented immigrants.[2]

At the same time, the Court left in force Section 2B, which requires law enforcement officers to check the immigration status of those they have in custody who they suspect might be unlawfully present.[3] Also left in place were provisions of SB 1070 that were not appealed after the district court ruling in the case, including one that prevents localities within Arizona from enacting "sanctuary" ordinances to resist federal enforcement.

Appeals courts that heard cases regarding SB 1070's copycat laws – in Alabama, Georgia, Indiana, South Carolina, Utah, and cities like Hazelton, Pennsylvania, and Farmers Branch, Texas – also struck down most provisions in those laws based on the high court ruling in *Arizona*.[4] Those enactments contained some novel provisions that were not covered by the *Arizona* opinion, like Alabama's invalidation of contracts entered into by unauthorized immigrants or Fremont, Nebraska's rental ordinance penalizing landlords who rented to undocumented persons. Nevertheless, the Supreme Court has declined to separately weigh in on the unconstitutionality of those policies, and has let the various appeals court rulings remain the last word on those provisions. As a result, on the specific issue of rental ordinances, the Supreme Court left in place a circuit split between the Eighth Circuit, which upheld the policy, and the Fifth and Third Circuits that invalidated similar policies. Further, the lack of Supreme Court review over the contracting provision leaves open the possibility that other states down the road could attempt similar tactics, even if it is disallowed in the Eleventh Circuit.

Beyond the issues raised by Arizona SB 1070 and its progeny, other restrictionist avenues remain legally open as well. In *U.S. Chamber of Commerce v. Whiting*, the Court gave its blessing to state employer sanctions laws that require the use of E-verify by private employers. With that authority several states now have E-verify laws of some kind, with some applying to only public employers, or companies doing business with the state, or larger employers, and others, like Arizona's, applying to most private businesses. In addition, nothing in recent case law has changed the leeway provided by the 1996 welfare law to states, allowing them to restrict welfare provision to several classes of immigrants. Using that leeway, Arizona maintains laws with strict verification requirements for public assistance. In addition, the state denies in-state tuition rates to undocumented students at public universities. More broadly, the total effect of restrictionist laws in states such as Arizona or Alabama cannot be measured solely in terms of legally viable policies. Through their various enactments, enforcement posture, and political rhetoric, these states have clearly signaled their inhospitability to noncitizens, especially undocumented immigrants.

While states and localities retain some legal space to maneuver in the area of immigration restriction, the political restraints on the exercise of that authority are another important piece of the story. Kris Kobach, FAIR, and other important restrictionist actors have remained relatively quiet since 2012, but are certain to be conceiving of new opportunities and innovative means to achieve their policy vision. Most recently, Kobach was a lead figure in the suit by several states and state officials – all Republican controlled – attempting to enjoin President Obama's expansion of administrative relief for classes of undocumented immigrants. And, certainly, state-level restrictionism and enforcement remain popular in particular conservative jurisdictions, where talk of immigration, especially unauthorized migration, can galvanize the electorate and boost candidates adopting hard-line positions. Importantly, however, some jurisdictions that initially embraced enhanced enforcement policies have reconsidered them in light of political backlash, monetary cost, or both. A prominent example in this regard is Colorado SB 90, an immigration enforcement law enacted four years prior to SB 1070, and containing a provision similar to SB 1070's un-enjoined Section 2B. Despite its legal viability, the Colorado legislature repealed the policy in 2014.

More generally, the tide of restrictionist and enforcement-heavy regulations began to wane in 2012, soon followed by a rising tide of state-level integrationist laws (which we discuss in Chapter 5). The constitutional and statutory leeway for these pro-immigrant state and local enactments is broad, as many are either agnostic to immigration status or are in line with federal statutory authority. In this emerging state-level trend, states and localities are providing driver's licenses and municipal identification cards to undocumented immigrants, providing in-state tuition rates and financial assistance to undocumented students, resisting federal enforcement efforts to the extent possible, and some are even considering creative methods of providing health and other welfare benefits to undocumented persons. States like California are allowing unauthorized immigration to get professional licenses, while others like New York are contemplating proposals on state citizenship that would dramatically reconfigure present-day notion of political rights and membership.

In the end, the immigration federalism landscape looks radically different in 2015 than it did just a decade or two prior. States and localities are now undoubtedly important players in the immigration policy landscape. Some key provisions of restrictionist laws, such as state employment verification and denial of public benefits, remain constitutionally and politically viable, while a slew of pro-integration laws, ranging from enforcement resistance to the provision of in-state tuition and driver's licenses, seem to have become hardened features of immigration federalism that are here to stay, at least for the foreseeable future.

## WHAT'S NEXT FOR STATES AND LOCALITIES?

States and localities are situated to remain important players in the national immigration policy landscape in a way that they were not positioned to be just a mere twenty, or even ten, years ago. California policies, almost all exclusively integrationist over the past ten years, are a marked departure from the state's pioneering foray into immigration restrictionism with Prop. 187 in 1994. Now, as then, California remains home to the nation's highest immigrant population, percentage of population that is foreign born, and highest undocumented population.[5] Its policies not only mark out important ideological ground on immigration policy, they also affect the lives of the most number of immigrants, both documented and undocumented. California and five other states – Texas, Florida, New York, New Jersey, and Illinois – account for 60 percent of the unauthorized population in the United States, and are also the states with the highest immigrant populations generally. The state and local politics of places such as California, New York, and Illinois have led the integrationist movement of the past few years and likely will remain so into the foreseeable future.

But the importance and future viability of immigration federalism is not determined by demographics alone. For example, the partisan future of Texas and Florida might signal a corresponding shift in their policies on immigrant integration and immigration enforcement. The future of states and localities in immigration policy also depends a great deal on what the federal government chooses to do, or is able to produce, in the coming years. Future congressional action – similar to the assumption of federal power in the late 1800s, or the attempt to expressly preempt state employer sanctions laws in 1986, or the statutory leeway for state and local participation enacted in 1996 – can, in large measure, dictate the legal scope and breadth of state and local participation. Undoubtedly, some states may still seek to push against established federal statutory or constitutional boundaries with claims of inherent state sovereignty, or with the desire to oppositionally defy what appear to be established limits on their authority. But such actions are more likely to occur in the absence of clear legislative mandates, than in their existence. Congressional lawmaking can thus choose to staunch trends through extensive "field-claiming," or express preemption; it can choose to accommodate and foster trends through express allowances in statute; and, it can even provide for state and local participation, but on terms, and within bounds, wholly mediated by the federal government.

While all of these opportunities for federal policymaking vis-à-vis states and localities are possible, none are probable in the near future. Congressional deadlock and stalemate on immigration matters appears to be set to continue through, at minimum, the next cycle of federal elections, but could continue for much longer. The partisanship and polarization we identified in Chapter 4 as providing the ripe political context for state and local proliferation applies at the federal level as well. Unlike the bipartisan federal enactments of the twentieth century, including the major immigration overhauls of 1965, 1986, and 1996, since 2001, immigration has become a highly partisan issue with no political middle for compromise, a condition that is likely to remain through at least the next round of redisctricting in 2021.[6] Under such conditions, the potential for Congress to significantly address state-level trends – either to blunt them or to bless them – is remote.

What seems clear, however, is that the longer Congress waits to overcome the various veto pivots and procedural hurdles to enacting comprehensive immigration reform, the more normalized the several extant forms of state and local immigration policy become. Echoing the administratively diffi-cult transition from state to federal primacy in the late 1870s–1890s, the next round of federal legislative action on immigration will be forced to recog-nize, incorporate, and account for state and local preferences and policies. In short, the new federal regime, if and when it arrives, is bound to be shaped by our new immigration federalism; by integrationist policies in places like California and New York, and possibly by the restrictionism of places like Arizona and Alabama. To put it most simply: comprehensive immigration reform is unlikely to wipe out key features of our current framework of immi-gration federalism.

Going beyond Congress, states and localities are also increasingly playing a critical role in shaping executive branch policies on immigration. In an era of extended congressional stalemate, and bitter partisan contests between the White House and Congress, the president's role in setting immigration policy has been more prominent than ever. This is especially true in a time of divided government, when the Obama administration's Democratic plat-form on immigration has clashed with Congress's Republican leadership. The president's prerogatives became a prominent doctrinal concern in *Arizona v. United States*, with the executive branch's enforcement priorities playing a key role in the Court's determination that Arizona's SB 1070 conflicted with federal policy. More boldly, presidential action in the form of DACA in 2012 and the Deferred Acton for Parental Accountability (DAPA) in 2014 have fomented state and local action both consonant with, and in opposition to, the president's policy goals. On the one hand, most states enacted driver's license policies facilitating the provision of licenses to DACA recipients, and some went even further, extending licenses to undocumented immigrants more generally. Importantly, some of those state enacted policies will endure well past the deferred action periods granted by DACA, showing how executive action can have lasting effects on state policies toward immigrants.

States and localities can also play a more direct role in aiding or hindering executive action on immigration. After the Obama administration pronounced an expansion of deferred action in 2014, a coalition of twenty mayors from across the country – all members of the Democratic Party – met in New York City to discuss ways in which their respective localities could facilitate the implementation of DAPA and enact programs at the local level inuring to the benefit of the DAPA and DACA beneficiaries. At the same time, twenty-six Republican state officials filed suit against the Department of Homeland Security, alleging that the president had exceeded his constitutional authority in granting such large-scale administrative relief. As this book goes to print, that lawsuit has already had a significant effect, as a federal court in Texas enjoined the president's 2014 attempt at administrative relief. Even if that ruling is eventually overturned on appeal, it still showcases the potential for states to counter and check executive immigration policymaking.[7]

Thus, in the new immigration federalism landscape, during a period of polarized politics and congressional stalemate, states and localities appear poised to act as both entrenchers of executive policy visions and as potential checks on the exercise of executive power. Of course, as with other aspects of immigration federalism, this process, too, promises to remain highly partisan and subject to further evolution. Generally speaking, we would expect that, in this period of high partisan divisions, states and localities led by officials from the president's party will seek ways to entrench the president's vision, while those led by members of the out-party will likely seek to undermine or resist those very same policies.[8]

Apart from this recently appreciated ability for states and localities to act as surrogate arms of congressional or presidential will, the new immigration federalism also forces us to rethink the purpose of federalism and its utility. If we accept emerging accounts of federalism that stress the possibilities of horizontal federalism – that is, interactions among states rather than just with the federal government – we will increasingly see national policy battles waged on state and local turf. Consistent with our quantitative empirical findings debunking the myth that demography and policy challenges have spurred subfederal action, immigration federalism in coming years will continue to reflect deep partisan divisions nationally, within each state, and across various states. Thus, in the short term, we predict that immigration federalism will substitute for immigration nationalism.

To conclude, both the presence and the role of immigration federalism have changed considerably in the past decade, and have done so in ways that will have lasting effects on the creation and direction of future American immigration policy. Immigration federalism has the potential to do any or all of the following: In the realm of public policy, it can substitute for national legislation and policy debates, allowing partisans to instantiate competing visions of ideal immigration policy, including supporting or resisting executive action and federal enforcement. Next, in the realm of scholarly understanding, immigration federalism can push us toward a reexamination of citizenship with respect to national, state, and local governments, and toward a more critical understanding of the links between immigration restriction, racial anxiety, and discrimination. Finally, developments in immigration federalism will likely shape any future attempts at comprehensive immigration reform, as Congress will have to take into account existing policies and practices at the state and local level.

As this book goes to press, Congress remains unable to vote on, let alone pass, any comprehensive federal immigration reform. However, states and localities have remained active in the immigration arena, generating several policies before, during, and after the seminal case of *Arizona v. United States* in 2012. These policies reflect the American citizenry's diversity of competing perspectives on the divisive issue of immigration, as national policy battles get fought in these local arenas. As it turns out, Arizona's immigration laws, and the various Supreme Court cases they spawned, were important milestones in immigration federalism but they were by no means the end of the journey. The same holds true for the kinds of pro-integration developments we have seen in the last two years, including those policies initiated at the state level and those developed in reaction to the exercise of presidential authority. Action on immigration federalism continues apace, with partisan dynamics, separation of powers, issue entrepreneurship, and political mobilization likely to provide many more twists and turns in the years to come.

# Appendix C

## Statistical Analysis of State Immigrant Integration Laws

Using the same underlying state-level demographic data that we had in Appendix B, we ran logistic regressions against three outcomes: whether or not the state provided driver's licenses to all unauthorized immigrants (Table C.1), whether or not it provided in-state tuition (Table C.2), and whether or not it provided for financial assistance (public and/or private financial aid) for unauthorized residents (Table C.3). Other outcomes, such as the provision of public assistance for higher education or access to professional licensing cover too few cases for us to test for the statistical significance of key factors using a multivariate regression.

**Table C.1** *Logistic regression estimations of expanded access to driver's licenses*

| Factor | Regression estimation | (P) value |
|---|---|---|
| Republican control of state legislature | −4.034** | 0.048 |
| Growth of unauthorized population (2000 to 2007) | −0.027 | 0.108 |
| White poverty | −0.424 | 0.225 |
| Black poverty | −0.144 | 0.255 |
| Agriculture jobs (share of total) | −0.416 | 0.363 |
| Hispanic share of population | 0.174** | 0.04 |
| Naturalized share of electorate | −0.590* | 0.068 |
| Constant | 10.039** | 0.05 |
| *Observations* | 50 | |
| *Pseudo-R-squared* | 0.45 | |

\* significant at 10%; \*\* significant at 5%; \*\*\* significant at 1%, based on two-sided t-tests. Significance (p) values in brackets.

*Analysis of State Immigrant Integration Laws*

**Table C.2** *Logistic regression estimations of access to in-state tuition*

| Factor | Regression estimation | (P) value |
|---|---|---|
| Republican control of state legislature | −1.554* | 0.099 |
| Growth of unauthorized population (2000 to 2007) | −0.006 | 0.527 |
| White poverty | −0.270 | 0.269 |
| Black poverty | 0.085 | 0.291 |
| Agriculture jobs (share of total) | 0.162 | 0.504 |
| Hispanic share of population | 0.095 | 0.109 |
| Naturalized share of electorate | 0.404 | 0.145 |
| Constant | −1.951 | 0.582 |
| *Observations* | 50 | |
| *Pseudo-R-squared* | 0.45 | |

* significant at 10%; ** significant at 5%; *** significant at 1%, based on two-sided t-tests. Significance (p) values in brackets.

**Table C.3** *Logistic regression estimations of access to higher education financial assistance*

| Factor | Regression estimation | (P) value |
|---|---|---|
| Republican control of state legislature | −1.800 | 0.251 |
| Growth of unauthorized population (2000 to 2007) | −0.023 | 0.284 |
| White poverty | −0.094 | 0.77 |
| Black poverty | 0.039 | 0.746 |
| Agriculture jobs (share of total) | 0.089 | 0.816 |
| Hispanic share of population | 0.126* | 0.036 |
| Naturalized share of electorate | 0.129 | 0.63 |
| Constant | −2.879 | 0.569 |
| *Observations* | 50 | |
| *Pseudo-R-squared* | 0.45 | |

* significant at 10%; ** significant at 5%; *** significant at 1%, based on two-sided t-tests. Significance (p) values in brackets.

# Notes

## CHAPTER 1

1   Chamber of Commerce of the United States v Whiting, 131 S. Ct. 1968 (2011) (upholding the Legal Arizona Workers Act); Arizona v United States, 132 S. Ct. 2492 (2012) (striking down three of four challenged provisions of SB 1070); Arizona v Inter-Tribal Council of Arizona, 133 S. Ct. 2247 (2013) (striking down state proof-of-citizenship requirement for voter registration). This was not the first time that Arizona's laws affecting immigrants had reached the Supreme Court – in 1915, the Court had invalidated an Arizona law requiring employers to hire native-born workers, and in 1971, the Court struck down an Arizona welfare restriction on noncitizens.

2   Brief Of Business Organizations As *Amici Curiae* in Support Of Petitioners, Chamber of Commerce of the United States et al. v Michael B. Whiting et al. (2010) (no. 09–115).

3   Brief For the United States As *Amici Curiae* in Support Of Petitioners, Chamber of Commerce of the United States et al. v Michael B. Whiting et al. (2010) (no. 09–115).

4   Brief *Amici Curiae* Of Representative Romano L. Mazzoli, Senator Arlen Specter, and Representative Howard L. Berman in Support Of Petitioners, Chamber of Commerce of the United States et al. v Michael B. Whiting et al. (2010) (no. 09–115).

5   Brief Of The Service Employees International Union as *Amici Curiae* in Support Of Petitioners, Chamber of Commerce of the United States et al. v Michael B. Whiting et al. (2010) (no. 09–115).

6   Brief for Amicus Curiae Immigration Reform Law Institute as *Amici Curiae* in Support Of Respondents, Chamber of Commerce of the United States et al. v Michael B. Whiting et al. (2010) (no. 09–115).

7   Brief of States, Missouri, Alabama, Arkansas, Kansas, Louisiana, Michigan, Mississippi, Nebraska, North Dakota, South Carolina, Tennessee, Utah, and Virginia as Amici Curiae In Support Of Respondents, Chamber of Commerce of the United States et al. v Michael B. Whiting et al. (2010) (no. 09–115).

8   McClatchy Newspapers. "Justices Back Arizona Policy on Illegal Workers." *Pittsburg Tribune* ("The ruling will make it easier for states to pass similar laws, even though immigration is traditionally a federal responsibility.") May 27, 2011.

9  Gerald Neuman, *The Lost Century of Immigration Law 1776–1875*, 93 COLUM.
   L. REV. 1833 (1993).
10 In legal scholarship, several insightful contributions from prominent commentators
   have illuminated this subgenre within the immigration law field. As an illustrative,
   but certainly incomplete list, see, e.g., Hiroshi Motomura, IMMIGRATION OUTSIDE
   THE LAW (Oxford 2014); Strange Neighbors: The Role of States in Immigration
   Policy (Carissa Byrne Hessick and Gabriel J. Chin, eds.) (NYU Press 2014); Kevin
   Johnson, *State and Local Efforts to Regulate Immigration*, 46 GEORGIA L. REV.
   609 (2012); Peter Spiro and Kit Johnson, *Immigration Preemption after United
   States v. Arizona (Debate)*, 161 UNIV. PENN. L. REV. ONLINE 100 (2014); Stella
   Elias Burch, *The New Immigration Federalism*, 74 OHIO ST. L. J. 703 (2013); Rick
   Su, *The States of Immigration*, 54 WILLIAM & MARY L. REV. 1339 (2013); Cristina
   Rodriguez, Law and Borders, Democracy: A Journal of Ideas (Summer 2014);
   Cristina Rodriguez, *The Significance of the Local in Immigration Regulation*, 106
   MICH. L. REV. 567 (2008); Jennifer M. Chacon, *The Transformation of Immigration
   Federalism*, 21 WILLIAM & MARY BILL OF RIGHTS J. 577 (2012); Margaret Hu,
   *Reverse-Commandeering*, 46 U.C. DAVIS L. REV. 535 (2012); Huyen Pham and
   Pham Hoang Van, *The Economic Impact of Local Immigration Regulation: An
   Empirical Analysis*, 31 IMMIGR. AND NATIONALITY L. REV. 687 (2010); Michael
   A. Olivas, *Immigration-Related State and Local Ordinances: Preemption, Prejudice,
   and the Proper Role for Enforcement*, 2007 U. CHI. LEGAL FORUM 27 (2007); Peter
   Schuck, *Taking Immigration Federalism Seriously*, 2007 U. CHI. LEGAL FORUM 57
   (2007); Rose Cuison Villazor, *What Is a Sanctuary?*, 61 SMU L. REV. 133 (2008);
   Clare Huntington, *The Constitutional Dimensions of Immigration Federalism*, 61
   VANDERBILT L. REV. 787 (2008); Juliet P. Stumpf, *States of Confusion: The Rise
   of State and Local Power over Immigration*, 86 NORTH CAROLINA L. REV. 1557
   (2008); Michael Wishnie, *State and Local Police Enforcement of Immigration
   Law*, 4 UNIV. OF PENNSYLVANIA J. CONST. L. 1084 (2004); Daniel J. Tichenor
   and Alexandra Filindra, *Raising Arizona v. United States: Historical Patterns of
   American Immigration Federalism*, Lewis & Clark L. Rev. 16 (2012): 1215; Pratheepan
   Gulasekaram and Karthick Ramakrishnan, *Immigration Federalism: A Reappraisal*,
   88 N.Y.U. L. REV. 2074 (2013); Stephen H. Legomsky, *Immigration, Federalism,
   and the Welfare State*, 42 UCLA L. REV. 1453 (1995). For social science schol-
   arship, see Paul G. Lewis and S. Karthick Ramakrishnan, *Police Practices in
   Immigrant-Destination Cities: Political Control or Bureaucratic Professionalism?*
   URBAN AFFAIRS REVIEW 42, no. 6 (2007): 874–900; Lorrie A. Frasure and Michael
   Jones-Correa, *The Logic of Institutional Interdependency: The Case of Day
   Laborer Policy in Suburbia*, Urban Affairs Review 45, no. 4 (2010): 451–482; Daniel
   J. Hopkins, *Politicized Places: Explaining Where and When Immigrants Provoke
   Local Opposition*, American Political Science Review 104, no. 01 (2010): 40–60;
   Monica Varsanyi, ed., Taking Local Control: Immigration Policy Activism in U.S.
   Cities and States, Stanford, CA: Stanford University Press, 2010; Paul G. Lewis,
   Doris Marie Provine, Monica W. Varsanyi, and Scott H. Decker, *Why do (some)
   City Police Departments Enforce Federal Immigration Law? Political, Demographic,
   and Organizational Influences on Local Choices*, Journal of Public Administration
   Research and Theory (2012): 1–25; Tom K. Wong, *287 (g) and the Politics of Interior
   Immigration Control in the United States: Explaining Local Cooperation with*

*Federal Immigration Authorities*, Journal of Ethnic and Migration Studies 38, no. 5 (2012): 737–756; Michael Jones-Correa and Els de Graauw, *The Illegality Trap: The Politics of Immigration & the Lens of Illegality*, Daedalus 142, no. 3 (2013): 185–198.

11  This figure includes both restrictive and permissive legislation, and excludes vetoed bills and legislative resolutions that are non-binding.

12  Hiroshi Motomura, IMMIGRATION OUTSIDE THE LAW (Oxford 2014) (entitling Chapter 1, "Undocumented or Illegal?" and exploring the indeterminacy of the legal/illegal characterization of unauthorized migration).

13  Mohawk Industries, Inc. v. Norman Carpenter, 130 S.Ct. 599 (2009) (Justice Sotomayor's majority opinion using the term "undocumented immigrant"); Emily Guskin, *"Illegal," "Undocumented," "Unauthorized,": News Media Shift Language on Immigration*. Pew Research Center, June 17 (2013) (noting media shift to "undocumented" or "unauthorized").

## CHAPTER 2

1  *See* Pratheepan Gulasekaram and Karthick Ramakrishnan, *Immigration Federalism: A Reappraisal*, 88 N.Y.U. L. REV. 2074 (2013) (using the term "the new immigration federalism" to describe restrictionist state legislation post-9/11); Stella Elias Burch, *The New Immigration Federalism*, 74 OHIO ST. L. J. 703 (2013) (discussing the "new immigration federalism" after Arizona v. United States).

2  David Rubenstein, *Immigration Structuralism: A Return to Form*, 8 DUKE J. CONST. L. AND PUB. POL'Y 81, (2013).

3  An Act to Establish an Uniform Rule of Naturalization, Sess. II, ch. 3, 1 Stat. 103 (as enacted by 1st Cong., Nov. 26, 1790).

4  An Act to Establish an Uniform Rule of Naturalization, Sess. II, ch. 19, 20, 1 Stat. 414 (as enacted by 3rd Cong., Jan. 29, 1795); An Act to Amend the Act, entitled "An Act to Establish an Uniform Rule of Naturalization," Sess. II, ch. 54, 1 Stat. 566 (as enacted by 5th Cong., June 17, 1798) (extending residency period to fourteen years); *see also*, 8 U.S.C. § 1427 (establishing current residency time for naturalization as five years).

5  An Act Concerning Aliens, Sess. II, ch. 58, 1 Stat. 577 (as enacted by 5th Cong., June 25, 1798).

6  An Act Respecting Alien Enemies, Sess II, ch. 66, 1 Stat. 570 (as enacted by 5th Cong., July 6, 1798).

7  An Act Regulating Passenger Ships and Vessels, Sess. II, ch. 47, 3 Stat. 488 (as enacted by 15th Cong., Mar. 2, 1819).

8  An Act Regulating Passenger Ships and Vessels, Sess. II, ch. 47, 3 Stat. 488 (as enacted by 15th Cong., Mar. 2, 1819) (establishing standards to be followed by ships carrying putative immigrants); 1855 Passenger Act, Sess. II, ch. 213, 10 Stat. 715 (as enacted by 33rd Cong., Mar. 3, 1855).

9  ANNA O. LAW, AN ASSESSMENT OF IMMIGRATION FEDERALISM IN THE NINETEENTH CENTURY, https://www.utexas.edu/law/calendar/uploads/UT_Law_Visit.pdf (Sept. 2013).

10  An Act to Regulate the Carriage of Passengers in Steamships and Other Vessels, Sess. II, ch. 213, 10 Stat. 715 (as enacted by 33rd Cong., Mar. 3, 1855).

11 An Act to Prohibit the "Coolie Trade" by American Citizens in American Vessels, Sess. II, ch. 27, 12 Stat. 340 (as enacted by 37th Cong., Feb. 19, 1862).

12 An Act to Encourage Immigration, Sess. I., ch. 246, 13 Stat. 385 (as enacted by 38th Cong., July 4, 1864); *see generally*, John Higham, *American Immigration Policy in Historical Perspective*, 21 Law and Contemp. Probs. 213 (1956).

13 Gerald Neuman, *The Lost Century of Immigration Law (1776–1875)*, 93 Colum. L. Rev. 1833 (1993); Daniel J. Tichenor & Alexandra Filindra, *Raising Arizona v. United States: Historical Patterns of American Immigration Federalism*, 16 Lewis & Clark L. Rev. 1215, 1223–34 (2012).

14 Arizona v. United States, 132 S.Ct. 2492, 2511–13 (Scalia, J., concurring in part and dissenting in part) (citing to eighteenth- and early nineteenth-century cases, statutes, and secondary sources).

15 Neuman, *supra* note 13 at 1866–80; *see also* Gerald L. Neuman, Strangers to the Constitution: Immigrants, Borders and Fundamental Law (1996), 24–29; Law, *supra* note 9 at 41–42.

16 Neuman, *supra* note 13 at 1859–65.

17 Chae Chan Ping v. United States, 130 U.S. 581 (1889); Fong Yue Ting v. United States, 149 U.S. 698 (1893).

18 Law, *supra* note 9 at 37–46.

19 U.S. Const. art. I, § 9, cl. 1 ("The migration or importation of such persons as any of the states now existing shall think proper to admit shall not be prohibited by the Congress prior to the year one thousand eight hundred and eight.").

20 Law, 19th Century Immigration Federalism at 38.

21 Even on naturalization, Congress in the early 1800s allowed state and local courts to be considered equivalent to federal district courts for purposes of naturalization (see D. M. Dewey, The Naturalization Laws of the United States, (1855), p. 33).

22 *See* Law, 19th Century Immigration Federalism at 21–30; *see also* Hidetaka Hirota, *The Moment of Transition: State Officials, the Federal Government, and the Formation of American Immigration Policy*, 99 J. Am. Hist. 1092 (2013); Tichenor and Filindra, supra n. 13 at 1225.

23 *See* Richard M. Valelly, The Two Reconstructions: The Struggle for Black Enfranchisement (2004). Even with the end of Reconstruction in 1877, the federal government remained strong with respect to immigration regulation because white Southern resistance to federal power was preoccupied with maintaining political power and social control over blacks, and comparatively much less concerned about immigration policy.

24 Aristide R. Zolberg, A Nation by Design, 166 (2005) ("In his December 1863 address to Congress, President Abraham Lincoln called for the establishment of a 'system for the encouragement of immigration.'") (citation omitted).

25 *Id.*; Hiroshi Motomura, Immigration Outside the Law 34 (Oxford Univ. Press 2014) ("The western states' enormous needs for cheap and ample labor led the federal government to negotiate the Burlingame Treaty with China in 1868.").

26 New York v. Miln, 36 U.S. 102 (1837) (upholding New York City law that imposed a bond on shipmasters of vessels arriving with immigrants as a valid exercise of state police powers).

27 Henderson v. City of New York, 92 U.S. 259 (1875) (striking down laws that required a bond or commutation from the shipmasters for arriving passengers at ports of entry); Chy Lung v. Freeman, 92 U.S. 275 (1875) (striking down California law requiring bond or commutation for arriving "lewd or debauched women"); The Passenger Cases, 48 U.S. 283 (1849) (striking down New York and Massachusetts laws that taxed arriving passengers at their ports of entry).

28 *See* Law, 19th Century Immigration Federalism at 33; Tichenor and Filindra, 16 Lewis & Clark L. Rev. at 1232 (citing Daniel J. Tichenor, Dividing Lines: The Politics of Immigration Control in America 69 (2002)); Hirota, The Moment of Transition, 99 J. Am. Hist. at 1097 ("The ban on the capitation tax also signified the loss of states' financial resources previously used for, among other related expenses, the maintenance of foreign paupers and sick immigrants at charitable institutions. Immediately after the Henderson decision, immigration officials in Atlantic Seaboard states campaigned to secure national immigration legislation as a substitute for state passenger laws."); *see also* William S. Bernard, *Immigration: History of U.S. Policy, in* HARVARD ENCYCLOPEDIA OF AMERICAN ETHNIC GROUPS 486–95 (Stephen Thernstrom ed., 1980).

29 *See generally* Law, 19th Century Immigration Federalism; Hirota, *The Moment of Transition*, 99 J. AM. HIST. 1092; Bernard, Immigration: History of U.S. Policy, in Harvard Encyclopedia of American Ethnic Groups.

30 Importantly, those classified as American Indian from those territories were not granted U.S. citizenship, although these persons had been granted citizenship by Mexico prior to the Treaty of Guadalupe Hidalgo. Richard Griswold del Castillo, THE TREATY OF GUADALUPE HIDALGO: A LEGACY OF CONFLICT, 69–72 (1990).

31 Lucy Salyer, LAWS HARSH AS TIGERS: CHINESE IMMIGRANTS AND THE SHAPING OF MODERN IMMIGRATION LAW, 7 (1995).

32 See, e.g., Tichenor and Filindra, 16 Lewis & Clark L. Rev at 1226–27 (listing milestones in California's anti-Chinese political and social movements). It should be noted, however, that while California was the epicenter of such anti-Chinese laws, jurisdictions across the country reflected this same prejudice. Earl M. Maltz, *The Federal Government and the Problem of Chinese Rights in the Era of the Fourteenth Amendment*, 94 HARV. J. L. AND PUB. POL'Y 223 (1994); Stuart C. Miller, THE UNWELCOME IMMIGRANT: THE AMERICAN IMAGE OF THE CHINESE 1785–1882, 165–75 (1969).

33 Mark Kanazawa, *Immigration, Exclusion, and Taxation: Anti-Chinese Legislation in Gold Rush California*, 65 J. ECON. HIST. 779 (2005); Higham, *American Immigration Policy in Historical Perspective*, 21 LAW AND CONTEMP. PROBS. at 215–17.

34 Salyer, Laws Harsh as Tigers at 7–15; Kanazawa, *Immigration, Exclusion, and Taxation*, 65 J. ECON. HIST. 779.

35 *See Lin Sing*, 20 Cal. 534; *Tiburcio Parrott*, 1 F. 481 (striking down a state law imposing criminal sanctions on anyone employing a Chinese or Mongolian person); *Ah Chong*, 2 F. 733 (striking down state law prohibiting Chinese from obtaining fishing licenses as a violation of the U.S. Constitution).

36 Charles J. McClain, IN SEARCH OF EQUALITY: THE CHINESE STRUGGLE AGAINST DISCRIMINATION IN NINETEENTH CENTURY AMERICA (1994).

37 Additional Articles to the Treaty between the United States and China, of June 18, 1858 (generally known as the "Burlingame Treaty of 1868"), U.S.-P.R.C., July 28, 1868, 16 Stat. 739, T.S. No. 48, *available at* http://librarysource.uchastings.edu/library/research/special-collections/wong-kim-ark/16%20Stat.%20739.pdf (last visited July 6, 2014).

38 Maltz, The Problem of Chinese Rights, 17 Harv. J. L. and Pub. Pol'y at 226–27. According to Maltz, compromise over that provision was achieved when provisions were added to eliminate the possibility of naturalization for those migrants.

39 Salyer, Laws Harsh as Tigers at 9–14.

40 Civil Rights Act of 1870, ch. 114, §§ 16–17, 16 Stat. 140, 144 (1870); *see* Lucas Guttentag, *The Forgotten Equality Norm in Immigration Preemption: Discrimination, Harassment, and the Civil Rights Act of 1870*, 8 DUKE J. CONST. L. AND PUB. POL'Y 1, 10 (2013) (arguing that the Civil Rights Act of 1870 enshrines an equality norm in federal statutes that should be considered when evaluating the preemptive effect of federal laws on restrictive immigration regulations like Arizona's SB 1070). Notably, however, the Chy Lung case (discussed *infra*) did not rely on the Civil Rights Act of 1870, and the Act has not, by itself, been dispositive in any immigration federalism case.

41 Kerry Abrams, *Polygamy, Prostitution, and the Federalization of Immigration Law*, 105 COLUM. L. REV. 641, 671–76; *see* An Act to Prevent the Kidnapping and Importation of Mongolian, Chinese, and Japanese females, for Criminal or Demoralizing Purposes, Act of Mar. 18, 1870, ch. 230, 1869–70 Cal. Stat. 330.

42 An act to Prevent the Importation of Chinese Criminals and to Prevent the Establishment of Coolie Slavery, Act of Mar. 18, 1870, ch. 231, 1870 Cal. Stat. 332.

43 Abrams, *Polygamy, Prostitution, and the Federalization of Immigration Law*, 105 COLUM. L. REV. at 676–77.

44 *Id.*

45 *See* Chy Lung, 92 U.S. 275.

46 *Id.* at 280.

47 *See* Kerry Abrams, *Plenary Power Preemption*, 99 VA. L. REV. 601, 614–15 (2013).

48 See Gulasekaram and Ramakrishnan, *Immigration Federalism: A Reappraisal*, 88 N.Y.U. L. REV. at 2083–90.

49 Chy Lung, 92 U.S. at 280.

50 Henderson v. Mayor of the City of New York, 92 U.S. 259 (1875) (striking down law requiring shipmasters to post a bond or pay a fee for every disembarking noncitizen passenger). Relying on constitutional provisions that provide Congress sole authority over the conduct of commerce with foreign countries, the Court concluded: "We are of the opinion that this whole subject has been confided to Congress by the Constitution.... Whether, in the absence of such action, the States can, or how far they can, by appropriate legislation, protect themselves against actual paupers, vagrants, criminals, and diseased persons ... we do not decide." *Id.* at 274.

51 Clare Huntington, *The Constitutional Dimensions of Immigration Federalism*, 61 VAND. L. REV. 787 (2008).

52 Cal. Const. Art. XIX (1879); see also, Motomura, Immigration Outside the Law 35; Tichenor and Filindra, 16 Lewis & Clark L. Rev. at 1234 and n. 153.

53 Leon E. Aylsworth, *The Passing of Alien Suffrage*, 25 Am. Pol. Sci. Rev. 114, 114–16; Motomura, Immigration Outside the Law 68.

purporting to authorize states to similarly restrict noncitizens' access to certain public benefits).

130 S. 735, Pub. L. No. 104–132, 110 Stat. 1214 (as enacted by 104th Cong., Apr. 24, 1996) (requiring the mandatory detention of noncitizens convicted of a range of offenses).

131 *See* 8 U.S.C. § 274 (current version at 8 U.S.C. § 1324 (2005)) (providing state enforcement authority for the crime of smuggling undocumented immigrants).

132 8 U.S.C. § 1601, et. seq.

133 8 U.S.C. §§ 1621(d), 1623(a).

134 See, e.g., William Finnegan, "Sheriff Joe," *The New Yorker*, July 20, 2009 (profiling Sheriff Joe Arpaio of Maricopa County, Arizona, the self-styled "America's Sheriff"); Jessica Chasmar, "Arizona Gov. Brewer Blasts 'Imperial' Obama for Failing to Secure Border," *The Washington Times*, July 8, 2014.

135 California Secretary of State. 1994. *November 8, 1994 General Election Statement of Vote*, available at https://www.sos.ca.gov/elections/sov/1994-general/ (last visited January 15, 2015).

136 California absorbed about half of all defense personnel cuts in the country during the early 1990s and lost upwards of 375,000 defense contracting jobs (Yousur Alhlou, "California Economy to Take Hit from Defense Cuts," *San Francisco Chronicle*, February 13, 2012).

137 Mark Baldassare. 1998. WHEN GOVERNMENT FAILS: THE ORANGE COUNTY BANKRUPTCY. Berkeley: San Francisco: University of California; Public Policy Institute of California.

138 Dan Morain, "A FATHER'S BITTERSWEET CRUSADE," *Los Angeles Times*, March 7, 1994.

139 Gebe Martinez and Doreen Carvajal, "Creators of Prop. 187 Largely Escape Spotlight," LOS ANGELES TIMES, September 4, 1994.

140 Ibid.

141 Paul Feldman, "Figures Behind Prop. 187 Look at Its Creation," *Los Angeles Times*, December 14, 1994.

142 University of California, Hastings College of the Law. 1994. *Illegal Aliens. Ineligibility for Public Services. Verification and Reporting. Initiative Statute*, available at http://repository.uchastings.edu/cgi/viewcontent.cgi?article=2103&context=ca_ballot_props (last visited January 15, 2015).

143 LULAC v. Wilson, 908 F. Supp. 755 (C.D. Cal. 1995).

144 Statement from California Attorney General Bill Lockyer, *Attorney General Lockyer Files Agreement Ending Major Challenges to Proposition 187* (July 29, 1999), available at http://oag.ca.gov/news/press-releases/attorney-general-lockyer-files-agreement-ending-major-challenges-proposition-187 (last visited, July 6, 2014); *see also* Nicole E. Lucy, *Mediation of Proposition 187: Creative Solution to an Old Problem? Or Quiet Death for Initiatives?*, 1 PEPP. DISP. RESOL. L.J. 123 (2001).

145 Interviews with Federation for American Immigration Reform (FAIR), January 31, 2012, NumbersUSA, March 6, 2012, and America's Voice, April 20, 2012.

146 Patrick J. McDonnell, 1994, op. cit.

147 Patrick J. McDonnell, "Anti-Illegal Immigration Proposition Fails to Qualify for Arizona Ballot," LOS ANGELES TIMES, July 15, 1996.

148 Arizona v. United States, 104 F.3d 1095 (9th Cir. 1997); California v. United States, 104 F.3d 1086 (9th Cir. 1997); Chiles v. United States, 69 F.3d 1094 (11th Cir.1995). Texas, New York, and New Jersey filed similar lawsuits. The lawsuits were dismissed by federal courts and the U.S. Supreme Court refused to hear the cases. Texas v. United States, 106 F.3d 661 (5th Cir. 1997) (affirming the dismissal of Texas's claims); New Jersey v. United States, 91 F.3d 463 (3d Cir. 1996) (affirming thedismissal of New Jersey's claims); Padavan v. United States, 82 F.3d 23 (2d Cir. 1996) (affirming the dismissal of New York's claims).

149 Tichenor and Filindra, 16 Lewis & Clark L. Rev. at 1235.

150 Patrick J. McDonnell, "Prop. 187 Found Unconstitutional by Federal Judge," *L.A. Times*, Nov. 15, 1997, available at http://articles.latimes.com/1997/nov/15/news/ mn-54053 (last visited July 6, 2014).

151 S. Karthick Ramakrishnan and Thomas J.Espenshade, *Immigrant Incorporation and Political Participation in the United States*, International Migration Review 35:870–910 (2001); Adrian D. Pantoja, Ricardo Ramirez, and Gary M. Segura, *Citizens by Choice, Voters by Necessity: Patterns in Political Mobilization in Naturalized Latinos*, 54 Political Research Quarterly 729–750 (2001).

152 Melanie Mason and Patrick McGreevy, *Latino Lawmakers Move to Reverse Decades of Anti-Immigrant Legislation*, Los Angeles Times, June 22, 2014.

## CHAPTER 3

1 Jerry Gillam. "California Laws '94." *Los Angeles Times*, December 31, 1993. http:// articles.latimes.com/1993-12-31/news/mn-7154_1_law-enforcement/2.

2 Mark Arax. "Stronger Rules on English in Signs Pushed by Council." *Los Angeles Times*, December 5, 1985. http://articles.latimes.com/1985-12-05/news/ ga-633_1_sign-ordinance. For a more extended treatment on Monterey Park, see Saito, Leland T. Race and Politics: Asian Americans, Latinos, and Whites in a Los Angeles Suburb. University of Illinois Press, 1998.

3 David W. Chen. "Karaoke Crackdown Stirs Ethnic Anger in Palisades Park." *New York Times*, September 8, 1996, sec. N.Y. / Region. http://www.nytimes .com/1996/09/08/nyregion/karaoke-crackdown-stirs-ethnic-anger-in-palisades-park .html.

4 Robert Hanley. "Debating the Language of Signs; New Jersey Towns Tell Asian-Owned Stores: Advertise in English, Too." *New York Times*, April 9, 1996, sec. N.Y. / Region. http://www.nytimes.com/1996/04/09/nyregion/debating-language-signs-new-jersey-towns-tell-asian-owned-stores-advertise.html.

5 8 U.S.C. § 1357*g (U.S. Immigration and Customs Enforcement, Fact Sheet: Delegation of Immigration Authority Section 287(g) Immigration and Nationality Act.

6 Colorado S.B. 90, C.R.S. §§29-29-101 – 103 (2006).

7 City of San Bernadino, Illegal Immigration Relief Act Ordinance, §§ 4, 5, 6, 7, and 8, available at www.ailadownloads.org/advo/SanBernadinoIllegal ImmigrationOrdinance.pdf

8   Cristina Rodriguez, Muzaffar Chisti, and Kimberly Nortman, TESTING THE
    LIMITS: A FRAMEWORK FOR ASSESSING THE LEGALITY OF STATE AND LOCAL
    IMMIGRATION MEASURES at pp. 2–3, Migration Policy Institute, Washington, DC
    (2007).
9   See A Review of State Immigration Legislation in 2005, NAT'L CONFERENCE
    OF STATE LEGISLATURES (2007), http://www.ncsl.org/research/immigration/
    immigrant-policy-project-state-legislation-117.aspx (reporting bills and resolutions
    passed or pending in the states in 2005).
10  Arizona v. Inter Tribal Council of Arizona, Inc., 133 S. Ct. 2247, 2252 (2013).
    Subsequently, Arizona and Kansas petitioned the U.S. Election Assistance
    Commission to approve bifurcated registration procedures, which would allow the
    state to impose its tougher citizenship proof requirements for state elections. The
    states sought judicial review of the Election Assistance Commission decision, and
    in March 2014, the district court ruled the Commission must change the federal
    registration form to permit states to require documentary proof. Kobach v. U.S.
    Election Assistance Comm'n, 13-CV-4095-EFM-TJJ, 2014 WL 1094957 (D. Kan.
    Mar. 19, 2014). The U.S. Election Assistance Commission immediately appealed to
    the 10th circuit, and a stay was granted on May 19 pending appeal. Kobach v. U.S.
    Election Assistance Comm'n, Appellate Case 14-3062 and 14-3072 (10th Cir. May
    19, 2014) (order granting a motion to stay the district court order pending appeal).
11  Ariz. Proposition 200, Arizona Taxpayer and Citizen Protection Act, A.R.S.
    § 46-140.01 ("Verifying applicants for public benefits") (2004) available at http://apps
    .azsos.gov/election/2004/Info/PubPamphlet/english/prop200.htm
12  Montana Legislative Referendum 121 (2012). The law was struck down by a fed-
    eral court primarily because the state – similar to California with Prop. 187 –
    was making up its own definition of "illegal aliens" who were ineligible for state
    benefits. Associated Press, "Judge Strikes Down Montana's Illegal Alien Benefits
    Law," GOPUSA, July 3, 2014 available at http://www.gopusa.com/news/2014/07/03/
    judge-strikes-down-montanas-illegal-alien-benefits-law/.
13  8 U.S.C. § 1622. For a critique that this particular form of federal law is better
    characterized as discrimination-enabling, see Michael J. Wishnie, Laboratories of
    Bigotry? Devolution of Immigration Power, Equal Protection, and Federalism, 76
    N.Y.U. L. Rev. 493 (2001).
14  8 U.S.C. § 1621 (d).
15  Aliessa v. Novello, 96 N.Y.2d 418 (N.Y. Ct. of App. 2001).
16  Soskin v. Reinertson, 353 F.3d 1242 (10th Cir. 2004).
17  See James P. Smith and Barry Edmonston, eds., THE NEW AMERICANS: ECONOMIC,
    DEMOGRAPHIC, AND FISCAL EFFECTS OF IMMIGRATION (Washington: National
    Academies Press, 1997); Amanda Levinson, Immigrants and Welfare Use,
    Migration Policy Institute (2002), available at http://www.migrationpolicy.org/
    article/immigrants-and-welfare-use#OVERVIEW; Peter H. Schuck, Taking
    Immigration Federalism Seriously, 2007 University of Chicago Law Forum at
    60–1; Marshall Fitz, Philip E. Wolgin, and Patrick Oakford, "Immigrants Are
    Makers, Not Takers," Center for American Progress, February 8, 2013, available
    at   http://www.americanprogress.org/issues/immigration/news/2013/02/08/52377/
    immigrants-are-makers-not-takers/.

18  See Stella Burch Elias, *The New Immigration Federalism*, 74 OHIO STATE LAW JOURNAL 703 (2013).

19  Guaman v. Velez, 432 N.J. Super. 230 (N.J. App. Div. 2013), aff'd Guaman v. Velez, No. A-87-13 073371 (N.J. Mar. 30, 2015). See also, Matthew Bultman, NJ High Court Leaves Alone New-Immigrant Health Care Ban, Law360, Mar. 30, 2015.

20  Arizona House Bill 2779, 48th Leg. 1st reg. sess. (Ariz. 2007).

21  8 U.S.C. § 1324a(h)(2) (preempts state sanctions on the employment of unauthorized aliens, "other than through licensing and similar laws").

22  See U.S. CITIZENSHIP AND IMMIGRATION SERVICES, "What Is E-Verify?" available at http://www.uscis.gov/e-verify/what-e-verify (last accessed July 2014).

23  Chamber of Commerce of U.S. v. Whiting, 131 S. Ct. 1968, 1974 (2011).

24  *The State of the States: E-Verify Bills 2012*, NATIONAL IMMIGRATION LAW CENTER (2012) available at http://www.nilc.org/stateeverifypolicyresrces.html; *E-Verify*, NATIONAL CONFERENCE OF STATE LEGISLATURES (2012) available at http://www.ncsl.org/research/immigration/everify-faq.aspx#2012%20State%20Action.

25  REAL ID Act, 49 U.S.C. § 30301 note § 202(c)(2)(B)(viii).

26  *Countdown to Real ID*, NAT'L CONFERENCE OF STATE LEGISLATURES (Feb. 7, 2014) at http://www.ncsl.org/research/transportation/count-down-to-real-id.aspx; Daniel C. Vock, "Real ID Is Slowly Changing State Drivers' Licenses," USA TODAY, January 22, 2014; Jo Ingles, *Ohio Delays Joining Real ID Because of Concerns of Federal Overreach*, 89.7 KWSU, December 9, 2013, available at http://www.wksu.org/news/story/37638.

27  Michael Csere, ISSUANCE OF DRIVER'S LICENSES TO UNDOCUMENTED IMMIGRANTS, CONNECTICUT OFFICE OF LEGISLATIVE RESEARCH 2013-R-0194 (Hartford, CT: 2013), available at http://www.cga.ct.gov/2013/rpt/2013-R-0194.htm.

28  Plyler v. Doe, 457 U.S. 202, 213 (1982).

29  Ala. Code § 31-13-27; Kevin R. Johnson, *Immigration and Civil Rights: Is the "New" Birmingham the Same as the "Old" Birmingham?*, 21 WM. & MARY BILL RTS. J. 367, 392 (2012).

30  Ala. Code § 31-13-2.

31  *Undocumented Student Tuition: Overview*, NAT'L CONFERENCE OF STATE LEGISLATURES (May 5, 2014) at http://www.ncsl.org/research/education/undocumented-student-tuition-overview.aspx; *Basic Facts about In-State Tuition for Undocumented Immigrant Students*, NATIONAL IMMIGRATION LAW CENTER (June 2014) at http://www.nilc.org/basic-facts-instate.html.

32  *Id.*

33  See, e.g., Lozano v. Hazleton, (3rd Cir. 2013) (discussing the city's Illegal Immigration Relief Act Ordinance, 2006–40); Gray v. City of Valley Park, 567 F.3d 976 (8th Cir. 2009) (upholding city Ordinance 1722 that prohibits business entities within the city from knowingly employing unauthorized aliens).

34  Hazleton, Pa., Ordinance 2006–18 (Sept. 21, 2006), available at https://www.aclu.org/files/pdfs/immigrants/hazleton_secondordinance.pdf; Farmers Branch, Tex., Ordinance 2903 (Jan. 22, 2007), available at http://www.americanbar.org/content/dam/aba/publishing/insights_law_society/news4.authcheckdam.pdf; Fremont, Ne., Ordinance 5165 (June 21, 2010), available at http://www.fremontne.gov/DocumentCenter/Home/View/770; Escondido, California Ordinance No. 2006–38R, An Ordinance Establishing Penalties For the Harboring of Illegal

Aliens in the City of Escondido (Oct. 18, 2006) available at http://www.cooley.com/ Escondido.

35  Colorado SB 90, Colo. Rev. Stat. § 29-29-101, et. seq. The law required local enforcement officers to report suspected undocumented immigrants to federal authorities, prohibited towns and localities from enacting "sanctuary" ordinances, and provided for financial penalties against local law enforcement agencies that failed to comply with the law. After significant controversy over its costs and efficacy, the law was repealed in April 2013. See, e.g., Kathy A. White and Lucy Dwight, *Misplaced Priorities: SB 90 & the Costs to Local Communities, A Report for the Colorado Center on Law and Policy,* Dec. 1, 2012; "Colorado Repeals Its Immigration Law," *Fox News Latino,* Apr. 27, 2013.

36  Harriet McLeod, "South Carolina, Rights Groups Settle Immigration Law Challenge," REUTERS, Mar. 3, 2014, available at http://www.reuters.com/ article/2014/03/04/us-southcarolina-immigration-idUSBREA2305220140304; Michael McNutt, "Oklahoma House Passes Anti-illegal Immigrant Bill," NEWSOK, Mar. 11, 2011 available at http://newsok.com/anti-illegal-immigrant-bill-passes-house/article/3547553; "Groups Seek Injunction against Alabama Immigration Law," *Fox News Latino,* July 22, 2011 at http://latino.foxnews.com/ latino/news/2011/07/21/groups-seek-injunction-against-alabama-immigration-law/; Patrik Jonson, "Far from Mexican Border, Georgia Mulls Arizona-Style Immigration Crackdown," CHRISTIAN SCIENCE MONITOR, Apr. 14, 2011 *at* http://www.csmonitor .com/USA/Politics/2011/0414/Far-from-Mexican-border-Georgia-mulls-Arizona-style-immigration-crackdown.

37  S.B. 1070, § 1, 49th Leg., 2d Reg. Sess. (Ariz. 2010), *enjoined in part by* Arizona v. United States, 132 S. Ct. 2492 (2012).

38  The "anti-harboring" section of the law was eventually declared unconstitutional by a federal court, and in 2014, the Supreme Court refused to hear an appeal from the decision of the lower court in that case. See Valle del Sol v. Whiting, CV 10-1061-PHX-SRB, 2012 WL 8021265 (D. Ariz. Sept. 5, 2012) *aff'd sub nom.,* Valle del Sol Inc. v. Whiting, 732 F.3d 1006 (9th Cir. 2013) (upholding trial court decision) *cert. denied,* 134 S. Ct. 1876 (2014).

39  S.B. 1070, §§ 2(B) (Ariz. 2010).

40  *Id.* at § 6.

41  *Id.* at § 3.

42  *Id.* at §§ 5(C).

43  The Beason-Hammon Alabama Taxpayer and Citizen Protection Act, H.B. 56, § 2 (2011).

44  H.B. 56 § 27(a).

45  H.B. 56 §§ 8 and 28.

46  THE NEW AMERICANS: ECONOMIC, DEMOGRAPHIC, AND FISCAL EFFECTS OF IMMIGRATION, (James P. Smith and Barry Edmonston, eds., 1997). CE: Washington, DC, National Academies Press.

47  Cristina Rodriguez, *The Significance of the Local in Immigration Regulation,* 106 MICH. L. REV. 567, 609 (2008).

48  Clare Huntington, *The Constitutional Dimension of Immigration Federalism,* 61 *Vand. L. Rev.* ("[M]ore punitive immigration measures often, although not always, are enacted in areas new to receiving significant populations of non-citizens.") 806 (2008).

49 Jill   Esbenshade. Division and Dislocation: Regulating Immigration through Local Housing Ordinances. Washington DC: Immigration Policy Center, American Immigration Council (2007).

50 See, e.g., Alex Kotlowitz, "Our Town," *New York Times*, N.Y. Times Magazine, August 5, 2007.

51 Ben Casselman, *Immigration Is Changing Much More Than the Immigration Debate*, FiveThirtyEight, July 9, 2014 ("[P]eople experience immigration on a local, not a national, level. And immigration, including undocumented immigration, is spreading to parts of the country where it was relatively rare just a few years ago.") available    at   http://fivethirtyeight.com/features/immigration-is-changing-much-more-than-the-immigration-debate/.

52 See Peter Skerry, *Many Borders to Cross: Is immigration the Exclusive Responsibility of the Federal Government?*, 25 Publius at 2 (1995); "California Sues U.S. Government over Costs Tied to Illegal Aliens," N.Y. *Times*, May 1, 1994; Pete Wilson, "Securing Our Nation's Borders," *The Social Contract* (1994).

53 Gov. Janet Napolitano, Statements in Press Release accompanying signing of the Legal Arizona Workers Act, H.B. 2779 (July 2, 2007) available at http://jurist.org/paperchase/2007/07/arizona-governor-signs-tough-sanctions.php.

54 8 U.S.C. §§ 1101, et. seq. (defining, inter alia, the class of persons who are unlawfully present, and the process and standards for their discovery and removal).

55 Statement by Governor Jan Brewer on the signing of Senate Bill 1070, Apr. 23, 2010, available at http://newamericamedia.org/2010/04/statement-by-governor-jan-brewer-signing-senate-bill-1070.php; *see also*, Press Release, State of Arizona Executive Office of Janet Napolitano Governor, *Governor Signs Employer Sanctions Bill* (July 2, 2007) ("Immigration is a federal responsibility, but I signed HB 2779 because it is now abundantly clear that Congress finds itself incapable of coping with the comprehensive immigration reforms our country needs.").

56 U.S. Office of the White House. *Remarks by the President on Comprehensive Immigration    Reform.*   http://www.whitehouse.gov/photos-and-video/video/president-obama-comprehensive-immigration-reform#transcript.

57 See, e.g., Statement of Hon. Louis Barletta, Mayor, City of Hazelton, Pa., Comprehensive Immigration Reform: Examining the Need for a Guest Worker Program: Hearing Before the S. Comm. on the Judiciary, 109th Cong. 11–13 (2006).

58 *See* Hazelton, PA City Ordinance 2006–18, "City of Hazleton Illegal Immigration Relief Act Ordinance." The subsequent litigation challenging the ordinance, however, resulted in enjoinment of the law. Lozano v. City of Hazleton (3d Cir. 2010) 620 F.3d 170 *cert. granted*, judgment vacated sub nom. (U.S. 2011) 131 S.Ct. 2958. The U.S. Supreme Court forestalled a final decision on the case by remanding it to the federal appeals court for consideration in light of the Court's recent decision in Chamber of Commerce v. Whiting, 131 S.Ct. 1968 (2011). *See* City of Hazleton, Pa. v. Lozano (2011) 131 S.Ct. 2958. In Whiting, the Court upheld an Arizona law requiring businesses in the state to verify the legal status of their employees. *See* Whiting, 131 S.Ct. 1968, 1985–86.

59 Paul Vitello, "As Illegal Workers Hit Suburbs, Politicians Scramble to Respond," New York Times, October 6, 2005; Bob Dart, "Minutemen Shadow Town's Day Labor Site," Atlanta Journal-Constitution, April 6, 2006.

60 Audrey Singer, *"The Rise of New Immigrant Gateways."* BROOKINGS INSTITUTION (2004).

61 Els de Graauw et al., *Funding Immigrant Organizations: Suburban Free Riding and Local Civic Presence*, AM. J. OF SOCIOLOGY, VOL. 119, NO. 1, Oct. 11, 2013 pp. 75–130, http://www.jstor.org/stable/10.1086/671168?origin=JSTOR-pdf; Charles T. Clotfelter, Helen F. Ladd, and Jacob L. Vigdor, *New Destinations, New Trajectories? The Educational Progress of Hispanic Youth in North Carolina*, 83 CHILD DEV., Sept. 11, 2012 available at http://onlinelibrary.wiley.com/doi/10.1111/ j.1467-8624.2012.01797.x/abstract; Audrey Singer, Susan Wiley Hardwick, and Caroline Brettell, TWENTY-FIRST CENTURY GATEWAYS: IMMIGRANT INCORPORATION IN SUBURBAN AMERICA (Brookings Institution Press, 2008).

62 A significant difference between our study here and prior academic explorations of the subnational immigration regulation phenomenon is our insistence in expanding the data set of municipalities and states as broadly as possible. Here, we do not rely on isolated comparisons between selected places to draw broad conclusions. Indeed, given the number of potentially competing explanations, we cannot rely on a few case studies to explicate the relative importance of each – in statistical parlance, we would confront a "degrees of freedom" problem, where the number of potentially explanatory factors exceed the number of cases being explained. Thus we have created databases of state and municipal legislation and enriched them with other contextual data.

63 Huntington, *Immigration Federalism*, 61 Vand. L. Rev. 787.

64 *See, e.g.*, Brewer, Statement on S.B. 1070, *supra* note 102 ("We in Arizona have been more than patient waiting for Washington to act. But decades of federal inaction … have created a dangerous and unacceptable situation."); Kim Chandler, *Immigration Law Sponsors Say Issue Isn't Going Away; Opponents Say It's Time for Alabama to "Move On,"* AL.COM (Apr. 29, 2013, 6:05 PM), http://blog.al.com/ wire/2013/04/alabama_immigration_law_sponso.html (discussing a statement made by Republican State Senator Scott Beason contending that "[t]he reason we have this problem is the federal government will not do its job"); Valerie Richardson, *"Arizona's AG: Court's Ruling Is 'A 70% Win,'"* WASH. TIMES, June 25, 2012, at A4 (citing a remark by Democratic U.S. Senate candidate Richard Carmona that "SB 1070 is the product of the federal government's failure to act").

65 Pub. L. No. 104–208, 110 Stat. 3009–546, 575–92 (1996) (expanding grounds for removal, reducing judicial review of removal, reducing opportunities to seek relief from removal, and expanding list of offenses with mandatory immigration detention).

66 Pub. L. No. 104–132, 110 Stat. 1214, 1273–77 (1996) (requiring the mandatory detention of noncitizens convicted of a range of offenses).

67 Pub. L. No. 104–193, 110 Stat. 2105, 2260–70 (1996) (limiting eligibility of noncitizens for federal public benefits and purporting to authorize states to similarly restrict noncitizens' access to certain public benefits).

68 Arizona v. United States, 132 S. Ct. 2492, 2522 (2012) (Scalia, J., concurring in part and dissenting in part) (referencing Arizona's argument that the federal enforcement efforts over the last decade had left Arizona's border comparatively neglected).

69 We discuss the relevant evidence and analysis later in this chapter.

70 Authors' analysis of American Community Survey 5-year file 2005–9.

71 "NCSL 2011 Report on State Immigration Laws," NATIONAL CONFERENCE OF STATE LEGISLATORS, available at http://www.ncsl.org/default.aspx?TabId=23960.

72 *Id.*

73 Alex Kotlowitz, "Our Town," NEW YORK TIMES MAGAZINE, August 5, 2007.

74 We use "recent immigrants" as a proxy measure for the likelihood of a high unauthorized migrant population. It is not possible to attain accurate data on numbers of unauthorized migrants in most municipalities, but we expect recent immigrants to be composed of a high percentage of unauthorized migrants. In addition, using this broader description accounts for the "new destinations" trope in current restrictionist discourse.

75 Karthick Ramakrishnan and Paul Lewis, *Immigrants and Local Governance: The View from City Hall*, PUBLIC POLICY INSTITUTE OF CALIFORNIA (2005).

76 Samuel P. Huntington, *The Hispanic Challenge*, 141 FOREIGN POL'Y, 30, 30–45 (2004).

77 Figures on the foreign-born proportion of Latino adults and adult citizens are derived from the 2008 Current Population Survey Voter Supplement. Latino voter opinion on immigration has been shown to be consistently for legalization, and against enforcement, in surveys by the Pew Hispanic Center and by Latino Decisions. Mark Hugo Lopez and Susan Minushkin, *Hispanics See Their Situation in U.S. Deteriorating; Oppose Key Immigration Enforcement Measures*, PEW HISPANIC CENTER, (Sept. 18, 2009), http://www.pewhispanic.org/2008/09 /18/2008-national-survey-of-latinos-hispanics-see-their-situation-in-us-deteriorati ng-oppose-key-immigration-enforcement-measures/; Sylvia Manzano, *One Year after SB1070: Why Immigration Will Not Go Away*, LATINO DECISIONS, May 9, 2011, http://latinodecisions.wordpress.com/2011/05/09/one-year-after-sb1070-why-immigration-will-not-go-away/.

78 Manzano, *op. cit.* (Latino Decisions tracking poll results from April 2011).

79 George Borjas, "Immigrants In, Wages Down," NATIONAL REVIEW, April 25 2006.

80 Claudine Gay, *Seeing Difference: The Effect of Economic Disparity on Black Attitudes toward Latinos*, 50 AM. J. POL. SCI., NO. 4, 982–97 (October 2006). (finds that African Americans who live in places "where Latinos are materially better off than blacks harbor more negative stereotypes about the group.").

81 We are aware, of course, that state preemption of local ordinances may occur and that our hypotheses and conclusions on this factor must be constrained by that possibility. Localities may sometimes be limited in their policy-making activity by state laws that expressly preclude or require local participation. Two important recent examples in California are AB1236 (2011), which prohibits localities from mandating that businesses use E-verify as a condition of licensing or government contracts, and AB976 (2007), which prohibits localities from passing ordinances that require landlords to verify the immigration status of their tenants. We will examine intrastate immigration dynamics in future research.

82 See, e.g., Heather Gerken, *Federalism All the Way Down*, 124 HARV. L. REV. 4, 24 (2009) ("Zoning commissions and school communities ... often feature robust rates of local participation and influence the basic building blocks of our communal life.").

83 The restrictive ordinances in our sample include measures whereby local governments use their official capacities to enforce federal immigration laws or to
address perceived negative societal consequences of illegal immigration. Illegal
Immigration Relief Act (IIRA) ordinances and variants of them constitute the
majority of these restrictive measures. IIRAs commonly refer to the fiscal and
governance challenges arising from the presence of illegal immigrants. The
pro-immigrant ordinances in our sample include resolutions and mandates that
express opposition to immigration raids and restrictionist national legislation, those
barring the use of public funds to enforce immigration laws, and those with explicit
"sanctuary" policies whereby local officials do not inquire about legal status and do
not notify immigration authorities about the status of individuals unless they are
convicted of serious crimes.

84 We use CLARIFY to simulate the effects on the dependent variable of changes in
each individual variable while holding other variables at their means. *See* Michael
Tomz, Jason Wittenberg, and Gary King, *CLARIFY: Software for Interpreting and
Presenting Statistical Results*, 8 JOURNAL OF STATISTICAL SOFTWARE 1–30 (2003).

85 S. Karthick Ramakrishnan and Paul G. Lewis, IMMIGRANTS AND LOCAL
GOVERNANCE: THE VIEW FROM CITY HALL, SAN FRANCISCO, CA: PUBLIC
POLICY INSTITUTE OF CALIFORNIA (2005).

86 Cf. Michael Mintrom, *Policy Entrepreneurs and the Diffusion of Innovation*, 41 AM.
J. POL. SCI. 738, 765 (1997) (noting the effects of strong union opposition).

87 When we break down the factor of city size further, into small, medium, and large
cities (with populations of up to 50,000; from 50,001 to 200,000; and greater than
200,000, respectively), we find that restrictive ordinances are most likely to be
found in medium-sized cities.

88 Alternatively, it could reflect measurement error in our data, where proposed legislation is less likely to gain media coverage and the attention of advocacy groups.
Given the limitations of publicly available data, we are not able to adjudicate
between these differences.

89 2007 ENACTED STATE LEGISLATION RELATED TO IMMIGRANTS AND IMMIGRATION,
NATIONAL CONFERENCE OF STATE LEGISLATURES, 2–34 (rev. Jan. 31, 2008),
http://www.ncsl.org/print/immig/2007Immigrationfinal.pdf.

90 The legislative summaries were coded on an ordinal scale of 1:"low impact" and
2:"high impact" on immigrant rights and/or access to benefits, based on the provision's likely effects on immigrant life chances and the number of immigrants likely
to be affected.

91 Past research on local government policies toward immigrant integration indicates
that the ideological and partisan leanings of governing institutions and the electorate play important roles in motivating immigration policy. For instance, in a 2003
survey of more than 300 California cities, Ramakrishnan and Lewis found that
municipal governments with Republican-leaning electorates and conservative city
councils were less likely to provide translation of city hall documents and interpretation services in public meetings. While much of the municipal legislative
attempts in 2006 and 2007 focused on restrictive measures instead of outreach to
immigrant residents, we believe that partisanship at the local level would still have
played a significant role – albeit in the direction of promoting restrictive measures
instead of hindering permissive ones.

92 We use two different measures of partisanship for the state and local levels. At the state level, we are able to obtain the kind of partisanship that is perhaps most relevant for legislation, namely the proportional strength of Republicans in the legislature. In some instances, the partisanship of the electorate varies from party control of the legislature, so we also obtain an alternate measure of party support based on the state's vote share of the prior presidential election. At the municipal level, many jurisdictions have nonpartisan elections, and we do not have comprehensive and reliable data on party control in places that have partisan local elections. Thus, we use county-level data from the presidential election, allowing us to identify municipalities in "Republican areas" and "Democratic areas." Using this right-left measure presents two challenges: First, while it would be ideal to also include measures of party registration, such data are not readily available across states (and, indeed, are not public information in several states). Nevertheless, given the relatively high correlation between Democrat-Republican party identification and presidential vote choice, the latter can serve as an adequate measure of partisanship at the local level. The second challenge is that we are using information on "proportion Republican" at the county level but information on ordinances at the municipality level. The error associated with this measure is related to a municipality's share of the county population. We ran an alternative, weighted least squares model based on the municipality's share of the total county population. This correction for heteroskedasticity does not invalidate findings regarding the significance of partisanship at the local level.

93 These are based on our data collection, which we describe in Appendix A.

94 State party registration data obtained from the California Secretary of State (https://www.sos.ca.gov/elections/ror/ror-pages/15day-gen-06/hist-reg-stats.pdf). Local party registration data for municipalities obtained from the firm Aristotle, Inc.

95 Phil Willon, "Conservative Inland Empire Cities Crack down on Illegal Workers," *Los Angeles Times*, February 14, 2011.

96 This was evident in Arizona as far back as 2004 and 2006, as long-standing Republican incumbents such as Congressman Jim Kolbe faced competitive primary elections by challengers focusing on immigration and border-control issues. *See* Joseph Lelyveld, "The Border Dividing Arizona," *New York Times*, October 15, 2006.

97 We report findings based on the partisanship of electorates in order to provide a comparable basis of comparison to our local partisanship measures. The results on partisanship are similar when using measures of party control of the state legislature.

98 We utilize a resource available via FindLaw that summarizes current state-level policies and code it on the same restrictive to permissive scale (low to high) as in our analysis of enacted legislation in the 2005–2007 period. State Immigration Laws, *FindLaw*, http://immigration.findlaw.com/immigration-laws-and-resources/state-immigration-laws/. Data is current as of December 31, 2011.

99 These figures are means (averages). The corresponding median figures are 1.72% for restrictive ordinance cities, and 0.16% for cities in the nation as a whole.

100 Local party registration data for municipalities obtained from the voter statistics firm Aristotle, Inc.

101 This compares to 57% of states with a Republican majority of voters in 2004.

## CHAPTER 4

1 Laura Sullivan, *Prison Economics Helped Drive Immigration Law*, Morning *Edition* (2010) October 28, 2010. Notably, NPR has retracted one of the central claims made in the piece regarding the role of the Corrections Corporation of America. http://www.npr.org/2010/10/28/130833741/prison-economics-help-drive-ariz-immigration-law.

2 Martin Luther King III & Richard Trumka, *Alabama's Immigration Law: Jim Crow Revisited*, CNN.COM, 2011, http://www.cnn.com/2011/11/17/opinion/trumka-king-civil-rights-alabama/index.html (last visited Feb 23, 2012).

3 Daniel Gonzalez, "SB 1070 Backlash Spurs Hispanics to Join Democrats," THE ARIZONA REPUBLIC, June 8, 2010. ("Arizona is different [from California] in that … the Latino vote is lower, about 12 percent versus 21 percent.")

4 Michael Mintrom, *Policy Entrepreneurs and the Diffusion of Innovation*, 41 AM J. POL. SCI. 738, 765–66 (1997); Cass R. Sunstein and Timur Kuran, *Availability Cascades and Risk Regulation*, 51 STAN. L. REV. 683 (1999); Catherine L. Carpenter, *Legislative Epidemics: A Cautionary Tale*, 58 BUFF. L. REV. 1.

5 John W. Kingdon, AGENDAS, ALTERNATIVES, AND PUBLIC POLICIES. (1984); Frank Baumgartner AND Bryan D. Jones, AGENDAS AND INSTABILITY IN AMERICAN POLITICS (1993).

6 Sunstein and Kuran, *Availability Cascades and Risk Regulation*, 51 STAN. L. REV. 683 (1999).

7 Judith Resnick, Federalism(s) Forms and Norms: Contesting Rights, Deessentializing Jurisdictional Divides, and Temporizing Accomodations, in NOMOS LV: FEDERALISM & SUBSIDIARITY (James Fleming, Ed., NYU 2014); Orbach et al. *Arming States' Rights: Federalism, Private Lawmakers, and the Battering Ram Strategy*, 52 ARIZ. L. REV. 1161 (2010).

8 Jessica Bulman-Pozen, Partisan Federalism, 127 Harv. L. rev. 1077 (2014); Larry D. Kramer, *Putting the Politics Back into the Political Safeguards of Federalism*, 100 COLUM L. REV. 215 (2000).

9 Larry D. Kramer, *Understanding Federalism*, 47 Vand. L. Rev. 1485, 1528 (1994); Larry K. Kramer, *Putting the Politics Back into the Political Safeguards of Federalism*, 100 COLUM. L. REV. 215 (2000); Laura Meckler, The GOP's Immigration Dilemma, Wall St. J., Feb. 26, 2013 ("For House Republicans, the issue is particularly treacherous. Attracting Hispanic votes is an imperative for presidential candidates, but most House Republicans represent overwhelmingly white districts safely in GOP hands; the most serious political threat they will face is a primary challenge from someone more conservative.").

10 Kramer, *Understanding Federalism*, 47 VAND. L. REV. at 1528. To be clear, we are adopting Kramer's observations about the structural and institutional ties between subfederal and federal political processes, which are influenced heavily by party affiliation. We do not adopt his understanding of the nature of political parties themselves, which Kramer argues are nonideological or constructed for the primary purpose of winning elections. Indeed, our work suggests that at least on some issues – including immigration – it is precisely the ideological cohesiveness of the party platform that helps coerce connectedness between national and subnational

lawmakers. See also, Jessica Bulman-Pozen, *Partisan Federalism*, 127 HARV. L. REV. 1077 (2014) (also critiquing Kramer's view of parties).

11 Kramer, Understanding Federalism, 47 Vand. at 1528; Kramer, *Putting the Politics Back*, 100 COLUM. L. REV. 215.

12 Kramer, *Putting the Politics Back*, 100 COLUM. L. REV. 215; see Meckler, "The GOP's Immigration Dilemma," *Wall St. J.*, Feb. 26, 2013; see also Cristina Rodriguez, *Negotiating Conflict through Federalism: Institutional and Popular Perspectives*, 123 YALE L. J. 2094 (2014) (noting that federalism provides opportunities for realization of personal ambition for state and local politicians).

13 Joseph Lelyveld, "The Border Dividing Arizona," *N.Y. Times Mag.*, Oct. 15, 2006 (discussing challenge to GOP Congressman Jim Kolbe in his primary campaign from challengers focusing on immigration and border issues).

14 See Rodriguez, *Negotiating Conflict through Federalism*, 123 YALE L.J. at 2120 (noting that subfederal actors "traffic" in the rhetoric of federal failure).

15 Sunstein and Kuran, *Availability Cascades*, 51 STAN. L. REV. 683 (arguing that cognitive biases – like susceptibility to availability cascades, in which limited, available information becomes dominant and accepted – that affect officials and those advocating for change can lead to suboptimal policy outcomes); Cindy D. Kam and Robert A. Mikos, *Do Citizens Care about Federalism? An Experimental Test*, 4 J. EMP. L. STUDIES 589 (arguing that framing of problems by "elites" affects how citizenry views a problem and its solution).

16 Mintrom, *Policy Entrepreneurs*, 41 AM. J. POL. SCI. 738; Sunstein and Kuran *Availability Cascades*, 51 STAN. L. REV. 683.

17 Resnik, Federalism(s) Forms and Norms 364–370.

18 The extent to which parties can prevent "strange bedfellow" coalitions depends, to some extent, on whether the issue at hand has one dimension on which parties can differentiate, or two dimensions that typically lead to instability in decisionmaking (Daniel Tichenor, DIVIDING LINES, 2002). On issues of low public salience, such as tax policy, congressional logrolls along committee lines and interest group access can play more prominent roles (R. Douglas Arnold, THE LOGIC OF CONGRESSIONAL ACTION (1990).

19 John W. Kingdon, AGENDAS, ALTERNATIVES, AND PUBLIC POLICIES. (1984).

20 Our counterfactual analysis suggests that without the work of these vital actors, the immigration landscape – both nationally and subnationally – would appear drastically different. That is, without these actors, we would expect to have passed comprehensive immigration reform, and decreases in subnational immigration policymaking.

21 Sunstein and Kuran, *Availability Cascades*, 51 STAN. L. REV. at 687 (describing social agents who understand availability heuristics and attempt to trigger availability cascades to achieve policy goals); Michael Mintron, *Policy Entrepreneurs and the Diffusion of Innovation*, 41 AM. J. POL. SCI. 738, 739 (1997) (identifying policy entrepreneurs as a class of policy actors who seek dynamic policy change, and noting that policies are more likely to be considered and approved when such actors are present); Roderick M. Hills, 82 N.Y.U. L. REV. 1, 21 (2007); Heather K. Gerken, *Federalism All the Way Down*, 124 HARV. L. REV. 4, 17 (2010); Eric Talley, *Precedential Cascades*, 73 S. CAL. L. REV. 87, 90 (1999) (describing persons who are eager to exploit group pathologies to achieve an end); Harold H. Koh,

*Bringing International Law Home*, 35 Hous. L. Rev. 623 (1998) (describing the influence of norm entrepreneurs in changing domestic attitudes about equality); Barak Y. Orbach et al., *Arming States Rights: Federalism, Private Lawmakers, and the Battering Ram Strategy*, 52 Ariz. L. Rev. 1161, 1163 (2010) (discussing the work of private lawmakers who use gun rights as a policy vehicle to effect a broader states' rights platform). Indeed, even the use of the term "entrepreneur" to describe that population has been prominent in the literature. Both legal and political science commentators have identified the work and importance of "availability entrepreneurs," "policy entrepreneurs," "political entrepreneurs," "social entrepreneurs," "norm entrepreneurs," and "private lawmakers" in galvanizing lawmaking; Judith Resnik, Federalism(s) Forms and Norms, in NOMOS LV (NYU Press 2014); Judith Resnik et al., *Ratifying Kyoto at the Local Level: Sovereigntism, Federalism, and Translocal Organizations of Government Actors (TOGAs)*, 50 Ariz. L. Rev. 709 (2008).

22 *See, e.g.*, Mintron, *Policy Entrepreneurs*, 41 Am. J. Pol. Sci. at 739–41; Orbach et al., *Private Lawmakers*, 52 Ariz. L. Rev. at 1167; Sunstein and Kuran, *Availability Cascades*, 51 Stan. L. Rev. at 714.

23 Orbach et al., 52 Ariz. L. Rev. at 1163 (noting that federal policies in immigration are prime targets for private lawmakers) and at 1166 (identifying former law professor, and now elected official, Kris Kobach as a private lawmaker in the immigration field).

24 See, e.g., Hills, *Against Preemption*, 82 N.Y.U. L. Rev. at 36 ("Few with influence in the political process care about promoting state power as an end in itself."); *Contra* Orbach et al., *Private Lawmakers*, 52 Ariz. L. Rev. at 1170, 1178 (arguing that private lawmakers in the gun rights area use those laws as a way to return the Supreme Court to a pre–New Deal congressional power jurisprudence).

25 The Immigration Reform Law Institute, the legal arm of the Federation for American Immigration Reform, challenged the provision of in-state tuition for unauthorized immigrant students [David Savage, "Justices Allow Tuition Deals for Illegal Residents," South Florida Sun-Sentinel, June 7, 2011] and municipal identification cards for all city residents regardless of their immigration status [John Coté, "Judge Rules for ID Cards", San Francisco Chronicle, September 15, 2008].

26 Cristina Rodriguez, *Law and Borders*, Democracy: A Journal of Ideas (Summer 2014).

27 Cindy D. Kam and Robert A. Mikos, *Do Citizens Care about Federalism? An Experimental Test*, 4 J. Emp. L. Studies 589, 592–601 (2007).

28 Cf. Id. at 601 (noting that the federalism rhetoric of politicians is salient in influencing voter attitudes toward federal legislation).

29 Pew Research Center, Illegal Immigration: Gaps Between and Within Parties, December 6, 2011, http://www.people-press.org/2011/12/06/illegal-immigration-gaps-between-and-within-parties/.

30 Peter J. Spiro, "Be Careful What You Wish For," N.Y. *Times*, Room for Debate, Oct. 4, 2011 (arguing that Alabama's law, driving out immigrants, will force the state to learn the importance of immigrants to its economic well-being); Patrik Jonsson, "Why Republicans Are Doing an About-Face on Tough Alabama Immigration Law," The Christian Science Monitor, November 16, 2011, available at,

http://www.csmonitor.com/USA/Politics/2011/1116/Why-Republicans-are-doing-an
-about-face-on-tough-Alabama-immigration-law; ("Prof. Samuel Addy at the Center
for Business and Economic Research at the University of Alabama recently predicted that HB 56 will reduce the Alabama economy by $40 million as income and
spending by both illegal and legal Hispanic immigrants will decline. What's more,
employers face troves of fresh paperwork and licensing requirements to comply with
the law that they say will potentially hurt business."); PBS Newshour, Alabama's
Immigration Law: Assessing the Economic, Social Impact, transcript, Oct. 13, 2011,
http://www.pbs.org/newshour/bb/business/july-dec11/alimmigration_10-13.html.

31  Ruben G. Rumbaut et al., _Debunking the Myth of Immigrant Criminality:_
_Imprisonment among First- and Second-Generation Young Men_, MIGRATION
INFORMATION SOURCE (June 2006) available at http://www.migrationinformation
.org/Feature/display.cfm?id=403.

32  Randal C. Archibold, "On Border Violence, Truth Pales Compared to Ideas,"
_NEW YORK TIMES_, June 19, 2010).

33  _Cf._ Sunstein and Kuran, 51 STAN. L. REV. at 714 (noting that the objectively
weaker side may triumph by exploiting cognitive biases); Catherine L. Carpenter,
_Legislative Epidemics: A Cautionary Tale_, 58 BUFF. L. REV. 1, 37, 56 (2010).

34  Carpenter, 58 BUFF. L. REV. at 29.

35  Hills, _Against Preemption_, 82 N.Y.U. L. REV. at 21 ("State and local politicians,
however, are natural policy entrepreneurs who can significantly influence what
sorts of conditions are publicly recognized as problems.... The entrepreneur can
transform a social condition that everyone has taken for granted into a problem that
must be addressed by recategorizing the issue and offering different comparisons
for judging whether the issue is being acceptably handled.").

36  Carpenter, _Legislative Epidemics_, 58 BUFF. L. REV. at 40.

37  Mintrom, _Policy Entrepreneurs_, 41 AM. J. POL. SCI. at 739, 760.

38  _Immigration Challenge: September 6, 2001_, NEWSHOUR WITH JIM LEHRER, Sept.
6, 2001 (Representative Tancredo discussing his opposition to various aspects of
then-proposed immigration reforms).

39  Carl Hulse and Jim Rutenberg, "Bush Faces Resistance on Immigration," N.Y.
_TIMES_, May 17, 2006; _Lou Dobbs Tonight_ June 5, 2007, CNN transcripts.

40  M. E. Sprengelmeyer, "Debate on Immigration Bill in Congress Pleases Tancredo
after Years of Pushing the Issue: Littleton Republican Has Ear of GOP Leadership,"
DENV. ROCKY MTN. NEWS, Dec. 16, 2005 (On Thursday [during a House vote on
Rep. Sensenbrenner's employment verification bill], [Tancredo] had a direct line
to Republican leadership because without the support of his hard-line immigration
caucus, it was unlikely they could pass anything to appease an increasingly vocal
part of the Republican base.").

41  Jeff Zeleny, "THE 2008 CAMPAIGN – Rep. Tancredo of Colorado Enters G.O.P.
Presidential Race," N.Y. _TIMES_, April 3, 2007 ("His intention is to force other
Republican candidates, particularly Senator John McCain of Arizona, former
Gov. Mitt Romney of Massachusetts and former Mayor Rudolph W. Giuliani of
New York, to address illegal immigration.")

42  H.AMDT.294, Bill Summary & Status – 110th Congress (2007–2008), THE
LIBRARY OF CONGRESS (THOMAS), http://thomas.loc.gov/cgi-bin/bdquery/
z?d110:HZ294: (last visited Jan 4, 2012).

43 Beverly Wang, "Tancredo Targets New Hampshire 'Sanctuary State' Bill," THE DENVER POST, September 5, 2007.

44 H.RES.839.IH, Bill Text – 109th Congress (2005–2006), THE LIBRARY OF CONGRESS (THOMAS), http://thomas.loc.gov/cgi-bin/query/z?c109:H.RES.839:

45 US Fed News Service, Including US State News, *Lawmakers Introduce All-Encompassing National Security Begins at Home Illegal Immigration Reform Package*, High Beam Research, March 21, 2007, http://www.highbeam.com/doc/1P3-1346939381.html.

46 Luige del Puerto, "Tancredo Forms Group Opposing Pearce Recall," ARIZONA CAPITOL TIMES, July 25, 2011. (Tancredo's Team America PAC, whose singular focus is on eliminating illegal immigration to the United States, set up a fundraising committee in 2011 to defend Russell Pearce, Arizona State Senator and chief architect of the state's SB 1070 law); Gary Nelson, "Pearce Basks in Adulation at Rally," THE ARIZONA REPUBLIC, October 17, 2011.

47 Résumé of Kris Kobach, Kansas Secretary of State: http://www.kssos.org/forms/administration/Kobach_Bio_Resume.pdf.

48 Eric Schmitt, "Administration Split on Local Role in Terror Fight," NEW YORK TIMES, April 29, 2002. ("Critics are also upset that Mr. Ashcroft have given ... Kobach a leading role in developing the delicate policy even though Mr. Kobach, 36, is only a White House Fellow on temporary assignment to the Justice Department this year."). A 2002 Office of Legal Counsel Memorandum advances the position taken by Kobach. Memorandum from Jay S. Bybee, Ass't Attorney Gen., U.S. Dep't of Justice, to John Ashcrosft, Attorney Gen., U.S. Dep't of Justice, Non-Preemption of the Authority of State and Local Law Enforcement Officials to Arrest Aliens for Immigration Violations, Apr. 3, 2002.

49 Kris W. Kobach, *Reinforcing the Rule of Law: What States Can and Should Do to Reduce Illegal Immigration*, 22 GEORGETOWN IMMIGRATION L. REV. (2008); Kris W. Kobach, *Attrition through Enforcement: A Rational Approach to Illegal Immigration*, 15 TULSA J. OF COMP. & INT. L. (2008); Kris W. Kobach, *Immigration, Amnesty, and the Rule of Law*, 36 HOFSTRA L. REV. 1323 (2008); Kris W. Kobach, *The Quintessential Force Multiplier: The Inherent Authority of Local Police to Make Immigration Arrests*, 69 ALBANY L. REV. 179 (2005).

50 Kobach, *Immigration Amnesty and the Rule of Law*, 36 HOFSTRA L. REV. at 1324.

51 Kobach, *Immigration, Amnesty, and the Rule of Law*, 36 HOFSTRA L. REV. at 1326.

52 Kobach, *The Quintessential Force-Multipler*, 36 HOFSTRA L. REV. at 201–33 (making the doctrinal case for state and local immigration enforcement authority); Kobach, *Attrition through Enforcement*, 15 TULSA J. COMP. & INT. L. at 156–63 (arguing for more robust and comprehensive federal enforcement efforts to create self-deportation by undocumented persons).

53 Kent Jackson, "Top Court Gives City 2nd Chance," STANDARD SPEAKER, June 7, 2011, (noting that Kobach, attorney for Hazleton, was encouraged by the Supreme Court's Whiting decision, arguing that it "put Hazleton on very strong ground" for remand consideration in front of the Third Circuit).

54 See, for instance, the expanded scope of Alabama's HB 56 in 2011, which passed one year after Arizona's SB 1070. Ian Gomez, "States Make Daily Life Harder for Illegal Immigrants," USA TODAY, December 20, 2011.

55 George Talbot, "Kris Kobach, the Kansas Lawyer behind Alabama's Immigration Law," PRESS-REGISTER (Mobile, AL), October 16, 2011.

56 Indeed it is likely that a homegrown effort would have avoided post-enactment hand-wringing, and a vow by the Alabama Governor to revisit and amend the legislation to cure several economic and social issues it has created for the state.

57 Mitt Romney Press Release, *Mitt Romney Announces Support of Kansas Secretary of State Kris Kobach* (2012), http://www.presidency.ucsb.edu/ws/?pid=99028 ("Kris has been a true leader on securing our borders and stopping the flow of illegal immigration … I look forward to working with him to take forceful steps to curtail illegal immigration and to support states like South Carolina and Arizona that are stepping forward to address this problem.")

58 George Talbot, *op. cit.*

59 Mitt Romney Press, *op. cit.*

60 Robert Pear, "Little-Known Groups Claims a Win on Immigration," N.Y. TIMES, July 15, 2007; Nicole Gaouette, "Immigration Bill Ignites a Grass-Roots Fire on the Right: The Activist Group NumbersUSA May Be Getting Too Loud for Congress to Ignore," LOS ANGELES TIMES, June 24, 2007.

61 http://www.fairus.org/about (last visited April 23, 2015).

62 Paul Feldman, "Group's Funding of Immigration Measure Assailed," LOS ANGELES TIMES, September 10, 1994 ("When former federal immigration chief Nelson helped write the initiative last year, he was a Sacramento lobbyist for the Federation for American Immigration Reform, a national organization that advocates sealing the nation's borders and reducing immigration."). Note, however, that the ballot sponsors denied that the organization was directly involved.

63 Ibid. This view was reiterated in our author interview with FAIR senior staff member, March 2012 and author interview with Frank Sharry, America's Voice, April 2012.

64 Author interviews with FAIR senior staff member and Frank Sharry.

65 Interview with Frank Sharry, Executive Director of America's Voice (Apr. 12, 2012).

66 IRLI appealed the case of Martinez v. Board of Regents of the University of California to the U.S. Supreme Court, where it was dismissed. David Savage," Justices Allow Tuition Deals for Illegal Residents," SOUTH FLORIDA SUN-SENTINEL, June 7, 2011.

67 John Coté, "Judge Rules for ID Cards," SAN FRANCISCO CHRONICLE, Sept. 15, 2008.

68 See Roy Beck, THE CASE AGAINST IMMIGRATION (W.W. Norton 1996) (arguing that immigration adversely affects the U.S. labor market, the environment, and local community systems); NumbersUSA, About Us: Early History, available at http://www.numbersusa.com/content/learn/about/roy-beck-executive-director.html.

69 Jason Deparle, "The Anti-Immigration Crusader," NEW YORK TIMES, April 17, 2011.

70 Southern Poverty Law Center Intelligence Report, *The Puppeteer*, Vol. 106 (Summer 2002) ("The organized anti-immigration 'movement,' increasingly in bed with racist hate groups, is dominated by one man, John Tanton."); see also, Testimony of Roy Beck, House Immigration and Claims Subcommittee on the INS and EOIR, May 15, 2001.

71 Jason Deparle, *op. cit.* ("'One of my prime concerns,' [John Tanton] wrote to a large donor, 'is about the decline of folks who look like you and me.' He warned

a friend that 'for European-American society and culture to persist requires a European-American majority, and a clear one at that.'")

72 Robert Pear, "Little-Known Group Claims a Win on Immigration," New York Times, July 15, 2007.

73 Leonard Zeskind, "The New Nativism," The American Prospect, October 23, 2005.

74 Robert Pear, "Little-Known Group Claims a Win on Immigration," N.Y. Times, July 15, 2007 (quoting Frank Sharry, executive director of the national Immigration Forum as stating "Roy Beck takes people who are upset about illegal immigration for different reasons, including hostility to Latino immigrants, and disciplines them so their message is based on policy rather than race-based arguments or xenophobia."); see NumbersUSA.

75 Mallie Jane Kim, "After 9/11, Immigration Became About Homeland Security," U.S. News & World Report, September 8, 2011

76 Nicole Gaouette, "Immigration Bill Ignites a Grass-Roots Fire on the Right," Los Angeles Times, June 24, 2007.

77 Robert Pear, "Little-Known Group Claims a Win on Immigration," N.Y. Times, July 15, 2007.

78 Robert Pear, "Little-Known Group Claims a Win on Immigration," N.Y. Times, July 15, 2007.

79 The show was dubbed *Lou Dobbs Tonight* starting on June 9, 2003. We treat the inaugural year as June 9, 2003 to June 8, 2004.

80 Media Matters, *Fear & Loathing in Prime Time: Immigration Myths and Cable News* (May 21, 2008).

81 From 2004 to 2006, Sensenbrenner was covered in 119 shows, and the Minutemen were covered in 129 shows.

82 *Lou Dobbs Tonight*, May 4, 2007.

83 *Lou Dobbs Tonight*, May 4, 2007, available at http://transcripts.cnn.com/TRANSCRIPTS/0705/04/ldt.01.html (urging viewers to donate funds to subsidize Hazelton's legal defense of its immigration ordinance).

84 Erika Hayasaki, "Driver's License Plan Dropped," Los Angeles Times, Nov. 15, 2007.

85 Geoffrey C. Layman, Thomas M. Carsey, and Juliana Menasce Horowitz, *Party Polarization in American Politics: Characteristics, Causes, and Consequences*, 9 Annual Review of Political Science 83–110 (2006); Gary C Jacobson, *A Divider, Not a Uniter: George W. Bush and the American People: The 2006 Election and Beyond* (2008); Morris P. Fiorina and Samuel J. Abrams, *Political Polarization in the American Public*, 11 Annual Review of Political Science 563–88 (2008); Alan I. Abramowitz and Walter J. Stone, *The Bush Effect: Polarization, Turnout, and Activism in the 2004 Presidential Election*, 36 Presidential Studies Quarterly 141–54 (2006).

86 Thomas E. Mann and Norman J. Ornstein. It's Even Worse Than It Looks: How the American Constitutional System Collided with the New Politics of Extremism. New York: Basic Books, 2012.

87 Dale Krane, *The Middle Tier in American Federalism: State Government Policy Activism during the Bush Presidency*, 37 Publius 453 (July 2007).

88  H.R. 1: No Child Left Behind Act of 2001 passed in the House 384–45 and Senate
    91–8. See http://www.govtrack.us/congress/bill.xpd?bill=h107-1 (Summary of con-
    gressional voting for H.R. 1: No Child Left Behind Act of 2001).

89  H. J. Res. 114: Authorization for Use of Military Force Against Iraq Resolution of
    2002 passed the House 296–133 and Senate 77–23. See http://www.govtrack.us/
    congress/bill.xpd?bill=hj107-114 (summary of congressional voting for H. J. Res.
    114: Authorization for Use of Military Force Against Iraq Resolution of 2002).
    H.R. 1836: Economic Growth and Tax Relief Reconciliation Act of 2001 passed
    the House 230–197 and Senate 58–33. See http://www.govtrack.us/congress/bill
    .xpd?bill=h107-1836 (summary of congressional voting for H.R. 1836: Economic
    Growth and Tax Relief Reconciliation Act of 2001).

90  See http://www.govtrack.us/congress/vote.xpd?vote=h1986-872.

91  See http://www.govtrack.us/congress/vote.xpd?vote=s1996-108.

92  Eric Schmitt, "Two Amigos Visit Toledo and Court Its Mexicans," NEW YORK
    TIMES, Sept. 7, 2001.

93  Congressman Tancredo used various legislative maneuvers to force a two-thirds
    requirement that passed with one vote. See Robert Pear, "House Passes Immigrant
    Bill to Aid Mexico," New York Times, March 13, 2002.

94  Jason Deparle, "The Anti-Immigration Crusader," NEW YORK TIMES, April 17, 2011
    ("Numbers USA showed its force in 2002 when Republican leaders of the House
    backed a bill that would have allowed some illegal immigrants to remain in the
    United States while seeking legal status. Numbers USA set the phones on fire, and
    a majority of Republicans opposed it."I had people come up to me on the floor
    of the House saying, 'O.K., O.K., call off the dogs' – meaning Numbers USA,"
    said former Representative Tom Tancredo, a Colorado Republican who fought the
    bill.")

95  M.E. Sprengelmeyer, "Debate on Immigration Bill in Congress Pleases Tancredo
    after Years of Pushing the Issue: Littleton Republican Has Ear of GOP Leadership,"
    DENV. ROCKY MTN. NEWS, Dec. 16, 2005 (noting the necessity of GOP leadership
    taking heed of hard-line restrictionists because of the voting power of Tancredo's
    immigration caucus).

96  See, e.g., Hills, Against Preemption, 82 N.Y.U. L. REV. at 12 (The problem [of creat-
    ing national gridlock] is not that interest groups do not represent diffuse ideological
    interests. Rather, the problem is that nothing unifies these interests into coalitions
    capable of making policy."). To be clear, Hills expressly excluded immigration
    from his consideration, focusing instead on other regulatory areas. Our comments
    are orthogonal to his; not oppositional. We use this opportunity to showcase how
    some of the important considerations and theories one might defend with regard
    to federal legislation generally, may not neatly apply in the immigration context.

97  Victoria DeFrancesco Soto, "Strange Bedfellows in Arizona's Recall of
    Russell Pearce," DAILY GRITO, July 21, 2011, http://drvmds.com/2011/07/
    strange-bedfellows-in-arizona%E2%80%99s-recall-of-russell-pearce/ (Discussing
    coalition of Chamber of Commerce, the Church of Jesus Christ of Latter-day
    Saints and Latinos in opposition to SB 1070 and supporting recall of State Senator
    Russell Pearce).

98  Hills, Against Preemption, 82 N.Y.U. L. REV. at 12 ("[B]ecause enacting federal laws
    requires supermajorities to overcome presidential vetoes or senatorial filibusters, a

group of interests far smaller than a majority can block legislation.") (citing KEITH KREHBIEL, PIVOTAL POLITICS: A THEORY OF U.S. LAWMAKING 20–48 (1998)).

99 Hills, *Against Preemption*, 82 N.Y.U. L. REV. at 21 ("[I]ncumbent members of Congress may also regard political entrepreneurship as too risky, given the specialized communities that it might offend and the benefits of ... cultivating the personal vote.").

100 Clarence Page, "And, Now, the Pat and David Show," CHICAGO TRIBUNE, December 11, 1991.

101 Samuel Huntington's *The Hispanic Challenge* (2004) begins: "The persistent inflow of Hispanic immigrants threatens to divide the United States into two peoples, two cultures, and two languages."

102 See J.D. Hayworth, *Whatever It Takes: Illegal Immigration, Border Security, and the War on Terror.*

103 CNN's *Lou Dobbs Tonight* frequently made the linkages between state driver's licenses to illegal immigrants and terrorist threats to homeland security. See, for example, CNN *Lou Dobbs Tonight* (Oct 17, 2007): ("The governor ... will make it easier for law breakers of all sorts – including terrorists – to take advantage of New York State's driver's licenses.") http://transcripts.cnn.com/TRANSCRIPTS/0710/17/ldt.01.html.

104 Jennifer M. Chacón, *Unsecured Borders: Immigration Restrictions, Crime Control, and National Security*, 39 CONN. L. REV. 1827, 1853 (2007) (arguing that the removals of noncitizens were "depicted as national security policy. With regard to border enforcement efforts, the phrase – border security – has become a ubiquitous descriptive term.").

105 Mallie Jane Kim, "AFTER 9/11, IMMIGRATION BECAME ABOUT HOMELAND SECURITY," U.S. NEWS & WORLD REPORT, September 8, 2011; cf. Linda Bosniak, *Nativism*, in Immigrants Out! (Juan Perea, ed.) (arguing that the word "nativism" is not as important for what it means as what it does; that is, it delegitimizes points of view and takes them out of the bounds of rational debate).

106 Kobach, *The Quintessential Force Multiplier*, 69 ALBANY L. REV. 179.

107 Kobach, *The Quintessential Force Multiplier*, 69 ALBANY L. REV. at 179, and 179–93.

108 Federal law maintained racial barriers to naturalization, excluded based on national and racial origin, and recently called for special registration of certain middle-eastern migrants through its NSEERS program – a program architected, in part, by Kris Kobach, one of the immigration issue entrepreneurs we identify, during his stint with the Department of Justice. See Huntington, *Immigration Federalism*, 61 VAND. L. REV. 787; see generally, Hiroshi Motomura, *Immigration Outside the Law* (Oxford Univ. Press 2014).

109 Michael Wishnie, *Laboratories of Bigotry? Devolution of the Immigration Power, Equal Protection, and Federalism*, 76 N.Y.U. L. REV. 493, 553 (2001) (arguing that devolution of immigrant-related lawmaking power to the states would "erode the antidiscrimination and anti-caste principles that are at the heart of our Constitution.").

110 Letter Memorandum from Thomas E. Perez, Assistant United States Attorney General, to Mr. Bill Montgomery, County Attorney for Maricopa County, Arizona,

Re: United States' Investigation of the Maricopa County Sheriff's Office, Dec. 15, 2011 ("Based upon our extensive investigation, we find reasonable cause to believe that [the sheriff's office] engages in a pattern or practice of unconstitutional policing. Specifically, we find that [the sheriff's office] engages in racial profiling of Latinos; unlawfully stops, detains, and arrests Latinos.").

111 Media Matters Action Network. FEAR & LOATHING IN PRIME TIME: IMMIGRATION MYTHS AND CABLE NEWS. Washington, DC: Media Matters for America, May 21, 2008.

112 Louise Cainkar. HOMELAND INSECURITY: THE ARAB AMERICAN AND MUSLIM AMERICAN EXPERIENCE AFTER 9/11. 1st ed. New York: Russell Sage Foundation, 2009; Darren W. Davis and Brian D. Silver. *"Civil Liberties vs. Security: Public Opinion in the Context of the Terrorist Attacks on America."* AMERICAN JOURNAL OF POLITICAL SCIENCE 48, no. 1 (January 1, 2004): 28–46; Phyllis B. Gerstenfeld. *"A Time to Hate: Situational Antecedents of Intergroup Bias."* ANALYSES OF SOCIAL ISSUES AND PUBLIC POLICY 2, no. 1 (December 1, 2002): 61–67; Bill Ong Hing. *"Vigilante Racism: The De-Americanization of Immigrant America."* MICHIGAN JOURNAL OF RACE & LAW 7 (2002, 2001): 441; Jeffrey Kaplan. *"Islamophobia in America?: September 11 and Islamophobic Hate Crime 1."* TERRORISM AND POLITICAL VIOLENCE 18, no. 1 (2006): 1–33.

113 William Claiborne, "Immigration Foes Find Platform in Iowa; National Groups Fight Governor on Recruiting Workers from Abroad," THE WASHINGTON POST, Aug. 19, 2001.

114 CNN, "At Least 35 U.S. Troops Injured West of Baghdad. New Bush Immigration Plan Causes Controversy," CNN Newsnight, Aaron Brown (January 7, 2004).

115 Sergio Bustos, "The Three Amigos Introduce Bill to Legalize Illegal Immigrants," GANNETT NEWS SERVICE (July 28, 2003); Jim Behnke, "The Tres Amigos – Kolbe, Flake, McCain," SIERRA VISTA HERALD (Jan. 8, 2004).

116 Steven Wall, "Efforts against Illegal Immigrants Rise," SAN BENARDINO SUN, November 9, 2004.

117 Yes on Proposition 200 v. Napolitano, CV2004-092999 (Ariz. Super. Ct. 2004), Plaintiff's claims were dismissed by the trial court; however, on appeal, the Arizona Court of Appeal reversed the dismissal of the plaintiff's declaratory judgment action against the governor and allowed plaintiffs leave to file second amended complaint. *Yes on Prop 200 v. Napolitano* (Ariz. Ct. App. 2007) 215 Ariz. 458, 472; see also, *"Suit Filed over AG's Opinion on Public Benefits under Prop 200,"* ARIZONA REPUBLIC, November 19, 2004.

118 The increase in spending under the 2003 Medicare Prescription Drug Modernization Act was particularly galling to many conservative leaders and activists in the Republican Party. Craig Shirley and Donald Devine, "Karl Rove Is No Conservative, as His Memoir Shows," WASHINGTON POST, April 10, 2010.

119 Rachel Morris, "Borderline Catastrophe: How the Fight over Immigration Blew Up Rove's Big Tent," WASHINGTON MONTHLY, October, 2006.

120 Interview with Angela Kelley, former deputy director of the National Immigration Forum, February 2011 (notes on file with author).

121 F. James Sensenbrenner, Jr., *Rep. Gekas Introduces Compromise Immigration 245(i) Extension Legislation; Sensenbrenner Supports Expedited House Consideration Next Week* (2001) (Sensenbrenner called 245i a "fair piece of compromise

legislation that deserves passage. I believe this legislation strengthens families without unintentionally encouraging people to break the law.")

122 Jason Deparle," The Anti-Immigration Crusader," NEW YORK TIMES, April 17, 2011.

123 We note, however, that there have been some federal legislative efforts championed by issue entrepreneurs. Some, like the Secure Fences Act of 2006, were successful. Others, like the CLEAR Act were not.

124 Federation for American Immigration Reform, THE PUSH FOR AMNESTY FOR ILLEGAL ALIENS (2009) ("of the three legs of the stool [enforcement, improved legal flows, path to legalization], only one leg – law enforcement – makes sense and has broad public support.") http://www.fairus.org/site/News2?page= NewsArticle&id=22499&security=1601&news_iv_ctrl=1007.

125 Hills, *Against Preemption*, N.Y.U. L. REV. at 10–11 (describing holdups to federal legislation, including "Madison's Nightmare" of majority inaction enabling minority dominance (citing Richard B. Stewart, *Madison's Nightmare*, 57 U. CHI. L. REV. 335, 342 (1990)), and problems of collective action).

126 In its current and recent versions, comprehensive federal immigration reform proposals feature items anathema to the restrictionist vision, like the DREAM Act and increased legal immigration. Federation for American Immigration Reform, FAIR APPLAUDS SENATE DEFEAT OF THE "RECURRING" DREAM ACT AMNESTY (2007), http://www.fairus.org/site/News2?page=NewsArticle&id=16385.

127 See, for example, *Lou Dobbs Tonight*, October 5, 2006.

128 Eyal Press, "Do Immigrants Make Us Safer?"*THE NEW YORK TIMES MAGAZINE*, Dec. 3, 2006; Ruben G. Rumbaut et al., *Debunking the Myth of Immigrant Criminality: Imprisonment among First- and Second-Generation Young Men*, MIGRATION INFORMATION SOURCE (June 2006). Crime data by nativity or race is not available for the vast majority of (small) municipalities and counties in the United States, and thus cannot be incorporated into our analysis of local ordinances in Part I.

129 Randal C. Archibold, "On Border Violence, Truth Pales Compared to Ideas," THE NEW YORK TIMES, June 19, 2010. ("[T]he rate of violent crime at the border, and indeed across Arizona, has been declining, according to the Federal Bureau of Investigation.")

130 See, e.g., FAIR/CIS re: immigrant threat; Kitty Calavita, *The New Politics of Immigration: "Balanced-Budget Conservatism" and the Symbolism of Proposition 187*, 43:3 SOCIAL PROBLEMS 284–305 (August 1986); Ruben G. Rumbaut et al., *Debunking the Myth of Immigrant Criminality: Imprisonment among First- and Second-Generation Young Men*, MIGRATION INFORMATION SOURCE (June 2006) available at http://www.migrationinformation.org/Feature/display.cfm?id=403; Pratheepan Gulasekaram, *Subnational Immigration Regulation and the Pursuit of Cultural Cohesion*, U. CINN. L. REV. (2009) (arguing that anti-immigrant regulations impossibly and impermissibly attempt to protect perceived cultural values and commonalities).

131 See e.g., Cristina Costantini, *Does Immigration Fuel Crime? Without Statistical Consensus, Rhetoric and Fear Reign in Debate*, HUFFINGTON POST, Nov. 15, 2011; see Cunningham-Parmeter, *Forced Federalism*, 62 Hast. L. J. at 1710 ("in the public's mind, the empirical questions are already answered; aliens are bad for the economy).

132 See Harold Chang, *The Disadvantages of Immigration Restriction as a Policy to Improve Income Distribution*, 61 SMU L. Rev. 23 (Winter, 2008); Tamar Jacoby, *Immigration Nation*, FOREIGN AFFAIRS, November/December 2006.Note that we acknowledge findings that suggest some short-term economic losses concentrated at the local level (from medical care and other local public services). However, even accounting for those potential losses, evidence overwhelmingly shows the net welfare gains from increased immigration. Further, the objection of concentrated local losses could always be addressed through cross-subsidization schemes whereby federal windfalls could be distributed to specifically affected municipalities.

133 Ruben G. Rumbaut et al., *Debunking the Myth of Immigrant Criminality: Imprisonment among First- and Second-Generation Young Men*, MIGRATION INFORMATION SOURCE (June 2006) available at http://www.migration information.org/Feature/display.cfm?id=403.

134 Ruy Teixeira, *Public Opinion Watch*, CENTER FOR AMERICAN PROGRESS, Apr. 5, 2006, ("For example, in the most recent Time poll, 68 percent said illegal immigration was a very or extremely serious problem and, in a just-released Pew poll on immigration (PDF), 74 percent termed immigration a very big or moderately big problem, up from 69 percent in 2002. In the same Pew poll, 52 percent now say that 'immigrants today are a burden on our country because they take our jobs, housing and health care' (up from 38 percent in 2000), compared to 41 percent who say 'immigrants today strengthen our country because of their hard work and talents' (down from 50 percent in 2000).") available at http://www.american progress.org/issues/2006/04/b1531059.html.

135 See, for example, *Lou Dobbs Tonight*, October 5, 2006.

136 First Focus, *Public Support for the Dream Act* (2010) http://www.firstfocus.net/sites/default/files/dreampollbreakdown_0.pdf.

137 Professor Roderick Hills, analyzing the role of policy advocates in mobilizing federal action, compared such advocates to surfers, who wait for the right "wave of problems" and politics before he can engage. 81 N.Y.U. L. Rev. at 20. While it remains true, as Hills notes, that these entrepreneurs rely on the "right opportunities and incentives" – that is, in our framework, the right partisan conditions – we introduce a slight twist on his conception. We envision an active and deliberative role for the restrictionist issue entrepreneur, in creating opportunities and incentives. In our conception, congressional inaction does not cause the immigration entrepreneur to spring into action; rather, the entrepreneur presses for a national legislative stalemate when proposed federal policy is unlikely to yield all the outcomes desired by restrictionists. This may be especially true at this moment in jurisprudential history, given the Court's recent turn against campaign finance regulation. At least one scholar predicts that *Citizens United* is a boon to issue entrepreneurs, easing the funding of their campaigns. See Orbach et al., Arming States Rights, 52 Ariz. L. Rev. 1161. Thus, we might predict that entrepreneurs will now exponentially enhance their power and funding with each minor success. Sunstein and Kuran, 51 Stan. L. Rev. at 714 (noting that the phenomenon of an availability cascade feeds on itself, and that once successful, availability entrepreneurs will command greater resources); Orbach et al., 52 ARIZ. L. REV. at 1169 (arguing that private lawmakers' power and funding increase with each city that clones or enacts a suggested law).

138 Kris W. Kobach, "Another Amnesty? New Bill Hobbles Border States," N.Y. POST, June 16, 2011 available at http://nypost.com/2011/06/16/another-amnesty/.

139 Peter Slevin, "Deportation of Illegal Immigrants Increases under Obama Administration," THE WASHINGTON POST, July 26, 2010.

140 Pamela Constable and N. C. Aizenman, "Rally against Illegal Immigration Scheduled," THE WASHINGTON POST, April 22, 2007.

141 Jason Deparle, "The Anti-Immigration Crusader," NEW YORK TIMES, April 17, 2011.

142 Roger Hedgecock, Mexican Drug Cartels Control Parts of Arizona, HUMAN EVENTS, June 18, 2010. ("Think about it. A part of America is off limits to U.S. citizens because it is now controlled by an army of foreigners.").

143 Alan Gomez, "States Make Daily Life Harder for Illegal Immigrants," USA TODAY, Dec. 20, 2011 (Kobach continued by noting that the provision could have "much greater effect than some people might expect at first glance.").

144 See NumbersUSA, North Carolina Could be Next to Pass Statewide Immigration Law, Dec. 9, 2011 available at http://www.numbersusa.com/content/news/december-9-2011/north-carolina-could-be-next-pass-state-wide-immigration-law.html.

145 Jeff Amy, "GOP Takes Miss. House for 1st Time in Years," BOSTON GLOBE, November 1, 2011. In February 2012, the Mississippi Immigrant Rights Alliance noted that "with the Republicans in charge now for the first time ... [we] expect many anti-immigrant bills to come from that chamber." http://lawprofessors.typepad.com/immigration/2012/02/mississippi-republicans-up-to-no-good.html.

146 NumbersUSA, North Carolina Could Be Next to Pass Statewide Immigration Law, Dec. 9, 2011 available at http://www.numbersusa.com/content/news/december-9-2011/north-carolina-could-be-next-pass-state-wide-immigration-law.html.

147 Jeffrey M. Jones, More Americans Favor Than Oppose Arizona Immigration Law, GALLUP, April 29, 2010 http://www.gallup.com/poll/127598/americans-favor-oppose-arizona-immigration-law.aspx (last visited Jan 20, 2015).

148 Elizabeth Llorente, "Mitt Romney Touts Endorsement by Architect of Tough State Immigration Laws" FOX NEWS LATINO, January 11, 2012; Michael A. Memoli, "Romney Calls Arizona Immigration Law a Model for the Nation," LOS ANGELES TIMES, February 22, 2012.

## CHAPTER 5

1 Interview with America's Voice, March 2012; Interview with National Immigration Law Center, January 2014.

2 There were important contrasts, however, between restrictive and pro-integration strategies on proliferating state legislation, including whether or not they sought to derail national legislation that contained unpalatable provisions, and whether or not they relied on racial anxiety to achieve their aims. We discuss these distinctions in greater detail later in this chapter.

3 Pew Hispanic Center, U.S. UNAUTHORIZED IMMIGRATION POPULATION TRENDS, 1990–2012 (2014), http://www.pewhispanic.org/2014/12/11/unauthorized-trends/ (last visited Jan 18, 2015).

4  Pew Hispanic Center, U.S. Unauthorized Immigration Population Trends, 1990–2012 (2014), http://www.pewhispanic.org/2014/12/11/unauthorized-trends/ (last visited Jan 18, 2015).

5  Jeffrey S. Passel, D'Vera Cohn, and Ana Gonzalez-Barrera, Net Migration from Mexico Falls to Zero – and Perhaps Less (2012), http://www.pewhispanic .org/2012/04/23/net-migration-from-mexico-falls-to-zero-and-perhaps-less/ (last visited Jan 19, 2015).

6  Bureau of Labor Statistics, Seasonally Adjusted Unemployment Rate (2015), http://data.bls.gov/timeseries/LNS14000000 (last visited Jan 18, 2015).

7  Neil Shah, "Real Time Economics: Which States Have Worst Underemployment?," Wall Street Journal, July 30, 2012.

8  As we note in Chapter 6, the potential for pro-integration policy at the national level still remained viable through executive action, and this had significant implications for federalism as well. We elaborate on these ideas further in Gulasekaram and Ramakrishnan, The President and Immigration Federalism, 68 Fla. L. Rev. – (forthcoming 2016).

9  See, Adam B. Cox, Enforcement Redundancy and the Future of Immigration Law, 2012 Sup. Ct. Rev. 31 (2013); See also, Gulasekaram and Ramakrishnan, The President and Immigration Federalism (forthcoming 2015).

10  See Christina M. Rodriguez, Negotiating Conflict through Federalism: Institutional and Popular Perspectives, 123 Yale L.J. 2094, 2103 (2014); Gulasekaram and Ramakrishnan, The President and Immigration Federalism, 68 Fla. L. Rev. – (forthcoming 2016) (showing that federal government suits against state or local immigration policies are exceedingly rare).

11  Some of the other remaining provisions were left non-enjoined, such as the provision preventing localities from enacting sanctuary ordinances, and others became parts of subsequent lawsuits, like the provisions penalizing solicitation of work by day laborers and those penalizing the harboring or smuggling or undocumented persons.

12  See Chapter 6's discussion of the legal consequences of the new immigration federalism for citations to, and a fuller discussion of, these cases.

13  Valle del Sol v. Whiting, 709 F.3d 808 (9th Cir. 2013) (holding that sections of SB 1070 criminalizing the solicitation of work by day laborers interacting with people in vehicles violated the First Amendment).

14  Valle del Sol v. Whiting, 732 F.3d 1006 (9th Cir. 2013) (holding that the section of SB 1070 criminalizing the harboring and transporting of unauthorized immigrants in Arizona was both void for vagueness and preempted).

15  Dep't of Homeland Security Secretary Jeh C. Johnson, Memorandum re: Exercising Prosecutorial Discretion with Respect to Individuals Who Came to the United States as Children and with Respect to Certain Individuals Who Are the Parents of U.S. Citizens or Permanent Residents, Nov. 20, 2014.

16  Elizabeth Llorente, "Latinos Give Obama Higher Ratings on Immigration, Fox News Latino Poll Says," Fox News Latino, September 20, 2012.

17  Jennifer Merolla, S. Karthick Ramakrishnan, and Chris Haynes, "Illegal," "Undocumented," or "Unauthorized": Equivalency Frames, Issue Frames, and Public Opinion on Immigration, 11 Perspectives on Politics 789–807 (2013).

18  Julia Preston and John H. Cushman, Jr, "U.S. to Stop Deporting Some Immigrants," NEW YORK TIMES, June 15, 2012, http://www.nytimes.com/2012/06/16/us/us-to-stop-deporting-some-illegal-immigrants.html (last visited Jan 19, 2015).

19  U.S. Department of Education, *U.S. Secretary of Education Lauds President Obama's Immigration Announcement on Thirtieth Anniversary of Plyler v. Doe*, June 15, 2012, http://www.ed.gov/news/press-releases/us-secretary-education-lauds-president-obamas-immigration-announcement-thirtieth (last visited Jan 19, 2015).

20  CNN/ORC Poll, http://i2.cdn.turner.com/cnn/2012/images/10/02/rel11c.pdf (last visited Jan 19, 2015).

21  A Lexis-Nexis search for "Deferred Action for Childhood Arrivals" or DACA between July 1 and December 1, 2012 in major U.S. newspapers revealed 245 newspaper stories, while SB 1070 was covered in 58 news stories during the same time period. In addition to the dozens of human interest stories on DACA providing empathetic coverage, news stories on DACA also focused on what Mitt Romney might do if he won the election. (see Fox News Latino, "Mitt Romney Camp Says He Will Not Continue Deferred Action after Taking Office," FOX NEWS LATINO, October 13, 2012).

22  Elizabeth Llorente, "Mitt Romney Touts Endorsement by Architect of Tough State Immigration Laws" Fox News Latino, January 11, 2012.

23  See *Mitt Romney Announces Support of Kansas Secretary of State Kris Kobach* (January 11, 2012) http://www.presidency.ucsb.edu/ws/?pid=99028.

24  Fox News Latino, 2012, supra note 21.

25  New York Times, "President Exit Polls" (2012), http://elections.nytimes.com/2012/results/president/exit-polls (last visited Apr 2, 2014).

26  Asian American Justice Center, APIA Vote, and National Asian American Survey, *Behind the Numbers: Post Election Survey of Asian American and Pacific Islander Voters in 2012*, http://www.naasurvey.com/resources/Presentations/2012-aapipes-national.pdf (last accessed Jan 19, 2015).

27  New York Times, "President Exit Polls" http://elections.nytimes.com/2012/results/president/exit-polls.

28  Michael O'Brien, GOP Resistance to Immigration Reform Could Be Casualty of 2012 Election. NBC News, Nov. 9, 2012 available at http://nbcpolitics.nbcnews.com/_news/2012/11/09/15040894-gop-resistance-to-immigration-reform-could-be-casualty-of-2012-election?lite; Rebecca Elliott. "Grover Norquist, Rahm Emanuel: House Will Pass Immigration," POLITICO, July 15, 2013. http://www.politico.com/story/2013/07/immigration-grover-norquist-rahm-emanuel-94235.html.

29  Rachel Weiner, "Sean Hannity: I've 'Evolved' on Immigration," *Washington Post*, November 8, 2012. http://www.washingtonpost.com/blogs/post-politics/wp/2012/11/08/sean-hannity-ive-evolved-on-immigration/; Burgess Everett, "Bill O'Reilly Backs Immigration Deal," POLITICO, June 20, 2013.

30  National Conference of State Legislators, "2013 Immigration Report" (Washington, 2014), available at http://www.ncsl.org/research/immigration/2013-immigration-report.aspx.

31  David Olson, "Riverside County Supervisors Back Immigration Reform," *Riverside Press-Enterprise*, February 26, 2013.

32 Stephanie Czekalinski, *States Introduce Fewer Immigration Bills*, NATIONAL
   JOURNAL, May 23, 2012 (noting that several states were awaiting Court resolution
   on SB 1070 before passing similar legislation).

33 Although estimates vary – partly based on how one defines "sanctuary" – several
   dozen jurisdictions across the country maintain some form of what might reasonably be deemed a sanctuary policy. See Lynn Tramonte, DEBUNKING THE MYTH
   OF "SANCTUARY CITIES" (Washington: Immigration Policy Center, 2011) (stating
   that "more than 70 cities and states" maintain some form of noncooperation policy). Oregon and Utah maintain state-wide policies. H.B. 116, 2011 Gen. Ses. (West
   2011); Ore. Code Ann. St. Police §181.850 (West 2011). The sanctuary movement
   gained significant momentum during the 1980s, with religious organizations and
   cities responding to the concerns of Central American migrants facing deportation to countries that were then embroiled in civil conflicts. The Los Angeles
   Police Department had, starting in 1979, prohibited officers from commencing
   interactions or investigations solely to inquire about immigration status or to arrest
   immigrants for unlawful presence. See Bill Ong Hing, *Immigration Sanctuary
   Policies: Constitutional and Representative of Good Policing and Good Public
   Policy*, 2 U.C. IRVINE L. REV. 247 (2012); Rose Villazor, *What Is a Sanctuary?*, 61
   S.M.U. L. REV. 133 (2008). Decades after its implementation, the LAPD's policy
   withstood a post-1996 legal challenge, with a California state court ruling that local
   law enforcement need not administer or enforce federal immigration law. Sturgeon
   v. Bratton, 95 Cal. Rptr. 3d 718 (Ct. App. 2009).

34 San Francisco's sanctuary ordinance, first passed in 1985, but later modified in
   1989, specifies that local law enforcement officers and city agencies (e.g., school
   districts, public assistance institutions, public health clinics) would not aid federal
   enforcement efforts to the extent that such noncooperation was consistent with
   state and federal law. S.F. Bd. Of Supervisors Res. 1087–85 (1985, superseded by
   S.F. Admin. Code § 12H.2 (1989). In 1989, New York City's policy went even further, virtually prohibiting any direct contact between local law enforcement and
   federal agencies to identify or reveal undocumented status. City Policy Concerning
   Aliens, New York City Executive Order No. 124 (Aug. 7, 1989). Responding to
   New York City's type of sanctuary policy, the 1996 federal immigration law prohibited states from banning voluntary communication with federal agencies. 8 U.S.C.
   § 1373; 8 U.S.C. § 1644. In light of this law, a federal appeals court struck down the
   portion of New York City's law that prevented voluntary communication between
   local agents and immigration authorities. City of New York v. United States, 179
   F.3d 29 (2ᵈ Cir. 1999).

35 Cox and Rodriguez, *The President and Immigration Law*, 119 YALE L. J. 458,
   501–09 (2009); American Immigration Council, Executive Grants of Temporary
   Relief, 1956–Present (Oct. 2014).

36 See generally, Motomura, IMMIGRATION OUTSIDE THE LAW 46 (Oxford 2014);
   Rose Cuison Villazor, *What Is a "Sanctuary"?* 61 S.M.U.L. REV. 133 (2008).

37 City of New York v. United States, 179 F.3d 29 (2ᵈ Cir. 1999) (striking down N.Y.
   Executive Order No. 124, which prevented local officials from reporting suspected
   unlawfully present persons to federal immigration authorities). Exec. Order No.
   124 was implemented in 1989. The continued viability of the order required judicial assessment, however, when a provision of a federal statute enacted in 1996 (8

National Immigration Law Center, Basic Facts about In-State Tuition for Undocumented Students, (Washington, 2013), available at http://www.nilc.org/basic-facts-instate.html. Note that the Illinois financial aid scheme does not provide for state financial aid, but instead sets up a fund to which monies can be donated, from which undocumented students can receive assistance. See 110 IL Comp. St. 947 s. 67 ("Illinois DREAM Fund Commission").

82 Hawai'i Board of Regents, Michigan Board of Regents, Rhode Island Board of Governors.

83 See, e.g., California Education Code § 68130.5(a).

84 National Conference of State Legislatures, Undocumented Student Tuition: State Action, June 12, 2014, available at http://www.ncsl.org/research/education/undocumented-student-tuition-state-action.aspx.

85 National Conference of State Legislatures, Undocumented Student Tuition: State Action, June 12, 2014, available at http://www.ncsl.org/research/education/undocumented-student-tuition-state-action.aspx.

86 Martinez v. Regents of the University of California, 50 Cal. 4th 1277 (2010), cert. denied 131 U.S. S. Ct. 2961 (2011).

87 Alabama, Arizona, Georgia, Indiana, and South Carolina. Further, Alabama and South Carolina deny admission. National Conference of State Legislatures, "Undocumented Student Tuition: Overview."; National Immigration Law Center, Basic Facts about In-State Tuition for Undocumented Students.

88 8 U.S.C. § 1601 et. seq.

89 8 U.S.C. § 1622.

90 8 U.S.C. § 1621(d).

91 Audrey Singer, *Immigrants, Welfare Reform and the Coming Reauthorization Vote*, Migration Information Source (2002), http://www.migrationpolicy.org/article/immigrants-welfare-reform-and-coming-reauthorization-vote (last accessed Apr 23, 2015).

92 Wendy Zimmermann and Karen C. Tumlin, *Patchwork Policies: State Assistance for Immigrants under Welfare Reform*, Urban Institute (1999).

93 Rachel Fabi. 2014. "Undocumented Immigrants in the United States: Access to Prenatal Care." *The Hastings Center: Undocumented Patients Project.* September 29.

94 "MAPS: Health Coverage for Immigrant Children and Pregnant Women." 2015. *National Immigration Law Center.* January 6. http://www.nilc.org/healthcoveragemaps.html (last accessed April 22, 2015); Lisa Zamosky, *Healthcare Options for Undocumented Immigrants*, Los Angeles Times.

95 Caitlin Owens, California Bill Would Extend Health Insurance to Undocumented Immigrants, The National Journal, Apr. 9, 2015; California State Senate, SB-4, *Health Care Coverage: Immigration Status*, Amended version 04/06/2015, http://leginfo.legislature.ca.gov/faces/billNavClient.xhtml?bill_id=201520160SB4 (last accessed April 22, 2015).

96 Jordan Fabian, "Sergio Garcia: USA's First Undocumented Lawyer," *National Journal*, Jan. 6, 2014.

97 8 U.S.C. § 1621(d).

98 Cal. Bus. & Prof. Code § 6064 (b) (2014).

99 In re Sergio C. Garcia on Admission, S202512 (Cal. Jan. 2, 2014).

100 Florida Board of Bar Examiners Re: Question as to Whether Undocumented Immigrants Are Eligible for Admission to the Florida Bar, N. SC11-2568 (Fla. Mar. 6, 2014).

101 Katie Mettier, "Undocumented Immigrant Jose Godinez-Samperio Tells of Becoming a Lawyer," *Tampa Bay Times*, Oct. 21, 2014.

102 Kirk Semple, "Bar Exam Passed, Immigrant Still Can't Practice Law," N.Y. *Times*, Dec. 3, 2013.

103 Jennifer Medina, "Allowed to Join the Bar, but Not to Take a Job," N.Y. *Times*, Jan. 2, 2014.

104 "Undocumented Lawyer Sergio Garcia Hopes Efforts to Become an Attorney Inspire Others," *Fox New Latino*, Nov. 9, 2014.

105 Josie Huang, Immigrants without legal status able to apply for professional licenses in CA, Southern California Public Radio (2014), http://www.scpr.org/blogs/multiamerican/2014/09/29/17360/immigrants-professionally-licensed-california/ (last visited Jan 20, 2015).

106 The White House Task Force on New Americans, Strengthening Communities by Welcoming All Residents: A Federal Strategic Action Plan on Immigrant & Refugee Integration 17–19, Apr. 2015.

107 Interview with Chief of Staff, Office of California State Senator Ricardo Lara, April 17, 2015; California State Senate, SB-10 Immigration: Governor's Office of New Americans, http://leginfo.legislature.ca.gov/faces/billNavClient.xhtml?bill_id=201520160SB10 (last accessed April 22, 2015).

108 New York City, Mayor's Office of Immigrant Affairs, www.nyc.gov/html/imm/html/home/home.shtml.

109 The White House Task Force on New Americans, Strengthening Communities by Welcoming all Residents: 2.

110 The White House Task Force on New Americans, Strengthening Communities by Welcoming all Residents: 14.

111 The National Partnership for New Americans, NPNA Partners, available at http://www.partnershipfornewamericans.org/partners/ (last accessed April 22, 2015).

112 Welcoming America: Need and History, http://www.welcomingamerica.org/about-us/why-we-are-needed/ (last accessed April 22, 2015).

113 Welcoming America, Affiliate Introduction Packet, Appendix H: Sample Welcoming Resolution, http://www.welcomingamerica.org/wp-content/uploads/2011/11/Affiliate-Introduction-Packet-.pdf (last accessed April 22, 2015).

114 Welcoming Cities & Counties, "Commitment to Participate in the Welcoming Cities and Counties Project," available at the Welcoming America web site: http://www.welcomingamerica.org/wp-content/uploads/2013/01/Commitment-Form-Welcoming-Cities-and-Counties1.pdf. (last accessed April 22, 2015).

115 List available at Welcoming America: Welcoming Cities and Counties, http://www.welcomingamerica.org/get-involved/cities/ (accessed April 22, 2015).

116 Welcoming America: Welcoming Cities and Counties, http://www.welcomingamerica.org/get-involved/cities/ (accessed March 12, 2014).

117 Julia Preston. "Ailing Midwestern Cities Extend a Welcoming Hand to Immigrants." *The New York Times*, October 6, 2013.

118 Id.

119 Cities United for Immigration Action, available at http://citiesforaction.us/; Democratic Mayors Rally Support for Obama's Immigration Changes, Huffington Post, Dec. 9, 2014 available at http://www.huffingtonpost.com/2014/12/08/mayors-immigration-reform_n_6288446.html.

120 Cities United for Immigration Action, available at http://citiesforaction.us/.

121 Resnik, Federalism(s) Forms and Norms in Federalism and Subsidiarity: NOMOS LV 401–04.

122 Id; see also, Gulasekaram and Ramakrishnan, *Immigration Federalism: A Reappraisal*, 88 N.Y.U.L. Rev. at 2108–19 (discussing the influence of restrictionist issue entrepreneurs in being able to spread enforcement-heavy policies across multiple jurisdictions).

123 Josh Eidelson, "New York State Mulls Citizenship for Undocumented Workers," *Bloomberg BusinessWeek*, June 16, 2014; Room for Debate, "Is State Citizenship the Answer to Immigration Reform?" N.Y. *Times*, June 24, 2014 (with Peter L. Markowitz, Peter J. Spiro, Ted Ruthzier, and Rose Cuison Villazor, contributing various perspectives on the question).

124 Leon E. Aylsworth, *The Passing of Alien Suffrage*, 25 Am. Pol. Sci. Rev. 114, 114–16.

125 Jake Grovum, "Drawing Undocumented Immigrants Out of the Shadows," USATODAY, July 17, 2014

126 Id. (quoting Professor Peter Markowitz "The very nature of our dual-sovereign federal structure means that New York gets to decide who are New Yorkers."); see also Peter Markowitz, *Undocumented No More: The Power of State Citizenship*, 67 Stan. L. Rev. (forthcoming 2015).

127 See Leon A. Aylsworth, *The Passing of Alien Suffrage*, 25 Am. Pol. Sci. Rev. 114 (1931); see also, Jamin B. Raskin, *Legal Aliens, Local Citizens: The Historical Constitutional and Theoretical Meanings of Alien Suffrage*, 14 U. Penn. L. Rev. 1391 (1993).

128 Peter Spiro, Noncitizen Voting Makes Sense. Why Don't Liberals Agree? BloombergView (2013), http://www.bloombergview.com/articles/2013-06-19/noncitizen-voting-makes-sense-why-don-t-liberals-agree- (last visited Jan 20, 2015).

129 Interview with Professor Peter Markowitz, February 2, 2015.

130 California and Connecticut are the only states that have passed TRUST Acts, and they both have Democratically controlled legislatures. For analysis of municipal sanctuary policies, see S. Karthick Ramakrishnan and Tom Wong, "Partisanship, Not Spanish: Explaining Municipal Ordinances Affecting Undocumented Immigrants," in: State and Local Immigration Policy Activism in the U.S.: Interdisciplinary Perspectives 73–95 (Monica W. Varsanyi, ed., 2010).

131 Mostly, DACA recipients in almost every state were eligible for licenses pursuant to extant state legislation or administrative regulations that already provided licenses to those with deferred action and Employment Authorization Documents (EAD). DACA is, fundamentally, a large-scale deferred action program, with recipients eligible for EADs. Therefore, in many cases, it was a matter of clarifying that DACA recipients would be treated as other recipients of deferred action were already being treated under governing state policies.

132 U.S. Census Bureau, "State & County QuickFacts: Arizona," 2013. http://quickfacts.census.gov/qfd/states/04000.html.

133 The only exception was in 2000, when Democrats and Republicans each had 50% of the State Senate in Arizona. See National Conference of State Legislatures: State Partisan Composition, http://www.ncsl.org/research/about-state-legislatures/partisan-composition.aspx#Timelines (last accessed April 23, 2015).

134 See Alex Kotlowitz. "Our Town." *The New York Times*, August 5, 2007; Jay Newton-Small. "John McCain: Can He Mend Fences with the Right?" *Time*, October 8, 2009.

135 Boris Shor, "How U.S. State Legislatures Are Polarized and Getting More Polarized (in 2 Graphs)," THE WASHINGTON POST, January 14, 2014, http://www.washingtonpost.com/blogs/monkey-cage/wp/2014/01/14/how-u-s-state-legislatures-are-polarized-and-getting-more-polarized-in-2-graphs/ (last visited Jan 21, 2015).

136 Nolan McCarty, "What We Know and Don't Know about Our Polarized Politics," THE WASHINGTON POST, January 8, 2014, http://www.washingtonpost.com/blogs/monkey-cage/wp/2014/01/08/what-we-know-and-dont-know-about-our-polarized-politics/ (last visited Jan 21, 2015).

137 This was particularly true in the fall of 2014, as several Republican candidates began airing advertisements linking terrorism in Syria to potential security vulnerabilities in the U.S.-Mexico border. See Greg Sargent, "Tom Cotton: Terrorists Collaborating with Mexican Drug Cartels to Infiltrate Arkansas," THE WASHINGTON POST, October 7, 2014; Charles M. Blow, "ISIS, Deep in the Heart of Texas," *New York Times*, September 3, 2014; Michael S. Schmidt, "U.S. Pushes Back against Warnings That ISIS Plans to Enter from Mexico," *New York Times*, September 15, 2014.

138 Only in rare cases, such as the government shutdown, has the U.S. House relaxed the so-called Hastert Rule, where only legislation that has the support of a majority of the majority party will be allowed a floor vote.

139 Patrick McGreevy, "Assemblyman Tries Again on Licenses for Illegal Immigrants," *L.A. Times*, Feb. 25, 2012.

140 Albert Sabaté, Calif. Gov Jerry Brown vetoes TRUST Act, ABC News (2012), http://abcnews.go.com/ABC_Univision/News/calif-gov-jerry-brown-vetos-trust-act-immigration/story?id=17360224 (last visited Jan 21, 2015).

141 Interview with national pro-integration organization focused on state-level policies, January 2015.

142 Frank R. Baumgartner and Bryan D. Jones. AGENDAS AND INSTABILITY IN AMERICAN POLITICS. University of Chicago Press, 2010.

143 Even though the administration did not openly admit it, the conventional wisdom of the president's action on DACA was that it was a politically calculated move intended to appeal to Latino voters in advance of the 2012 presidential election, especially in light of prominent and sustained protests by pro-immigrant advocates. See Miriam Jordan, "Anatomy of a Deferred-Action Dream," WALL STREET JOURNAL, October 15, 2012 ("The policy has strengthened Mr. Obama's standing among Hispanic voters.").

144 Doug McAdam, POLITICAL PROCESS AND THE DEVELOPMENT OF BLACK INSURGENCY, 1930–1970 (1982); Frank R. Baumgartner and Bryan D Jones, AGENDAS AND INSTABILITY IN AMERICAN POLITICS (1993); John W. Kingdon, AGENDAS, ALTERNATIVES, AND PUBLIC POLICIES (1984).

145 These include particular foundations such as Carnegie Corporation of New York and the J. M. Kaplan Fund, as well as immigrant-rights funder collaboratives like Grantmakers Concerned with Immigrants and Refugees (GCIR) and the Four Freedoms Fund.

146 This shift in thinking among funders after the failure of the DREAM Act has been confirmed in several of our organizational interviews, including with National Immigration Law Center, Progressive States Network, and America's Voice.

147 As we note in Chapter 6, the potential for pro-integration policy at the national level still remained viable through executive action, and these had significant implications for federalism as well. We elaborate on these ideas further in Pratheepan Gulasekaram and S. Karthick Ramakrishnan, "The President and Immigration Federalism," 68 Fla. L. Rev. – (forthcoming 2016).

148 Interview with Suman Raghunathan, former Immigration Policy Specialist for Progressive States Network, January 25, 2015; Interview with Marielena Hincapie, National Immigration Law Center, January 11, 2015; Suman Raghunathan, PROGRESSIVE IMMIGRATION MEASURES PICK UP STEAM AT THE STATE LEVEL, IMMIGRATION IMPACT (2011), http://immigrationimpact.com/2011/02/14/ progressive-immigration-measures-pick-up-steam-at-the-state-level/ (last accessed Apr 23, 2015).

149 See Andrea Goodell, "Local Officials Discuss Their Faith in Immigration Reform," *Holland Sentinel*, February 23, 2014; Marjorie Cortez, "GOP Immigration Reform Standards a Cause for Optimism, Local Leaders Say," *Deseret News*, February 4, 2014.

150 Julia Preston, *The Big Money Behind the Push for an Immigration Overhaul*, THE NEW YORK TIMES, November 14, 2014; Ali Noorani, *New Approach by Conservatives on Immigration?*, CNN.com, February 27, 2012, http://www.cnn.com/2012/02/27/ opinion/noorani-conservative-immigration/index.html (last accessed Apr 23, 2015).

151 Sahil Kapur, *"Bibles, Badges and Business" Unite for Immigration Reform*, TALKINGPOINTSMEMO (2013), http://talkingpointsmemo.com/livewire/bibles-badges-and-business-unite-for-immigration-reform (last accessed Apr 23, 2015); Connie Marshner, *Bibles, Badges and Business*, NATIONAL CATHOLIC REGISTER, December 9, 2012; this pattern was also confirmed by all of our interviews with organizations focused on state-level efforts.

152 Melanie Mason and Patrick McGreevy, *Latino Lawmakers Move to Reverse Decades of Anti-Immigrant Legislation*, LOS ANGELES TIMES, June 22, 2014. Interestingly, however, the newest generation of Latino legislators in California (including State Senators Ricardo Lara and Pro Tempore Kevin de León) have been more likely than their predecessors to frame immigration policies as workforce issues rather than as predominantly civil rights issues, and have been more flexible in their approach to negotiating immigration policy in the state legislature (Interview with California state legislative staff member, April 2015). Thus, for example, while Senator Gil Cedillo had previously insisted on removing any identifying mark of immigrant status in his various legislative attempts at passing a driver's license bill, legislators in the Latino Legislative Caucus were willing to include that very provision in 2013 despite the opposition of several immigration rights advocates, calculating that they would need such a mark in order to

be compliant with the REAL ID Act and gain the Governor's signature (KXTV, *Late Amendments on Licenses, Fracking Draw Attention,* NEWS10, September 10, 2013, http://www.news10.net/story/news/politics/john-myers/2014/01/22/4761313/ (last accessed Apr 23, 2015).

153 Patrick J. McDonnell, *State Restored Most Aid Noncitizens Lost in '96,* LOS ANGELES TIMES, June 7, 1999, http://articles.latimes.com/1999/jun/07/news/mn-45020 (last visited Apr 23, 2015).

154 Robert Salladay & Jennifer Delson, *Gov. Vows to Veto Driver's License Bill,* LOS ANGELES TIMES, September 9, 2005.

155 Cathy Cha, *Lessons for Philanthropy from the Success of California's Immigrant Rights Movement,* NATIONAL PHILANTHROPY, http://ncrp.org/files/rp-articles/RP_Winter14-15.pdf (last accessed April 23, 2015).

156 Interview with Reshma Shamasunder, Director of California Immigrant Policy Center, March 2014. An illustrative example of both regional coordination and civil disobedience is the "undocumented caravan" that stopped in various places from San Diego to Sacramento, culminating in a sit-in in Governor Jerry Brown's office that coincided with vigorous lobbying efforts by other pro-immigrant organizations (See "Capitol Alert: Immigration Activists Stage Sit-in in Jerry Brown's Office" *Sacramento Bee,* July 2, 2013, http://blogs.sacbee.com/capitolalertlatest/2013/07/immigration-activists-stage-sit-in-in-jerry-browns-office.html; Gabriel San Ramon. "Undocumented Caravan Stops in OC Today along Its Statewide Pro-TRUST Act Trip." *OC Weekly,* June 26, 2013, http://blogs.ocweekly.com/navelgazing/2013/06/undocumented_caravan.php.).

157 National Partnership for New Americans: Members, http://www.partnership fornewamericans.org/partners/ (last accessed April 23, 2015). For several years, NPNA has organized national conferences to bring together various types of immigrant-serving organizations and local government officials to build new partnerships and to encourage cross-regional learning (The White House Task Force on New Americans, Strengthening Communities by Welcoming All Residents: A Federal Strategic Action Plan on Immigrant & Refugee Integration 17–19, Apr. 2015).

158 At the best of the state Department of Motor Vehicles (DMV), the state legislature did not include an emergency clause on driver's licenses. All other measures included emergency clauses with immediate implementation, rendering them immune to a referendum challenge. Andrea Silva, *Undocumented Immigrants, Driver's Licenses, and State Policy Development: A Comparative Analysis of Oregon and California,* Paper presented at the Annual Meeting of the Western Political Science Association, April 2, 2015

159 Aura Bogado, *Goodbye, Secure Communities. Hello, Priority Enforcement Program* COLORLINES (2014), http://www.colorlines.com/articles/goodbye-secure-communities-hello-priority-enforcement-program (last accessed Apr 23, 2015); National Day Laborer Organizing Network, *Immigrant Rights Groups Call For Transparency As They Serve Foia Request To Uncover The Truth About Ice's "Discontinuation" Of Secure Communities* (Press release), March 5, 2015 http://www.ndlon.org/en/pressroom/press-releases/item/1122-immigrant-rights-groups-call-for-transparency-as-they-serve-foia-request-to-uncover-the-truth-about-ice-s-discontinuation-of-secure-communities          (last accessed April 23, 2015).

160 For more on "de facto" state citizenship and comprehensive immigration reform, see S. Karthick Ramakrishnan and Allan Colbern, *The California Package Immigrant Integration and the Evolving Nature of State Citizenship*, policy matters: a publication of uc riverside school of public policy, 6 NO. 03, 2015.

## CHAPTER 6

1 U.S. Chamber of Commerce v. Whiting, 131 S.Ct. 1968 (2011).

2 Personal Responsibility and Work Opportunity Reconciliation Act, Pub. L. 104–193, 110 Stat. 2105, 104th Cong. (1996); 8 U.S.C. § 1622.

3 Illegal Immigration Reform and Immigrant Responsibility Act, Pub. L. 104–208, 110 Stat. 3009, 104th Cong. (1996); 8 U.S.C. § 1621(c) and 1623.

4 Jennifer M. Chacon, The Transformation of Immigration Federalism, 21 Wm. & Mary Bill Rts. J. 577, 598–605 (2012).

5 Chacon, Tranformation of Immigration Federalism, 21 Wm. & Mary Bill Rts. J. at 598.

6 Ernest A. Young, "The Ordinary Diet of the Law": The Presumption Against Preemption in the Roberts Court, 2011 Sup. Ct. Rev. 253, 259 (2011) (noting that after the New Deal and the change of Supreme Court justices in the late 1930s, "the Court's federalism doctrine has generally abandoned dual federalism's notion of separate spheres in favor of a regime of concurrent jurisdiction.").

7 Judith Resnik, FEDERALISM(S) FORMS AND NORMS IN NOMOS LV: FEDERALISM AND SUBSIDIARITY 366 (James Fleming, ed., NYU Press 2014).

8 Resnik, Federalism(s) Forms and Norms 365 ("The authorization of many points of law production through layered and redundant legislative, executive, and judicial systems enables norm entrepreneurs to shop systems to persuade similarly situated actors (such as executive officials, judges, and legislators from different levels) about the wisdom or legality of particular points of view – for or against, for example, openness toward new immigrants, state mandates for health care, or environmental regulation."); Heather K. Gerken and Ari Holtzblatt, The Political Safeguards of Horizontal Federalism, 113 Mich. L. Rev. 57, 63–4 (2014).

9 See, e.g., Jessica Bulman-Pozen and Heather K. Gerken, *Uncooperative Federalism*, 118 YALE L.J. 1256, 1261–62 (2009) (discussing autonomy and cooperative federalism models as competing theoretical frameworks for federalism); Margaret H. Lemos, *State Enforcement of Federal Law*, 86 N.Y.U. L. REV. 698, 744 (2011) ("Properly understood, federalism is a means to an end. A federal system is desirable not for its own sake, but because decentralized decision making is thought to have various desirable consequences."); Robert A. Schapiro, *Toward a Theory of Interactive Federalism*, 91 IOWA L. REV. 243, 266 (2005) ("[C]ommentators generally offer a variety of presumed benefits, clustering around five areas: responsive governance, governmental competition, innovation, participatory democracy, and resisting tyranny.").

10 Young, The Presumption Against Preemption in the Roberts Court, 2011 Sup. Ct. Rev. 253 (querying the continued salience of the presumption against preemption).

11 PEW RESEARCH CTR., UNAUTHORIZED IMMIGRANT POPULATION: NATIONAL AND STATE TRENDS, 2010, at 23 tbl. A3 (2011), *available at* http://www.pewhispanic.org/2011/02/01/unauthorized-immigrant-population-brnational-and-state-trends-2010/.

12  See N.M. SEC'Y OF STATE, VOTER REGISTRATION STATISTICS DATA (January 15, 2013), *available at* http://www.sos.state.nm.us/Elections_Data/Voter_Registration_Statistics_Data.aspx (providing voter registration statistics every two years).

13  See PEW RESEARCH CTR., UNAUTHORIZED IMMIGRANT POPULATION: NATIONAL AND STATE TRENDS, 2010, at tbl. A4.

14  See PEW RESEARCH CTR., UNAUTHORIZED IMMIGRANT POPULATION: NATIONAL AND STATE TRENDS, 2010 at 1.

15  See Chapters 3 and 4; *see also* Bulman-Pozen, 127 Harv. L. Rev. 1077, 1090 ("The centrality of partisanship instead points to [state contestation of federal policy] grounded in overlap and integration. Party politics means that state opposition need not be based on something essentially 'state' rather than 'national.'").

16  *See, e.g.*, Rodríguez, *The Significance of the Local*, 106 MICH. L. REV. at 617 (discussing how the demographic shifts caused by globalization and immigration impact parts of the country differently, and thus the viability of different immigration strategies may vary); Peter H. Schuck, *Taking Immigration Federalism Seriously*, 2007 U. CHI. L. FORUM 57, 68–83 (arguing that federal immigration policy might be better served if Congress authorized state authority in some policy areas, like employment-based admissions, state and local criminal justice systems integration, and employer sanctions); Peter J. Spiro, *Learning to Live with Immigration Federalism*, 29 CONN. L. REV. 1627, 1635–39 (2007) (noting that giving states space to enact their own subfederal anti-immigrant legislation relieves political pressure to promote those restrictive policies at the federal level).

17  *See, e.g.*, Clare Huntington, *The Constitutional Dimension of Immigration Federalism*, 61 VAND. L. REV. 787, 805–07 (2008) (explaining that subfederal lawmakers feel frustrated by perceived disproportionate burdens suffered as a result of illegal immigration); Erin F. Delaney, *In the Shadow of Article I: Applying a Dormant Commerce Clause Analysis to State Law Regulating Aliens*, 82 N.Y.U. L. Rev. 102, 103 (2007) ("Increase in state regulation has stemmed from two concomitant developments. The first is that the alien community has grown and has moved to new states unused to the societal pressures of immigration. The second change is the increased willingness of Congress to devolve the federal power over immigration to the states."); Matthew Parlow, *A Localist's Case for Decentralizing Immigration Policy*, 84 DENV. U. L. REV. 1061, 1071 (2007) ("Indeed, different states and local governments are affected in drastically different manners – both positively and negatively – by illegal immigration. Local governments should be able to respond accordingly, especially if the federal government is not meeting those communities' needs.").

18  See Chapters 3 and 4; *see also* Cass R. Sunstein, *Deliberative Trouble? Why Groups Go to Extremes*, 110 YALE L. J. 71 (2000) (showing how limited private information tends to make people follow others, and reach more extreme policy positions).

19  Rodríguez, 106 Mich. L. Rev. at 571.

20  See Rodríguez, 106 Mich. L. Rev. at 571, 611. For a more recent expression of Professor Rodriguez's important thoughts on, among other topics, immigration federalism, see Christina M. Rodríguez, *Negotiating Conflict through Federalism*, 123 YALE L.J. 2094 (2014) (arguing that federalism's utility is its ability to create a framework for expression of disagreement and a forum for negotiating conflict and arriving at consensus).

21 New State Ice Co. v. Liebmann, 285 U.S. 262, 311 (1932) ("[A] single courageous State may, if its citizens choose, serve as a laboratory; and try novel social and economic experiments without risk to the rest of the country.").

22 Keith Cunningham-Parmeter, *Forced Federalism: States as Laboratories of Immigration Reform*, 62 HASTINGS L.J. 1673,1693 (2011).

23 Cunningham-Parmeter, 62 Hastings L.J. at 1676–77.

24 Cunningham-Parmeter, 62 Hastings L.J. at 1714 ("[S]tate immigration regulations export costs in a number of ways."); Roderick Hills, *Against Preemption: How Federalism Can Improve the National Legislative Process*, 82 N.Y.U. L. REV. 1, 23–24 (2007) (listing immigration as an area "in which the risk of external costs are [sic] so high that preemption of state law ought to be presumed (and is, as a matter of judicial practice)").

25 *See* Villas at Parkside Partners v. City of Farmers Branch, 726 F.3d 524 (5th Cir. 2013) (Higginson, J., concurring) (suggesting that an ordinance that discouraged immigrants from living in Farmers Branch burdens other nearby municipalities); Cunningham-Parmeter, 62 Hastings L.J. at 1714–23; *see also* Josh Gerstein, *South Carolina Law Sparks Suit from Justice Department*, POLITICO (Oct. 31, 2011, 4:36 PM) http://www.politico.com/news/stories/1011/67274.html ("Pushing undocumented individuals out of one state and into another is simply not a solution to our immigration challenges." (quoting Assistant U.S. Attorney General Tony West)).

26 Gerken and Holtzblatt, Horizontal Federalism, 113 Mich. L. Rev. at 80–86.

27 *See* Cunningham-Parmeter, 62 Hastings L.J. at 1697–99 (discussing the necessity that other government bodies be able to duplicate the results of state experiments).

28 Cunningham-Parmeter, 62 Hastings L.J. at 1724; *cf.* Barak Y. Orbach et al., *Arming States' Rights*, 52 ARIZ. L. REV. 1161, 1180–83 (2010) (discussing the proliferation of cloned Firearms Freedom Acts in states across the country). To be clear, we have argued that the policies actually accrete punitive provisions from enactment to enactment. We argue that they are largely the same, with each subsequent jurisdiction and variation generally increasing enforcement possibilities.

29 *See generally* Cass R. Sunstein and Timur Kuran, *Availability Cascades and Risk Regulation*, 51 STAN. L. REV. 683 (1999) 29 (arguing that public discourse is distorted by responses to local preferences even in the face of reports and data that make the endorsed local claims suspect).

30 *See* Bulman-Pozen, 127 Harv. L. Rev. 1101 ("Often working together directly or through allied interests groups, ... state and federal politicians shuffle ideas and even bill text back and forth, seeking friendly partisan ground in which to plant their policies. The resulting policies are only 'state' or 'national' in the sense of their site of enactment, not their purposes or intended audiences."); Orbach et al., 52 Ariz. L. Rev. at 1182–83 (noting that although Firearms Freedom Acts vary in particulars, all have "remained faithful to the constitutional theories expressed in the original").

31 Rodriguez, 106 Mich. L. Rev. at 609; *see also* Huntington, 61 Vand. L. Rev. at 830–38; Parlow, 84 Denv. U. L. Rev.

32 Many of these ordinances, however, do demonstrate the social and economic pitfalls of local regulation. Several states have abandoned or reconsidered their enforcement-heavy approaches after enactment, and after experiencing the consequences of such laws. *See* Cunningham-Parmeter, 62 Hastings L.J. at 1711–12

264 *Notes to Pages 158–160*

(discussing the repeal of anti-immigrant laws in Oklahoma and Riverside, New Jersey, after the laws led to dramatic decreases in their migrant worker population).

33  Hills, 82 N.Y.U. L. Rev. at 4 ("Federalism's value, if there is any, lies in the often competitive interaction between the levels of government."). *But see* Bulman-Pozen, *Federalism as a Safeguard of the Separation of Powers*, 112 COLUM. L. REV. 459, 487("But when Congress grants administrative authority to both the states and the federal executive, an open-ended grant of authority may instead stimulate competition by empowering states to challenge the federal executive.").

34  See Bulman-Pozen, *Partisan Federalism*, 127 HARV. L. REV. 1077; Bulman-Pozen, *From Sovereignty and Process to Administration and Politics: The Afterlife of American Federalism*, 123 YALE L.J. 1920 (2014); Larry Kramer, *Putting the Politics Back into the Political Safeguards of Federalism*, 100 COLUM. L. REV. 215 (2000).

35  Professor Heather Gerken argues that SB 1070 led to federal engagement on immigration issues. Heather K. Gerken, *The Supreme Court, 2009 Term – Foreword: Federalism All the Way Down*, 124 HARV. L. REV. 6, 68 (2010) (arguing that Arizona's SB 1070 finally galvanized national debate and forced national elites to engage the issue). It is worth noting that the engagement Gerken cites in support of her argument is *federal judicial engagement*. Specifically, she explains how SB 1070 led the United States Department of Justice to sue Arizona.

36  See Orbach et al., 51 Ariz. L. Rev. at 1163 (describing the strategy of interest group focus on state and local lawmaking as a "battering ram" to break down the "walls" of federal policy, using the example of subfederal firearms bills).

37  See Orbach et al., 51 Ariz. L. Rev at 1163–64; *see also* Bulman-Pozen, *Federalism as a Safeguard of the Separation of Powers*, 112 COLUM. L. REV. at 483–89 (arguing that states, like Arizona with its immigration policy, are "goading" the federal government toward a particular policy goal, and "when state and federal policies clash, states cast themselves as faithful agents of Congress, seeking to carry out a statute as Congress intended, in contrast to a wayward federal executive branch").

38  See Cindy D. Kam and Robert A. Mikos, *Do Citizens Care about Federalism? An Experimental Test*, 4 J. EMPIRICAL LEGAL STUD. 589, 620 (2007) (presenting evidence that political elites' use of the tropes of trust in state government and federalism beliefs negatively influences support for federal policies).

39  See Bulman-Pozen and Gerken, *Uncooperative Federalism*, 118 YALE L.J. 1256, 1279–80 (2009) (using Patriot Act objections as an example of subfederal entities "challenging a national policy for violating the country's deeper commitments").

40  Gerken and Holtzblatt, Horizontal Federalism, 113 Mich. L. Rev. at 87.

41  See Chapter 5, pp. 89–90.

42  Sunstein and Kuran, *Availability Cascades and Risk Regulation*, 51 STAN. L. REV. at 715–28.

43  Sunstein and Kuran, 51 Stan. L. Rev. at 685–701 (discussing how availability cascades can generate widespread mistaken beliefs because of informational availability and reputational concerns, and the susceptibility of the public and elected officials to cognitive biases in information processes).

44  Sunstein and Kuran, 51 Stan. L. Rev. at 714; *see also* Cass R. Sunstein, *Deliberative Trouble? Why Groups Go to Extremes*, 110 YALE L.J. 71, 76 (2000) (describing how, in the absence of their own private information, people tend to follow others, and this process helps reach extreme policy positions); Eric Talley, *Precedential*

*Cascades*, 73 S. Cal. L. Rev. 87, 90 (1999) (discussing how "social entrepreneurs" are eager to exploit group pathologies).

45 Sunstein and Kuran, *supra* note 29, at 714.

46 Sunstein and Kuran, 51 Stan. L. Rev. at 687 (emphasis omitted).

47 Sunstein and Kuran, 51 Stan. L. Rev. at 691–703 (discussing policy responses to the health concerns regarding Love Canal in New York, the anxieties caused by pollutants such as Alar, and the 1996 crash of TWA Flight 800 as examples of availability errors and cascades in action).

48 *See* Catherine L. Carptenter, *Legislative Epidemics*, 58 Buff. L. Rev. 1, 8–10 (2010).

49 Carpenter, *Legislative Epidemics*, 58 Buff. L. Rev. at 13–21.

50 See Chapter 4 for our discussion of issue entrepreneurs.

51 *Model Laws*, Immigr. Reform L. Inst., *available at* http://www.irli.org/laws (last visited Aug. 27, 2013).

52 *See* Patrik Jonsson, "Why Republicans Are Doing an About-Face on Tough Alabama Immigration Law," *Christian Sci. Monitor* (Nov. 16, 2011), http://www.csmonitor .com/USA/Politics/2011/1116/Why-Republicans-are-doing-an-about-face-on-tough-Alabama-immigration-law ("Prof. Samuel Addy ... recently predicted that HB 56 will reduce the Alabama economy by $40 million as income and spending by both illegal and legal Hispanic immigrants will decline. What's more, employers face troves of fresh paperwork and licensing requirements ... that they say will potentially hurt business."); Peter J. Spiro, "Be Careful What You Wish For," N.Y. *Times* (May 14, 2012, 1:49 PM), http://www.nytimes.com/roomfordebate/2011/10/04/ should-alabama-schools-help-catch-illegal-immigrants/be-careful-what-you-w ish-for-alabama (arguing that Alabama's law, driving out immigrants, will force the state to appreciate their value); *NewsHour: Alabama's Immigration Law* (PBS Oct. 13, 2011), *transcript available at* http://www.pbs.org/newshour/bb/business/ july-dec11/alimmigration_10-13.html (discussing the adverse impact of HB 56 on the agriculture and construction industries).

53 *See* Spiro, *Learning to Live with Immigration Federalism*, 29 Conn. L. Rev. at 1636 ("Affording the states discretion to act on their preferences diminishes the pressure on the structure as a whole; otherwise, because you don't let off the steam, sooner or later the roof comes off.").

54 The limitation has to be defined in terms of the quantity of subfederal jurisdictions; substantively, it is difficult to suggest that Alabama's recent immigration law – which has had the effect of driving immigrant children out of school – is relatively harmless, even if it occurs only within an individual state.

55 Prior to the Supreme Court's decision in Arizona, Professor Spiro argued that "in the long run, immigrant interests will be better helped if the Supreme Court upholds S.B. 1070.... If the Supreme Court strikes down S.B. 1070, anti-immigrant constituencies will redouble their efforts to enact tougher laws at the federal level." Peter J. Spiro, "Let Arizona's Law Stand", N.Y. *Times*, Apr. 23, 2012, at A19.

56 *See* Spiro, *Learning to Live with Immigration Federalism*, 29 Conn. L. Rev. at 1637 and nn. 35, 37–38.

57 Spiro, *Learning to Live with Immigration Federalism*, 29 Conn. L. Rev. at 1635 ("A state disempowered from acting in its own jurisdiction will get its way at the

national level."); *id.* at 1630 ("One must look to the consequence of such suppression and the possibility that frustrated state preferences may actually prompt the effectuation of anti-alien measures at the federal level.").

58 *See* Chapter 4; *see also* Ramakrishnan and Gulasekaram, *The Importance of the Political in Immigration Federalism,* 44 ARIZ. ST. L.J. at 1445–50 (using qualitative empirical data to show the highly networked and coordinated work of immigration issue entrepreneurs at the federal and subfederal levels).

59 Kris W. Kobach, "Another Amnesty?: New Bill Hobbles Border States," N.Y. *Post,* June 15, 2011. Deriding a federal E-verify bill that would have produced a federal version of Arizona's E-verify law, Kobach argued that the federal mandate would "defang the only government bodies that are serious about enforcing immigration law – the states. The timing couldn't be worse. The bill stabs Arizona in the back, just after it won a victory in [Whiting v. Chamber of Commerce, re: Arizona's E-verify law].").

60 See Chapter 5, pp. 89–90.

61 *See* Peter J. Spiro, "Let Arizona's Law Stand," N.Y. *Times,* Apr. 23, 2012.

62 Here, we defend this claim only with regard to the time period we investigate (2000–2012).

63 *See* H.B. 488, 2012 Leg., Reg. Sess. (Miss. 2012); H.B. 56, 2011 Leg., Reg. Sess. (Ala. 2011) (codified in part at Ala. Code § 31-13 (LexisNexis 2011)); H.B. 87, 151st Gen. Assemb. (Ga. 2011); Hazleton, Pa., Ordinance 2006–18 (Sept. 21, 2006); Valley Park, Mo., Ordinance 1708 (July 17, 2006); S.B. 1070, 49th Leg., 2d Reg. Sess. (Ariz. 2010); Farmers Branch, Tex., Ordinance 2903 (2007).

64 Sunstein and Kuran, 51 Stan. L. Rev. at 687.

65 *Senator Lara Tries Again on Immigrant Health Care Bill,* KPCC SOUTHERN CALIFORNIA PUBLIC RADIO, December 1, 2014. (noting that the bill stalled in committee the prior year after some initial cost estimates of more than $350 million a year).

66 Patrick McGreevy, *Gov. Brown signs bill repealing unenforceable parts of Prop. 187,* LOS ANGELES TIMES, June 4, 2014 (quoting State Senator Kevin De León, "Today we remember the xenophobic sentiments that spurred Proposition 187, and we announce Senate Bill 396 to erase its stain from our law books.")

67 Judith Resnick, Federalism(s) Forms and Norms: Contesting Rights, Deessentializing Jurisdictional Divides, and Temporizing Accommodations, in Federalism and Subsidiarity NOMOS LV (James Fleming, Ed., NYU Press 2014) (noting the presence of norm entrepreneurs and collectives of government officials as important federalism actors); Jessica Bulman-Pozen, *Partisan Federalism,* 127 HARV. L. REV. 1107 (2013) (arguing that federalism provides the terrain for political parties to wage ideological and policy battles, and that party affiliation can be a stronger source of affiliation than can jurisdictional possibilities); Daryl J. Levinson and Richard H. Pildes, 119 Harv. L. Rev. 2311 (2006) (recognizing the role of political parties in vindicating separation of powers concerns).

68 Gerken and Holtzblatt, Horizontal Federalism, 113 Mich. L. Rev. at 80.

69 8 U.S.C. §1621(d) (conditions under which state benefit may be provided to unlawfully present persons); 8 U.S.C. § 1623(a) (condition under which postsecondary education benefits may be provided to unlawfully present persons).

70 Abbe Gluck, *Intrastatutory Federalism and Statutory Interpretation: State Implementation of Federal Law in Health Reform and Beyond*, 121 YALE L.J. 534 (2011)) (presenting a "legislation focused" theory of federalism). Gluck's primary example of the Affordable Care Act utilizes states as actual regulators and administrators of a federal scheme. In contrast, most immigration federalism contained in federal statutes provides for the possibility of state involvement, but does not empower them as regulators or administrators of federal law. Notable examples wherein states actually become regulators and agents of the federal government are programs like 287(g) and S-Communities, or its successor, the Priority Enforcement Program.

71 Cf. Rodriguez, *Negotiating Conflict through Federalism*, 123 YALE L.J. at 2129 (arguing that lawmaking power at the state and local level can translate into influence at the national level).

72 Young, The Ordinary Diet of the Law, 2011 Sup. Ct. Rev. at 264 ("In a world of concurrent power, federal legislation will frequently determine the actual allocation of responsibility between the federal and state authorities, and the courts are frequently called upon to interpret the allocation that Congress has established.").

73 Heather Gerken and Jessica Bulman-Pozen, *Uncooperative Federalism*, 118 YALE L.J. 1256 (2009).

74 127 Harv. L. Rev. 1107.

75 Resnik, Federalism(s) Forms and Norms 366.

76 See Christina Rodriguez, *Negotiating Conflict through Federalism*, 123 Yale L.J. at 2097–98.

77 See supra n. 147. (Kris W. Kobach, Another Amnesty?: New Bill Hobbles Border States, N.Y. Post, June 15, 2011. Deriding a federal E-verify bill that would have produced a federal version of Arizona's E-verify law, Kobach argued that the federal mandate would "defang the only government bodies that are serious about enforcing immigration law – the states. The timing couldn't be worse. The bill stabs Arizona in the back, just after it won a victory in [Whiting v. Chamber of Commerce, re: Arizona's e-verify law].").

78 Bulman-Pozen, *Partisan Federalism*, 127 HARV. L. REV. at 1123.

79 See generally, Bulman-Pozen, *Afterlife of American Federalism*, 123 YALE L.J. at 1933–46.

80 See generally, Gulasekaram and Ramakrishnan, The President and Immigration Federalism, 68 Fla. L. Rev. – (forthcoming 2016) (explaining how some executive actions can catalyze state-level policy making that helps entrench the executive policy); Ramakrishnan and Gulasekaram, "Immigration Federalism: Obama's Actions Likely to Spur State, Not Congress, to Act," *San Jose Mercury News*, Dec. 6, 2014 (Op-Ed); Ramakrishnan and Gulasekaram, "Driver's Licenses for Undocumented Immigrants," *San Jose Mercury News*, Oct. 12, 2013 (Op-Ed).

81 See Texas v. United States, No. 1:14-CV-254 (S.D. Tex. 2015) (finding that the state of Texas had standing, and enjoining the DAPA program).

82 Gerken and Holtzblatt, Horizontal Federalism, 113 Mich. L. Rev. at 80.

83 See, e.g., Leslie Berestein Rojas, Top Five Immigration Stories of 2010, #1: Arizona's SB 1070, Southern California Public Radio, Dec. 31, 2010 available at http://www.scpr.org/blogs/multiamerican/2010/12/31/7276/top-five-immigration-stories-of-2010-1-sb-1070/.

84 Without endorsing the Center for Immigration Studies report, as examples, see Steven A. Camarota, Welfare Use by Immigrant Households with Children: A Look at Cash, Medicaid, Housing, and Food Programs, Center for Immigration Studies, April 2011 available at http://cis.org/immigrant-welfare-use-2011; Marshall Fitz, Philip E. Wolgin, and Patrick Oakford, Immigrants Are Makers, Not Takers, Center for American Progress, Feb. 8, 2013 available at https://www.americanprogress.org/issues/immigration/news/2013/02/08/52377/immigrants-are-makers-not-takers/.

85 See Christina M. Rodriguez, *Negotiating Conflict through the Lens of Federalism,* 123 YALE L. J. at 2123–26.

86 Young, The Ordinary Diet of the Law, 2011 Sup. Ct. Rev. at 343.

87 See Chapter 2, pp. 47–59.

88 Erin F. Delaney, In the Shadow of Article I: Applying a Dormant Commerce Clause Analysis to State Laws Regulating Aliens, 82 N.Y.U. L. Rev. 102, 112 (2007).

89 Graham v. Richardson 403 U.S. 365 (1971) (prohibition on provision of state welfare benefits to noncitizens, including short-term lawful permanent residents); Foley v. Connelie, 435 U.S. 291 (1978) (upholding state ban on noncitizen employment as state troopers).

90 See Chapter 3, pp. 5–29; Chacon, Transformation of Immigration Federalism, 21 Wm. & Mary Bill Rts. J. at 598–605.

91 Arizona Senate Bill 1070, 49th Legis., 2nd Sess. § 1 (2010).

92 Alabama House Bill 56 § 2.

93 Jefferson Morley, The Man Behind Romney's "Self-Deportation" Plan, Salon, Feb. 22, 2012 (quoting from interview with Kobach) available at http://www.salon.com/2012/02/22/the_man_behind_romneys_self_deportation_dreams/.

94 United States v. Alabama, 691 F.3d 1269, 1294 (11th Cir. 2013).

95 Alabama, 691 F.3d at 1296.

96 Alabama, 691 F.3d at 1294 (emphasis added). But, even as that court recognized the doctrinal import of its categorization of the state law as immigration law, it buttressed its structural preemption conclusion by also applying an alienage framework and finding the law statutorily preempted by conflicting provisions in the INA.

97 Villas at Parkside Partners v. City of Farmers Branch, 726 F.3d 524 (5th Cir. 2013) (Dennis, J., specially concurring).

98 Villas at Parkside Partners v. City of Farmers Branch, 726 F.3d 524 (5th Cir. 2013) (Reavly, J., concurring in judgment). Despite these incantations of structural preemption principles apropos of state and local laws that act as "immigration laws," however, the Fifth Circuit ultimately applied alienage law analysis, using statutory preemption principles to find the rental ordinance invalid.

99 Keller v. City of Fremont, 719 F.3d 931 (8th Cir. 2013).

100 Gray v. City of Valley Park, 567 F.3d 976 (8th Cir. 2009).

101 Delaney, In the Shadow of Article I, 82 N.Y.U. L. Rev. at 110–12 (noting the difficulty of the categorical distinction between immigration law and alienage law).

102 Young, The Ordinary Diet of the Law, 2011 Sup. Ct. Rev. at 339–340; Delaney, In the Shadow of Article 1, 82 N.Y.U. L. Rev. at 110 ("The broad foreign affairs articulation of the national interest in a uniform immigration policy continues to underpin all types of preemption analyses in the immigration area.").

103 See, e.g., Rachel Rosenbloom, *The Citizenship Line: Rethinking Immigration Exceptionalism*, 54 B.C. L. REV. 1965 (2013); Jill E. Family, *Administrative Law through the Lens of Immigration Law*, 64 ADMIN. L. REV. 565 (2012); Peter J. Spiro, *Explaining the End of Plenary Power*, 16 GEO. IMMIGR. L. J. 339 (2002); Gabriel J. Chin, *Is There a Plenary Power Doctrine? A Tentative Apology and Prediction for Our Strange but Unexceptional Constitutional Immigration Law*, 14 GEO. IMMIGR. L. J. 257 (2000); Stephen H. Legomsky, *Immigration Law and the Principle of Plenary Congressional Power*, 1984 SUP. CT. REV. 255 (1985).

104 Arizona v. United States, 132 S.Ct. 2492, 2498 (2012).

105 Arizona, 132 S.Ct. at 2498–99.

106 See Chapter 2, pp. 57–59 for a general overview of preemption methodology; see also, Ernest A. Young, The Ordinary Diet of the Law: The Presumption Against Preemption in the Roberts Court, 2011 Sup. Ct. Rev. 253, 339 (2012) (citing Roderick Hills' work for the proposition that the Supreme Court's approach in Whiting was surprisingly conventional).

107 Arizona, 132 S.Ct. at 2509–10 ("[D]etaining individuals solely to verify their immigration status would raise constitutional concerns.... But §2(B) could be read to avoid these concerns.... This opinion does not foreclose preemption and constitutional challenges to the law as interpreted and applied after it goes into effect."); note that Professor Jennifer Chacon has sharply criticized the court's reasoning on this provision. Chacon, Transformation of Immigration Federalism, 21 Wm. & Mary Bill Rts J. at 609–13.

108 Kerry Abrams, *Plenary Power Preemption*, 99 VA. L. REV. 601, 624.

109 *See Arizona v. United States*, 132 S. Ct. 2492 (2012) (majority opinion of Kennedy, J.); *see generally* Abrams, *Plenary Power Preemption, supra* note 44, at 601 (arguing that "although the Arizona court purported to apply classic conflict and field preemption analysis, it was actually using a different form of preemption, one that gives particular weight to federal interests where questions of national sovereignty are at stake.").

110 Rice v. Santa Fe Elevator Corp, 331 U.S. 218 (1947). See Young, *The Ordinary Diet of Law:*, 2011 SUP. CT. REV. at 339 (2012) (noting that the Ninth Circuit opinion in Arizona v. United States declined to apply the presumption because the state was operating outside a traditional area of state regulation). Note that Young also presents an argument for the sustained salience of the presumption generally.

111 One might argue of course that the entire project of implied preemption analysis inherently involves hazy, or at least unexpressed, parameters.

112 Young, The Ordinary Diet of the Law, 2011 Sup. Ct. Rev. at 304.

113 Arizona v. United States, Brief for the United States, 2011 WL 5548708, Nov. 10, 2011, citing DHS Guidance on State and Local Governments' Assistance in Immigration Enforcement and Related Matters (Sept. 21, 2011).

114 Wyeth v. Levine, 555 U.S. 555 (2009) (quoting Medtronic v. Lohr, 518 U.S. 470, 485 (1996)).

115 Kris W. Kobach, *Reinforcing the Rule of Law: What States Can and Should Do to Reduce Illegal Immigration*, in STRANGE NEIGHBORS: THE ROLE OF STATES IN IMMIGRATION POLICY (G.J. Chin and Carissa Byrne Hessick, eds.) (NYU Press 2014); Gabriel J. Chin and Marc L. Miller, *Broken Mirror: the Unconstitutional*

*Foundation of New State Immigration Enforcement,* in Strange Neighbors; Margaret Hu, Mirror-Image Theory and Judicial Advicegiving in Immigration Policy (draft article, forthcoming 2016) (exploring both the genesis of mirror-image theory and long-term effects of the theory in judicial decision making).

116 Chamber of Commerce of the U.S. v. Whiting, 131 S. Ct. 1968, 1981 (2011).

117 This argument, however, would not cover all parts of SB 1070. Section 5(B), for example, created a legal sanction against the solicitation of unauthorized work, which the INA does not do. Therefore, even under mirror-theory, it is unlikely that 5(B) could be sustained.

118 Adam B. Cox, *Enforcement Redundancy and the Future of Immigration Law,* 2012 Sup. Ct. Rev. 31 (2013) (noting, for example, that the field of criminal law allows for redundant enforcement).

119 See Takahashi v. Fish & Game Comm'n, 334 U.S. 410, 421–22 (1948) ("It does not follow . . . that because the United States regulates immigration and naturalization in part on the basis of race and color classifications, a state can adopt one or more of the same classifications to prevent lawfully admitted aliens within its borders from earning a living in the same way as other state inhabitants."); Hines v. Davidowitz, 312 U.S. 52 (1941) (striking down the state registration scheme because the federal registration scheme occupied the entire field). Note, however, that one might argue that both cases, or at least Hines, was also implicitly based on the manner of federal enforcement compared to state enforcement.

120 *Arizona,* Brief for United States; Chin and Miller, Broken Mirror, in Strange Neighbors; *see generally,* Motomura, Immigration Outside the Law (arguing that federal policy, in operation, induces and tolerates significant unlawful presence).

121 8 U.S.C. § 1357(g) (authorizing federal government to enter into a "written agreement" with a state to allow qualified and trained state officers to perform investigations and detentions of noncitizens); 8 U.S.C. § 1252c (authorizing state officials to arrest and detain individuals who have illegally reentered the country after deportation); and 8 U.S.C. § 1324 (authorizing state officers to arrest those who might be smuggling, transporting, or harboring unlawfully present persons); see also, Chacon, Transformation of Immigration Federalism, 21 Wm. & Mary Bill Rts. J. at 595.

122 132 S.Ct. at 2499.

123 132 S. Ct. at 2517 (Scalia, J., concurring in part and dissenting in part).

124 See generally, Adam B. Cox and Christina M. Rodriguez, *The President and Immigration Law,* 119 Yale L. J. 458 (2009).

125 Cox, Enforcement Redundancy, 2012 Sup. Ct. Rev. at 32 (noting that several other regulatory areas have concurrent state and federal regulation or "enforcement redundancy" at the state level, and thus far have not been constitutionally challenged or found invalid).

126 On the question of preemptive power of non-binding executive guidance memoranda, see David S. Rubenstein, *Immigration Structuralism: A Return to Form,* 8 Duke J. L. & Pub. Pol. 81 (2013) (arguing that it is problematic to view such executive actions as "law" for federalism purposes, but not "law" for purposes of separation of powers analysis); see also, Roderick M. Hills Jr., *Arizona v. United States: The Unitary Executive's Enforcement Discretion as a Limit on Federalism,* 2012 Cato Sup. Ct. Rev. 189 (2013) (suggesting that the "presidential power to use

prosecutorial discretion to bar state enforcement of federal law ought to be narrowly construed."); Catherine Y. Kim, Immigration, Separation of Powers, and the President's Power to Preempt, 90 Notre Dame L. Rev. 691 (2014) (defending the preemptive authority of presidential prosecutorial discretion in the immigration field); Cox, *Enforcement Redundancy*, 2012 Sup. Ct. Rev. 32 (2013). On the question whether the president was rightfully within his constitutional and statutory authority in implementing large-scale deferred action programs in 2012 and 2014, see Balkinization, Symposium on Administrative Reform of Immigration Law, Nov. 26, 2014 (collected blog posts by several authors exploring the legality of Obama's 2014 deferred action program) available at http://balkin.blogspot .com/search?updated-max=2015-01-07T18:21:00-05:00; and compare Shobha Sivaprasad Wadhia, In Defense of DACA, Deferred Action, and the DREAM Act, 91 Tex. L. Rev. 59 (2013) with Robert J. Delahunty and John C. Yoo, 91 Tex. L. Rev. 2 (2013). See also, Peter J. Margulies, *Taking Care of Immigration Law: Presidential Stewardship, Prosecutorial Discretion, and the Separation of Powers*, 94 Boston U. L. Rev. 105 (2014) (advancing arguments for DACA, not from prosecutorial discretion powers, but from the president's responsibility of "stewardship").

127 Department of Homeland Security, Fixing Our Broken Immigration System through Executive Action – Key Facts, Jan. 5, 2015 available at http://www.dhs .gov/immigration-action. As this book goes to print, the 2014 expansion of deferred action is temporarily enjoined, with a district court in Texas finding that the state of Texas had standing to challenge the president's administrative action, and that on the merits, the deferred action program violated the "notice and comment" requirements of the Administrative Procedures Act. Texas, et al., v. Dep't of Homeland Security, No. 14-CV-254 (S.D. Tex. 2015).

128 Chacon, Transformation of Immigration Federalism, 21 Wm. & Mary Bill Rts. J. at 609–17.

129 Chacon, Transformation of Immigration Federalism, 21 Wm. & Mary Bill Rts. J. at 601 ("In the years immediately after September 11, 2001, the executive branch engaged in unprecedented expansions of state and local power in enforcement – an expansion that has ebbed in more recent years.").

130 Debra J. Saunders, "Free Pass for Sanctuary Cities?" *San Francisco Chronicle*, July 27, 2010.

131 See, e.g., Crane v. Napolitano, No. 14-10049 (5th Cir. Apr. 7, 2015) (finding that ICE agents and deportation officers did not have standing to challenge the Dep't of Homeland Security's DACA directive); Chiles v. United States, 69 F.3d 1094 (11th Cir. 1995) (concluding that state's lawsuit against the federal government for lax immigration enforcement was a political dispute, and not a legal one); but see, Texas v. Dep't of Homeland Security, No. 14-CV-254 (S.D. Tex. 2015) (finding standing for the state of Texas to challenge DHS 2014 deferred action program). As this book goes to print, that case is on appeal to the 5th Circuit.

132 See Texas, et al. v. Dep't of Homeland Security (S.D. Tex. 2015). Nearly half of Judge Hanen's lengthy opinion enjoining the President's 2014 deferred action program focused on establishing standing for the state of Texas, including the possibility of standing based on a theory of federal "abdication."

133 See Chapter 5, pp. 23–26.

134 Of course, Solicitor General decisions as to when to sue and when to forbear from suit or other involvement requires the weighing of many factors, both legal and political.

135 U.S. Const., Amdt. X ("The powers not delegated to the United States by the Constitution, nor prohibited by it to the states, are reserved to the states respectively, or to the people.").

136 *See* Garcia v. San Antonio Metropolitan Transit Authority, 469 U.S. 528 (1985) (stating that "the attempt to draw the boundaries of state regulatory immunity in terms of 'traditional governmental function' is not only unworkable but is also inconsistent with established principles of federalism").

137 New York v. United States, 505 U.S. 144 (1992) (reviving "state sovereignty" based in the Tenth Amendment as a constraint on Congress's power to direct state legislatures to enact certain types of laws); Printz v. United States, 521 U.S. 898 (1997) (striking down portions of the federal gun laws that commanded state and local law enforcement officials to conduct background checks on prospective handgun purchasers); *see generally,* Matthew D. Adler and Seth F. Kreimer, *The New Etiquette of Federalism: New York, Printz, and Yeskey,* 1998 SUP. CT. REV. 71 (1998). For a critique of the reasoning behind New York and Printz, see Neil S. Siegel, *Commandeering and Its Alternatives: A Federalism Perspective,* 59 VANDERBILT L. REV. 1629 (2006).

138 Legal scholar Margaret Hu suggests that the anti-commandeering principle can be used not just to preserve state noncooperation laws, but can be "flipped" to argue that state laws like SB 1070 have unconstitutionally "reverse commandeered" federal enforcement prerogatives. Hu, Reverse Commandeering, 46 U.C. Davis L. Rev. 535 (2012). Note that her argument appears to rely on defining an exclusive area of federal immigration authority.

139 See Chapter 5, pp. 29–31.

140 *See* South Dakota v. Dole, 483 U.S. 203 (1987) (upholding federal grant that conditioned highway funds to states on enactment of a twenty-one-year-old minimum drinking age law); *see generally,* Neil S. Siegel, *Commandeering and Its Alternatives: A Federalism Perspective,* 59 VANDERBILT L. REV. 1629 (2006).

141 See Chapter 5; Dep't of Homeland Security Secretary Jeh C. Johnson, Memorandum re: Secure Communities, Nov. 20, 2014 (discontinuing S-Comm, and noting that "governors, mayors, and state and local law enforcement officials around the country have increasingly refused to cooperate with the program, and many have issued executive orders or signed laws prohibiting such cooperation."). The memorandum also implemented the Priority Enforcement Program to replace S-Comm.

142 See Chapter 5, pp. 36–58; 8 U.S.C. §§ 1621(d), 1622 (setting eligibility requirements for public assistance programs, but allowing leeway for states to be more or less generous toward noncitizens, including unauthorized ones); Amanda Levinson, Immigrants and Welfare Use, Migration Policy Institute (2002). See also, Michael J. Wishnie, *Laboratories of Bigotry? Devolution of the Immigration Power, Equal Protection, and Federalism,* 76 N.Y.U. L. REV. 493 (2001) (arguing that Congress cannot devolve decision-making power to the states to enact welfare laws concerning noncitizens, and that such authority is likely to lead to anti-immigrant outcomes); REAL ID Act, 49 U.S.C. § 30301. Specifically on the issue of immigration

status, see 49 U.S.C. § 30301, note § 202(c)(2)(B)(viii). It is also worth noting that DHS has delayed the implementation and enforcement of many provisions of REAL ID as states have unevenly complied with it, and some have voiced their opposition to it. A recent DHS decision has now delayed implementation of key portions of the law until 2020. Interpreter Releases, DHS Postpones REAL ID Act Compliance Date to Oct. 2, 2020, 92 NO. 1 Interpreter Releases 3 (Jan. 5, 2015).

143 Martinez v. Regents of the University of California, 50 Cal. 4th 1277 (2010), cert. denied 131 S.Ct. 2961 (2011). For comprehensive and general information regarding higher education benefits, see Michael A. Olivas, The Law and Higher Education: Cases and Materials on Colleges in Court (3d Ed.) (2006).

144 In re Sergio C. Garcia on Admission, S202512 (Cal. 2014). The California legislature passed a law in September 2013 that specifically provided that undocumented applicants could become members of the California State Bar. The state's legislative action was intended to conform with federal law that permitted states to confer such licensing benefits pursuant to affirmative enactments after 1996.

145 See Gulasekaram and Ramakrishnan, The President and Immigration Federalism, 68 Fla. L. Rev. – (forthcoming 2016); Ramakrishnan and Gulasekaram, "Immigration Federalism: Obama's Actions Likely to Spur States, Not Congress, to Act," *San Jose Mercury News*, Dec. 6, 2014 (Op-Ed).

146 See Chapter 5, pp. 44–46 and 65–68.

147 See Peter J. Markowitz, *Undocumented No More*, 67 STAN. L. REV. – (forthcoming 2015) (defending the idea of state citizenship for undocumented persons, but noting "[T]he idea of a state asserting its authority to extend citizenship to nonfederal citizens will sound to many contemporary observers as a bold challenge to federal power."); Motomura, Immigration Outside the Law 169 ("The danger [of integration of unauthorized migrants into communities of state and local citizenship] is that integration into small-scale communities as sites of membership means that these communities will tolerate forms of discrimination that are inconsistent with constitutional protections for national citizenship.").

148 Of course, one might argue that state college attendance and degrees, driver's licenses, professional licensing, and other types of integrationist policies permitted by federal law also create these membership ties, albeit in a less formal manner than does the direct grant of "state citizenship."

149 Markowitz, Undocumented No More, 67 Stan L. Rev. – (pp. 13–16 in draft copy, discussing the "Constitutional Foundation of State Citizenship").

150 Markowitz, Undocumented No More, 67 Stan L. Rev. – (pp. 16–21 in draft copy, arguing that the Fourteenth Amendment establishes a floor, but not a ceiling, for state citizenship).

151 Heather K. Gerken, Justice Kennedy's Mad Genius: A New Take on Windsor v. United States, Balkination.com, Feb. 17, 2015 (blog post).

152 Harold H. Koh, *Equality with a Human Face*, 8 HAMLINE L. REV. 51, 55–56 (1985).

153 See, e.g., U.S. Const. Art. I (limiting congressional seats to citizens), Art. II (limiting the Presidency to natural born citizens), Amdt. IV § 1, cl. 2 (protecting the Privileges or Immunities of U.S. citizens). Mathews v. Diaz, 426 U.S. 67 (1976) (permitting federal discrimination on the basis of alienage); United States v. Brignoni-Ponce, 422 U.S. 873, 885–86 (1975) (finding that a border patrol stop

of a vehicle violated the Fourth Amendment, but concluding that federal officials may rely on "characteristic appearances of persons who live in Mexico", and stating that "Mexican appearance" can be a relevant factor in stopping a suspected immigration law violator);

154 *See* Chinese Exclusion Act of 1882, ch. 126, 22 Stat. 58 (excluding admission of Chinese laborers to the United States) (repealed 1943); Immigration Act of 1924, ch. 190, 43 Stat. 153 (establishing a quota system that limited immigration from Southern and Eastern Europe) (repealed 1952); Immigration Act of 1917, ch. 29, § 19, 39 Stat. 889, 890 (restricting immigration from Asia, and also known as the "Asiatic Barred Zone Act") (repealed 1952); Naturalization Act of 1870, ch. 254, 16 Stat. 254 (repealed 1943).

155 *See* 8 U.S.C. §§ 1152–1153 (providing yearly limitation of visas determined on a per-country basis, and providing formula for calculating visa allocation by country).

156 *See generally* Kevin R. Johnson, *The Intersection of Race and Class in U.S. Immigration Law and Enforcement*, 72 Law and Contemp. Probs. 1 (2009) (describing how U.S. immigration law excludes poor noncitizens of color); *see also* Bureau of Consular Affairs, U.S. Dep't of State, Visa Bulletin Vol. IX, No. 58, Immigrant Numbers for July 2013 (2013), *available at* http://www.travel.state.gov/visa/bulletin/bulletin_5993.html (illustrating the oversubscription of visa applicants from China, India, Mexico, and the Philippines).

157 Foley v. Connelie, 435 U.S. 291 (1978) (permitting the state to discriminate on the basis of alienage in hiring state troopers).

158 De Canas v. Bica, 424 U.S. 351 (1976) (upholding California's employer sanctions law for hiring of unauthorized workers).

159 See Chapter 2, pp. 24–26, describing provision that gave Chinese persons the same rights and protection of "citizens and subjects of the most favored nations."

160 Plyler, 457 U.S. at 223. Under well-established doctrine, categorizing legal classifications as affecting a "suspect class" (such as racial groups) triggers the Court's strictest judicial scrutiny, oftentimes resulting in the striking down of the state law. *Plyler* eschewed this traditional analytical category, instead resting its opinion on the innocence of the children and the potential for creating a permanent caste of uneducated residents if they were denied their important right to primary and secondary education.

161 Indeed, in *Toll v. Moreno*, a case decided the same term as was *Plyler*, the Court dealt with the state's ability to deny a certain group of temporary immigrants treatment as residents for the purpose of in-state tuition. In that decision, the Court concluded that its earlier alienage decisions, despite invoking equal protection standards, were better read as preemption cases. Toll v. Moreno, 458 U.S. 1, 11 n.16 (1982) (citing David F. Levi, Note, *The Equal Treatment of Aliens: Preemption or Equal Protection?*, 31 Stan. L. Rev. 1069 (1979)) (arguing that the Court's alienage decisions are better understood as preemption cases). See Chapter 2, pp. 91–92.

162 See Chapter 2, pp. 59–70 and 84–87.

163 Transcript of Oral Argument at 33–34, Arizona v. United States, 132 S. Ct. 2492 (2012) (No. 11–182), 2012 WL 1425227, at *33.

164 Transcript of Oral Argument, Arizona v. United States, 132 S. Ct. 2492 (2012) (No. 11–182), 2012 WL 1425227.

165 See Chapter 2, pp. 47–49, nn. 74 and 75.

166 Complaint, United States v. Maricopa County, No. 2:12-cv-00981-ROS (D. Ariz. May 10, 2012); Jerry Seper, "Justice Dept. Accuses Ariz. Sheriff Arpaio of Racial Profiling," Wash. *Times* (May 10, 2012), *see also* Melendres v. Arpaio, No. PHX-CV-07-02513-GMS, 2013 WL 2297173 (D. Ariz. May 24, 2013) (finding that class action plaintiffs were entitled to injunctive relief from Maricopa County Sheriff's Office for Fourth and Fourteenth Amendment violations and permanently enjoining the county from other enforcement actions).

167 Chacon, Transformation of Immigration Federalism, 21 Wm. & Mary Bill Rts. J. at 613.

168 Hiroshi Motomura, Immigration Outside the Law 145–54; Lucas Guttentag, *The Forgotten Equality Norm in Immigration Preemption: Discrimination, Harassment, and the Civil Rights Act of 1870*, 8 Duke J. Const. L. & Pub. Pol. 1 (2013). Professor (and current Senior Counselor to Director of U.S. Citizens and Immigration Services) Lucas Guttentag argues that the federal Civil Rights Act of 1870, with its requirement that "all persons within the jurisdiction of the United States" shall have the same enumerated rights "as is enjoyed by white citizens," provides a basis for differentiating integrationist and restrictionist laws. His theory is limited by the fact that courts have not ruled on that basis, and often do not address the Civil Rights Act in their opinions. Civil Rights Act of 1870, ch. 114, §§16–17, 16 Stat. 140, 144, codified at 42 U.S.C. § 1981. This tide may be changing, as a recent federal court took the federal Civil Rights Act of 1870 into account in ruling on a dispute between a DACA recipient and an insurance company that refused to hire him on account of his immigration status. Juarez v. Northwestern Mutual Life Insurance Co., (S.D.N.Y. Nov. 14, 2014) (denying defendants motion to dismiss and allowing plaintiff to proceed on his claim against the company).But cf. Rubenstein, Immigration Structuralism, 8 Duke J. Const. L & Pub. Pol. 81 (questioning this disparate treatment of integrationist laws on equality-based principles).

169 Motomura, Immigration Outside the Law 111–16.

170 Lozano v. City of Hazelton, 724 F.3d 297 (2013); Motomura, Immigration Outside the Law 133–35.

171 Chacon, Transformation of Immigration Federalism, 21 Wm. & Mary Bill Rts. J. at 579–80.

172 Washington v. Davis, 426 U.S. 229 (1976) (upholding the District of Columbia's recruiting process for police officers, which included a test that had racially disproportionate impacts on racial minorities, and ruling that claims of disparate impact were insufficient to state constitutional violations without evidence of discriminatory intent); Romer v. Evans, 517 U.S. 620 (1996) (striking down Colorado Amendment 2, which treated sexual orientation discrimination claims differently than all other discrimination claims, on the theory that the law evinced a bare desire to harm a politically unpopular group).

173 Cf. Villas at Parkside Partners v. City of Farmers Branch, No. 10-10751, 2013 WL 3791664, at *30 (5th Cir. July 22, 2013) (Higginson, J., concurring) ("I would point out that several other constitutional claims, under due process, equal protection, and the Privileges and Immunities and Commerce Clauses, were raised by the plaintiffs below but not reached by the district court.").

174 See, e.g., Michael A. Olivas, *Lawmakers Gone Wild?*, 61 S.M.U. L. Rev. 99, 131 (2008) (describing English-only laws and local ordinances requiring immigration

status check for residential rentals as "sure signs of an ethnic and national origin 'tax' that will be levied only on certain groups"); Michael A. Olivas, *The Political Efficacy of Plyler v. Doe*, 45 U.C. DAVIS L. REV. 1, 15 (2011) ("Blowback in affected communities and increased prejudice are sure to follow from sub-federal assumption of immigration powers.").

175  2010 Ariz. Sess. Laws 450 (changing SB 1070 text from "lawful contact" to "lawful stop, attention, or arrest" and removing "solely" from "may not solely consider race, color, or national origin"), *available at* http://www.azleg.gov/alispdfs/council/SB1070-HB2162.PDF.

176  Chapter 4, pp. 63–65.

177  *See, e.g.*, Muneer I. Ahmad, *A Rage Shared by Law*, 92 CAL. L. REV. 1261 (2004) (tracing a genealogy of racial violence post–September 11); Leti Volpp, *The Citizen and the Terrorist*, 49 U.C.L.A. L. REV. 1575 (2002) (discussing the racialized conception of those identified as "Middle Eastern, Arab, or Muslim" after September 11, regardless of citizenship status).

178  *See, e.g.*, United States v. South Carolina, 840 F. Supp. 2d 898, 905 (D.S.C. 2011) ("The South Carolina General Assembly took up the matter of state immigration legislation … because of a perceived failure of the United States to 'secure our southern border,' which 'really jeopardize[s] our national security.'" (citations omitted)), *modified*, 906 F. Supp. 2d 463 (D.S.C. 2012), *aff'd*, 720 F.3d 518 (4th Cir. 2013). Also see, more generally, Chapter 4 of this book on the work of restrictive issue entrepreneurs in shaping and exploiting post-9/11 concerns about national security.

179  City of Farmers Branch, Ordinance No. 2892 (Nov. 13, 2006). That ordinance was enjoined by a state court in Texas for technical reasons related to the faulty procedures used to pass it, and the City Council repealed it. A year later the City Council passed Ordinance 2952, which excluded the 9/11 and terrorist language of 2892. Ordiannce 2952 was eventually enjoined by a federal district court, with that ruling affirmed by the Fifth Circuit Court of Appeals. See Karen A. Herrling, District Court Strikes Down Texas Ordinance that Restricts Housing Based on Immigration Status, Catholic Legal Immigration Network, May 2010; see also, Jill Espbenshade, et al., Division and Dislocation: Regulating Immigration through Local Housing Ordinances, Special Report of the Immigration Policy Center (Summer 2007).

180  *See* J.D. HAYWORTH & JOSEPH J. EULE, WHATEVER IT TAKES: ILLEGAL IMMIGRATION, BORDER SECURITY, AND THE WAR ON TERROR, 5–8 (2006) (discussing the possibility of terrorists sneaking in through the U.S.-Mexico border).

181  CNN's *Lou Dobbs Tonight* frequently made the linkages between granting state driver's licenses to illegal immigrants and terrorist threats to homeland security. *See, e.g., Lou Dobbs Tonight* (CNN television broadcast Oct. 17, 2007), *transcript available at* http://transcripts.cnn.com/TRANSCRIPTS/0710/17/ldt.01.html ("The governor … will make it easier for law breakers of all sorts – including terrorists – to take advantage of New York State's driver's licenses.").

182  Maria Santana, Ebola fears spark backlash against Latino immigrants, CNN, Oct. 12, 2014; Martin Pengelly, "Texas Governor Rick Perry Warns of Migrants from Terrorist-Linked Nations," *The Guardian*, Aug. 3, 2014.

183 Jennifer M. Chacón, *Unsecured Borders: Immigration Restrictions, Crime Control, and National Security*, 39 CONN. L. REV. 1827, 1853 (2007) ("[R]emovals of non-citizens … can be, and frequently are, depicted as national security policy. With regard to border enforcement efforts, the phrase 'border security' has become a ubiquitous descriptive term.").

184 Chacon, Transformation of Immigration Federalism, 21 Wm. & Mary Bill Rts J. at 601.

185 *See, e.g.*, Volpp, *supra* note 275, at 1576 ("The stereotype of the 'Arab terrorist' is not an unfamiliar one. But the ferocity with which multiple communities have been interpellated as responsible for the events of September [11] suggests there are particular dimensions that have converged in this racialization.").

186 Chapter 4, pp. 61–69.

187 Dan Hopkins, "How Accents Influence the Immigration Debate," WASH. POST (Feb. 10, 2013, 12:16 PM), http://www.washingtonpost.com/blogs/wonkblog/wp/2013/02/10/how-accents-influence-the-immigration-debate/ (providing a summary by a political science professor of published work from various scholars on how aversion to foreign languages drives opposition to immigration, particularly among Republicans).

188 Ted Brader et al., *What Triggers Public Opposition to Immigration? Anxiety, Group Cues, and Immigration Threat*, 52 AM. J. POL. SCI. 959 (2008).

189 Karthick Ramakrishnan et al., Illegality, National Origin Cues, and Public Opinion on Immigration (2010) (working paper), *available at* http://polisci.osu.edu/sites/polisci.osu.edu/files/_illegality,%20national%20origin%20cues,%20and%20public%20opinion%20on%20immigration_.pdf (noting that Americans view Mexican immigrants less favorably than immigrants from other parts of the world).

190 *See id.* at 1 ("[R]acial affect, particularly with respect to negative attitudes towards Latinos, also play[s] a significant role in shaping public anxiety over immigration and immigration policy.").

191 Emily Ryo, Do Immigration Laws Shape our Attitude towards Latinos (draft under development, forthcoming 2015) (empirical work showing that both anti- and pro-immigration laws increase people's biases against Latinos, with anti-immigrant laws producing explicit attitudes toward Latinos).

192 See, e.g., Cass Sunstein, *On the Expressive Function of Law*, 144 U. PA. L. REV. 2021 (1996); Richard McAdams, *An Attitudinal Theory of Expressive Law*, 79 OREGON L. REV. 339 (2000).

193 *See* Washington v. Davis, 426 U.S. 229 (1976) (explaining that evidence of disparate impact alone is insufficient to satisfy the constitutional standard required for a finding of a racial classification).

194 *See* Hunter v. Underwood, 471 U.S. 222 (1985) (invalidating Alabama's felony disenfranchisement law based on evidence that the provision was created to disproportionately affect poor black citizens).

195 *See* Davis, 426 U.S. at 240–41 (describing cases holding that racial discrimination claims require showing a discriminatory purpose).

196 Motomura, *The Rights of Others: Legal Claims and Immigration Outside the Law*, 59 DUKE L.J. 1723, at 1743 (2010) (noting that "[a]n equal protection challenge would require proof of discriminatory intent, but a preemption challenge can

persuade some judges based on reasonable possibility of discriminatory intent," and commenting that the court in Lozano v. City of Hazleton, 496 F. Supp. 2d 477, 525–29 (M.D. Pa. 2007) might not have found the ordinance preempted had the plaintiffs not brought forth evidence of racial and ethnic bias).

197 *See* Ariz. Dream Act Coal. v. Brewer, No. 13 – 16248 (9th Cir. July 7, 2014). It is also important to remain aware of the limitations of this case. It did not decide that undocmented persons were a suspect class for equal protection purposes. Rather, the equality concern arose because the state offered licenses to some recipients of deferred action, but not to others. The court did not rule on the preemption claim, but Judge Christen, in concurrence, would have found for the challengers on preemption grounds as well.

198 *See* Civil Rights Act of 1964, 46 U.S.C. § 2000d (2006) (prohibiting discrimination in any program receiving federal assistance).

199 It is worth noting that not every case would be amenable to judicial consideration of individual liberty claims. For instance, the federal government may not have standing to advance equal protection claims in many cases. However, the vast majority of cases are brought by private individuals who would have standing to advance such claims, and in many cases involving the federal government, courts have consolidated companion cases involving private plaintiffs. *See, e.g.*, United States v. South Carolina, 840 F. Supp. 2d 898, 904 (D.S.C. 2011) (considering claims by a private party and the federal government against state immigration law), *aff'd*, 720 F.3d 518 (4th Cir. 2013).

CHAPTER 7

1 Certainly, the Patriot Act and its amendments, as well as the REAL ID Act, the Secure Fences Act, and aspects of VAWA amendments address discrete aspects of immigration. And, in the 113th Congress, the SAFE Act was being considered in the House. The SAFE Act would have made provisions for increased state and local involvement in immigration enforcement. https://www.congress.gov/bill/113th-congress/house-bill/4626/all-info.

2 The anti-smuggling law was actually first enacted by Arizona in 2005, but was modified and reenacted again as part of SB 1070. Before this recent ruling in November 2014, a district judge had already ruled that police could not arrest undocumented immigrants for the crime of "self-smuggling" under that law.

3 This "show me your papers" provision, however, is under attack in a currently pending case, with challengers claiming that the provision leads to lengthy detentions in violation of the fourth amendment and discriminatory police action against Latinos.

4 In addition, after the Eleventh circuit struck down most of Alabama's law, that state reached a settlement with the U.S. Department of Justice and advocacy groups to stop enforcing other aspects of its law, and agreed that police would not arrest, detain, or prolong the detention of any person solely to ascertain their immigration status.

5 Jeffrey S Passel and D'Vera Cohn, State Unauthorized Immigrant Populations, Pew Research, Hispanic Trends Project, Nov. 18, 2014; Jens Manuel Krogstad

and Micahel Keegan, 15 States with the Highest Share of Immigrants in their Population, Pew Research Center, May 14, 2014.

6 Griff Palmer & Michael Cooper, *Redistricting Helped Republicans Hold Onto Congress*, THE NEW YORK TIMES, December 14, 2012.

7 Prior state efforts have also been successful in influencing executive branch policies. As we detailed in Chapter 5, the detainer-resistance and TRUST Act movement in several counties and states led to the eventual dismantling of the Department of Homeland Security's S-Comm program in 2014. (Secretary of Homeland Secretaty Jeh S. Johnson, Memorandom re: Secure Communities, Nov. 20, 2014). As per the memorandum, DHS replaced S-Comm with the Priority Enforcement Program (PEP), which still requires state and local participation but in a seemingly less intrusive manner.

8 The state and local resistance to S-Comm, however, is a notable counter-example to this trend. It was mostly Democratic jurisdictions that resisted and undermined the program, which was being promoted by a Democratic administration. The program itself, however, was initiated by George W. Bush's Republican administration.

## APPENDIX A

1 *See* Magdalena Szumilas, *Explaining Odds Ratios*, 19 J. CAN. ACAD. CHILD ADOLESCENT PSYCHIATRY 227, 227–29 (2010) ("When a logistic regression is calculated, the regression coefficient ($b_1$) is the estimated increase in the log odds of the outcome per unit increase in the value of the exposure. In other words, the exponential function of the regression coefficient ($e^{b_1}$) is the odds ratio associated with a one-unit increase in the exposure.").

2 Michael Tomz et al., *ReLogit: Rare Events Logistic Regression*, GARY KING, http://gking.harvard.edu/relogit (last visited Aug. 31, 2013).

3 *See ReLogit: Rare Events Logistic Regression Package Description*, http://www.stanford.edu/~tomz/software/software.shtml (last visited Oct. 1, 2013).

## APPENDIX B

1 Information retrieved on January 12, 2012 from FindLaw, a Thomson Reuters resource on cases and statutes. *State Immigration Laws*, FindLaw, http://immigration.findlaw.com/immigration-laws-and-resources/state-immigration-laws/.

# Index